£4
British Topog/

architecture

LOCAL STYLES OF THE ENGLISH PARISH CHURCH

Consult the genius of the place in all
ALEXANDER POPE

Sir William Addison

Local Styles *of the* English Parish Church

B. T. Batsford Ltd.,
London

First published 1982

ISBN 0 7134 2564 4

Filmset in Monophoto Baskerville by
Latimer Trend & Company Ltd, Plymouth
and printed in Great Britain by
The Anchor Press Ltd
Tiptree, Essex
for the publishers
B. T. Batsford Ltd.
4 Fitzhardinge Street
London W1H 0AH

Contents

List of Illustrations

Acknowledgments

Since there are more than ten thousand ancient churches in England it would be impossible for anyone to visit and study them all. But the completion of *The Buildings of England* series by Sir Nikolaus Pevsner and his co-authors has made comparative studies of styles and features much more feasible than they have hitherto been. I cannot claim that I have visited every church named in this book; but I do claim that over a period of more than 60 years I have visited and revisited scores of them in most counties, and those I have been advised are the most characteristic in all. I am not an architect and do not write as one. For technical information I have relied on Pevsner and the other authorities I have named. There has been no embarrassment about this, because practically all the answers to the whys and wherefores of local styles of parish churches are historical, and local history has been a life-long passion with me. So while fully acknowledging my indebtedness to church architects and architectural historians who have written on the subject, my chief indebtedness is to the local historians, many of whom are personal friends, who have helped me to find what appear to be the most probable answers to local problems, and to the many incumbents who have been kind enough to discuss their churches with me.

I have conformed with the practice adopted for the new volumes of *The Victoria History of the Counties of England*, with which I have a long association, in retaining the pre-1974 county structure as the most reliable means of ensuring continuity in the study of local history.

Epping, 1982   W.A.

The author and publishers would like to thank the following for their permission to reproduce illustrations in this book: F. H. Crossley/Canon Ridgway (87); J. Dixon-Scott (31, 46); Leonard and Marjorie Gayton (90); A. F. Kersting (9, 10, 13, 16, 18, 19, 22–4, 30, 33, 35, 36, 39, 41, 42, 47, 48, 51, 52, 56, 60, 63, 68–70, 76, 79, 80, 89, 92, 94); National Monuments Record (50, 95, 96); Kenneth Scowen (20); Rev. E. V. Tanner (27); Reece Winstone (77). Figures 1–8 are from Arthur Stratton's *Introductory Handbook to the Styles of English Architecture, Part I* (Batsford, 1934). Nos. 11, 12, 14, 15, 17, 21, 25, 26, 28, 29, 32, 34, 37, 38, 40, 43, 44, 49, 53–5, 57–9, 61, 64–7, 71–5, 78, 81–6, 88, 91 and 93 are from the publishers' collection.

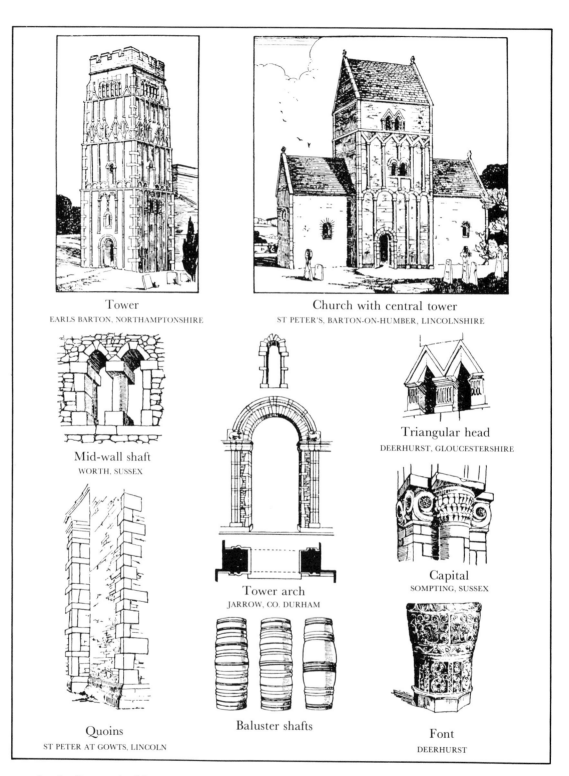

Tower
EARLS BARTON, NORTHAMPTONSHIRE

Church with central tower
ST PETER'S, BARTON-ON-HUMBER, LINCOLNSHIRE

Mid-wall shaft
WORTH, SUSSEX

Triangular head
DEERHURST, GLOUCESTERSHIRE

Tower arch
JARROW, CO. DURHAM

Capital
SOMPTING, SUSSEX

Quoins
ST PETER AT GOWTS, LINCOLN

Baluster shafts

Font
DEERHURST

1   Anglo-Saxon Architecture

1 Introduction

Surprisingly little has been written to explain how our English parish churches came to be built in so many different styles, ranging from the simple shepherds' churches on the Sussex Downs at one end of the scale to the stately wool churches of the Cotswolds and East Anglia at the other. Simply to divide these styles into Saxon, Norman, Transitional, Early English and the rest of them explains nothing. Yet once we gain clues to the origin of the various styles the subject becomes one of inexhaustible fascination.

The first surprise is that although the earliest Christian churches in England were built for one liturgical purpose they were in two distinct styles. The style introduced into Kent by St Augustine's missionaries was based on the Roman basilica and had an apsidal chancel for the altar. The style introduced into Northumbria by St Aidan's missionaries from Ireland was in the Celtic style, with a small square-ended chancel at the end of a tall rectangular nave. So already in the seventh century North was North and South was South. But it could not be said that never the twain should meet because before the end of the century St Wilfrid, Bishop of York, brought masons from Rome to build churches on the Roman plan at Hexham, Jarrow, and Ripon in contrast to the church on the Celtic plan which may still be seen at Escomb, County Durham.

Modifications of the two basic plans started with the division of the country into parishes,

a process that began earlier than is sometimes alleged. The word 'parish' is not derived from the Old French *paroche*, which made its first appearance in England in 1075, but from the Saxon *preost-scir*, 'priest shire', a territorial division that seems to have been conceived in 673 at the synod summoned by Archbishop Theodore, the first Primate of All England. But the theory that Theodore established a comprehensive parochial system has long been abandoned. It is now accepted that the Church was not fully organised within a parish framework until the end of the tenth century, when St Dunstan, as Archbishop of Canterbury, gave it a structure of head-minsters, middle-minsters, and lesser-minsters, with the provision that the lesser-minsters, which correspond with our parish churches, could have what St Dunstan called field-churches and we call chapels-of-ease. In these chapels-of-ease the Gospel could be preached, but there were strictly enforced limitations to the sacraments that could be administered in them. The most frustrating of these for centuries was that only parish churches could have burial grounds.

The wider distribution of churches on the Celtic than on the Roman plan would be partly due to the hill country of the North and West of England being more sparsely populated than the lowlands of the South-East, and partly to the greater missionary zeal of the Celtic saints, to which scores of preaching crosses and church dedications in the North and West continue to testify. Even in the east of England the influence of the missionaries from Northumbria extended rapidly down the coast from Lindisfarne to East Anglia, with churches being administered from Durham, York, Lincoln, and South Elmham, while from Glastonbury in the South Continental influences originating in the Rhineland radiated to produce a crop of cruciform churches, and to modify existing Celtic churches. We see the effect of this at Bradford-on-Avon in Wiltshire, where the Celtic nave and chancel were given projecting wings to conform with the plan that is thought to have been fully achieved at Breamore, between Fordingbridge and Salisbury. This Rhineland influence partly explains why the central tower remained a local style in Wessex and Wiltshire after it had been superseded in most regions by the western tower.

Survivors of the earliest types of churches are most numerous in one or other of three broad regions: the Saxon kingdoms of the South-East and the Celtic North and West of England. Outside these areas of greatest concentration there are many important strays, such as the early churches at Iffley in Oxfordshire, Stewkley in Buckinghamshire, and Adel in Yorkshire. Obviously the main factor in all survivals is the material of which the church was built. For the Celts good building material never presented problems. They occupied hill country where stone was abundant and they made use of whatever they could lay their hands on. The foundations of the earliest churches in Cornwall, for example, were often moorstone, broken up and carted from the tors, or wayside crosses. In lowland England timber was usually available. If not, the Anglo-Saxons raked flints from the fields through which they had driven their ploughs, or dredged pebbles from the streams. In East Anglia these drift materials, reinforced with any available rubble or Roman tiles, were set in mortar to build round towers, with skills acquired in sinking wells, which were round because country masons knew from experience that a ring is stronger

than a square if the material is poor.

Every part of the country had access to some form of building material, and these first churches continue to excite reverence and affection when their finer neighbours may only be admired. They belong, as no other buildings do, to the earth they appear to have grown out of as naturally as the trees that shade them or the yews along the churchyard path.

The extent to which these early churches were rebuilt in stone by the Normans suggests that in many places something more than need went into the reckoning. Not all the existing churches would be decayed. Many, like the nave at Greensted, near Ongar in Essex, might have survived for a thousand years. Given adequate protection from the weather oak is virtually indestructible. National prestige may well have been a major factor in the wholesale abandonment of timber, which had been the normal building material of the Anglo-Saxons and Jutes – races highly skilled as shipwrights and carpenters. The Normans preferred stone, not only because they regarded it as a superior material but because it gave them more scope for exhibiting the kind of craftsmanship in which they excelled, and which they displayed so exuberantly round the doorways of even their smallest churches.

Despite the parish church having gained its full legal status as the building designated for the administration of the rites of baptism, marriage, and burial before the Norman Conquest, Domesday is of limited value as a record of ancient churches. The reason for this is that the chief object of the Commissioners was the identification of sources of revenue, and only a proportion of parish churches qualified independently under that heading. But that does not explain why in some regions all the churches are recorded, in others none. The total number recorded is not more than 1,700, yet the number of ancient parishes already established in 1086 must have been between 10,000 and 12,000. We know that the figure varied little between the years 1300 and

Interiors

Chancel
IFFLEY, OXFORDSHIRE

Nave
ST PETER'S, NORTHAMPTON

Carved capitals
ST PETER'S, NORTHAMPTON

Pier arcade
LEOMINSTER, HEREFORDSHIRE

Scalloped capitals
TYPICAL EXAMPLES

Bases
TYPICAL EXAMPLES

Intersecting wall arcade
ST ALBAN'S ABBEY, HERTFORDSHIRE

W. SHEFFORD, BERKSHIRE

2 Norman architecture – late eleventh and twelfth century

1800, when the number was in excess of 12,000.

Over the country as a whole there was little church building during the half-century immediately after the Conquest. The new overlords were too busy dividing the country into manors, many of which were based on existing parishes. But as soon as they were firmly seated a large proportion of the Norman lords of manors built stone churches on their estates, where the sacraments could be administered by their personal chaplains as parish priests. We still see the effect of this in those parts of England where manorial influence was most assertive in the parish church being within a stone's throw of the manor house.

This feudal origin is important in studying style differentiation in parish churches because it introduced a secular element depending on wealth rather than piety. It is also the origin of the freehold of the parish priest in England being derived so often from feudal patronage, a feature which diminished during the period of monastic domination in the Middle Ages to reassert itself after the Dissolution, when the lay rector came into prominence. The title meant 'ruler' and Jane Austen's *Pride and Prejudice* has an imaginary picture of what this might give rise to in the satirised relationship between the compliant Rev. William Collins and the haughty and insolent Lady Catherine de Bourgh. Such extremes would be exceptional but they could exist, despite the fact that although the parish priest derived his living from the patron, his spiritual authority was derived from the bishop of the diocese, to whom alone he was responsible for his 'cure of souls'.

Since from the Norman Conquest onwards most churches were built in stone we need to have a general picture of England's stone structure, which inevitably became the chief factor in the differentiation of styles. The best building stone in England is in a loosely hung band of oolitic limestone extending for a distance of approximately 300 miles from Dorset in the South-West to Yorkshire in the North-East. It is from the quarries in this Jurassic Belt, as it is scientifically called, that the stone was taken to build practically all our most architecturally memorable churches, from the towers of Somerset at one end to the magnificent churches of Lincolnshire and Holderness at the other. The most beautiful of these stones are the honey-coloured Cotswold, and the Ketton of the Cambridge colleges, which take the light so serenely from the luminous East Anglian skies.

Blocks of blue limestone lie north of the Jurassic band across parts of Gloucestershire and Worcestershire, followed by ironstone in Northamptonshire and Rutland, while south of it runs the chalk Ridgeway from Salisbury Plain through Wiltshire, Berkshire and Hampshire to the Hog's Back, which links it with the downs of Surrey, Sussex, and Kent.

In the mountainous North the regions are more clearly defined. From the Trent to the Scottish border the vast majority of churches are built of the sombre carboniferous limestone of the Pennines, seen at its most dramatic in Matlock Vale and Dovedale. In the industrialised areas all too many of the churches have been over-restored – and incidentally it is odd that so inappropriate a word should be universally applied to the peculiar form of vandalism that became prevalent in the third quarter of the nineteenth century, since all ancient churches had already been genuinely restored or sympathetically altered repeatedly without local style being affected. Although to southern eyes carboniferous limestone may seem unattractive because of its tendency to gather grime, when seen in relation to the fells behind them, these northern churches, with their flagged roofs, and floors which were formerly strewn with rushes, have character and appeal which is all their own.

East of the carboniferous limestone and millstone grit are the wolds of Lincolnshire and Yorkshire, which are mainly of chalk and may be seen as the northern counterpart of the downland of southern England.

This ringing of changes, as it were, from one

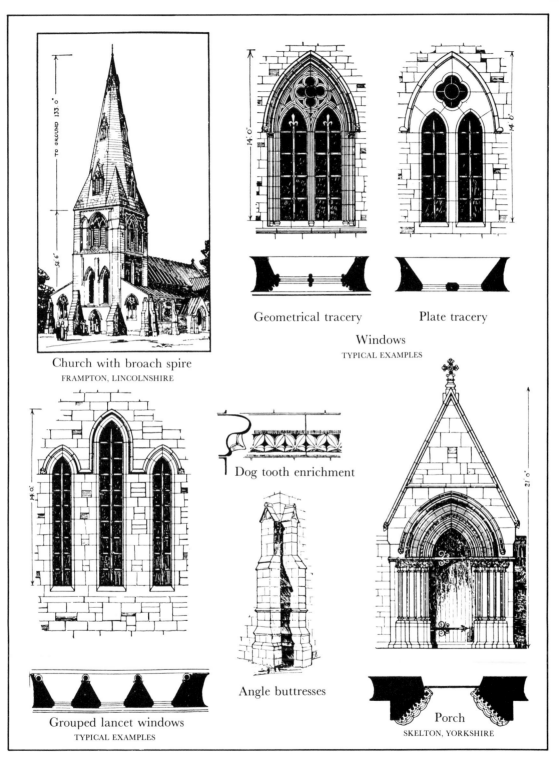

Church with broach spire
FRAMPTON, LINCOLNSHIRE

Geometrical tracery

Plate tracery

Windows
TYPICAL EXAMPLES

Dog tooth enrichment

Angle buttresses

Grouped lancet windows
TYPICAL EXAMPLES

Porch
SKELTON, YORKSHIRE

3 Early English architecture – thirteenth century

part of England to another is half the fascination of local styling. For example, the old red sandstone of Herefordshire and Devon comes through at St Bees in Cumberland to form a band across Cumbria as far as Kirkby Stephen, and the delight in finding it is increased by its close proximity to the Lakeland fells, the contrast matching the proximity of the old red sandstone of Devon to the granite of Cornwall. In both cases the granite dominates to produce over the region as a whole austere churches built in styles as ageless as the hills, dedicated to saints unheard of elsewhere.

Local masons trained in country skills found work in the scores, and eventually hundreds, of religious houses that started as cells of Continental abbeys, and from humble beginnings proliferated and prospered until during the thirteenth century the abbots were the largest employers of labour in England. Under guidance of the monks new skills were acquired which developed into the succession of sophisticated Gothic styles we now classify as Early English, Decorated, and finally Perpendicular. In those easy-going days the monks on their part were wise enough to leave ample scope for the expression of country wit and humour in the decoration of buildings reverently as well as professionally designed for the glory of God. So gargoyles still grin down on us from water spouts under the roofs of cathedral and collegiate churches, and subjects from medieval bestiaries look up from misericords from which the sacred offices were sung. These local masons and carpenters practised a vernacular art that we can only appreciate fully when we understand why it varied as dialects do from one district to another.

These carvings look so much more like illustrations of Chaucer's *Canterbury Tales* than of either the sobering prophecies of the *Old Testament* or the heavenly visions of the *New* that we may at times ask how these medieval workmen got away with them. With gargoyles, which often represent contemporary characters, the explanation must be that in an age in which life was short and limbs began to creak at 30 only the young could climb ladders to put roofs on naves, or scale towers to ensure that the spouts round the parapets cleared the walls.

In days when sons followed fathers in basic crafts for generations reactions to material were instinctive. The potentialities of every piece of local stone between a mason's knees was immediately apparent to him. Its limitations were equally apparent. So there was little risk of medieval masons making the kind of costly mistakes that we sometimes hear of architects making today. Even apart from this knowledge of what could be achieved in local material and what could not, the vernacular element was so strong that offences against the *genius loci* in building seem to have been virtually unthinkable in areas remote from Continental influences. It is, however, to be noted that this native element got less scope as the wealth and power of the Church increased. The thirteenth century was an age of relative security. England had emerged from the centuries of Saxon and Viking raids into one of serenity under the monastic symbol of the Crook. Along the Scottish and Welsh borders embattled towers continued to be built, with thick walls and iron-clad doors because the old traditions of the Church Militant were still strong there. In other parts of the country the heavily moulded arches of the Normans gave place to pointed arches that symbolised hands raised in prayer. Windows became larger and aisles were added to naves, or widened where they already existed, for processional use in bringing the liturgy to the congregations standing in the nave.

The pre-eminence of the Church in the thirteenth century meant that architectural styles were controlled by the religious orders, each with its own tradition brought over from the Continent. The main influence stemmed from the Benedictines, who got much of their stone from quarries in the Jurassic Belt, where many of their most important houses were built. Their wealth explains the magnificence

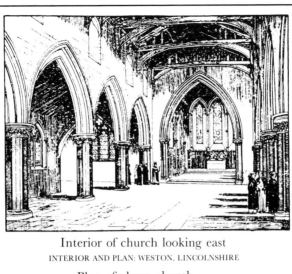

Interior of church looking east
INTERIOR AND PLAN: WESTON, LINCOLNSHIRE

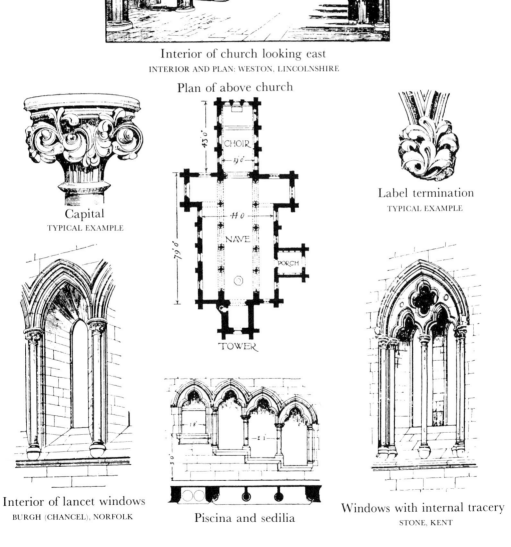

Plan of above church

Capital
TYPICAL EXAMPLE

Label termination
TYPICAL EXAMPLE

CHOIR

NAVE

PORCH

TOWER

Interior of lancet windows
BURGH (CHANCEL), NORFOLK

Piscina and sedilia

Windows with internal tracery
STONE, KENT

4 Early English architecture – thirteenth century

Church with parapet spire
HECKINGTON, LINCOLNSHIRE

Pierced parapet
HECKINGTON, LINCOLNSHIRE

Ball flower

Curvilinear tracery
HECKINGTON, LINCOLNSHIRE

Porch with angle buttresses
BYFIELD, NORTHAMPTONSHIRE

External niche
HOUGHTON-LE-DALE, NORFOLK

Traceried window

5 Decorated architecture – fourteenth century

of so many of the larger parish churches in both the west and east Midland counties. Tithe barns in rural parishes no less than churches testify to local prosperity, particularly where abbeys were able to obtain grants to hold fairs and markets. It must be remembered that it was the abbots who laid the foundations in their Cotswold sheep-walks for the rich clothiers who built, or rebuilt, what we call 'wool churches'. They were keen businessmen who were fully alive to the value of having a prosperous laity, since a tithe of what the land produced came back to them. They encouraged the craft guilds to endow chapels and set up altars in the aisles, and they did not scruple to import 'relics' without enquiring too closely into their alleged origin, knowing that if these could be suitably enshrined they would attract pilgrims from distant places. In fact, they invented the art – or craft – of tourist attraction.

Originally, one quarter of the tithe collected by the clergy was applied to the upkeep of the church fabric. Later the nave became the responsibility of the parishioners, leaving the clergy responsible for the chancel only. This is why the chancel is so often older than the nave, with the chancel-arch a kind of no-man's land between the two.

Under the ambitious Benedictines church-building became a major industry. Schools of masons and carpenters were established, usually linked with a cathedral or abbey church, and these were sent as freemasons and journeymen carpenters round the abbot's estates to enlarge and beautify the village churches. We can still trace the movement of some of the masons in the marks and devices they cut – usually in the form of a monogram – on any work of which they were particularly proud. Masons' marks are commoner than carpenters' because normally the mason had to work on the site from a block rudely cut out for its purpose at the quarry, whereas the carpenter could probably complete his job on a bench in his workshop and pass it on to a journeyman for fixing.

In contrast to the Benedictines, who built on the grand scale, and the Cluniacs, who sometimes sought to impress the people with their wealth by commissioning extravagant styles of ornamentation, the Cistercians despised worldliness and built in the simple styles we still see in the rural areas where most of their abbeys were built. No unscrupulous importation of 'relics' for them. This love of simplicity by the Cistercians and the Orders derived from them accounts for much of the contrast between town and village churches in such counties as Yorkshire, Herefordshire, Worcestershire, and Dorset. One clue to their influence is in the carving of pier capitals in either plain-scalloped or simple water-leaf designs. Despite the wealth the Cistercians accumulated from the sale of wool from their sheep-walks in Yorkshire and Cumbria, their masons continued to build churches as they built farmsteads and sheep folds.

The Augustinian canons were more missionary-minded, and it is remarkable how much their evangelical influence continues to colour the churchmanship of many of the counties they worked in. They were strong in Essex and Yorkshire. The Gilbertian sphere of influence was almost entirely confined to Lincolnshire and the borders of the adjoining counties. Perhaps the Order with the most obvious characteristic in its church styles was the Dominican, which as a great preaching Order built churches designed to accommodate large congregations – like the one of Blythburgh in Suffolk. Although all these Orders introduced styles that can be traced to Continental sources, their masons and carpenters formed themselves into local guilds that evolved their own distinctive variations wth the spontaneity that is so often the hallmark of the Englishman's work.

Secular bishops and lay benefactors came into the field decisively in the third quarter of the thirteenth century as a result of the Statute of Mortmain (1279) putting limits on the further granting of land to abbeys and priories. This statute specifically enjoined potential benefactors to endeavour to secure the future of their souls by bestowing wealth on their parish churches. So, as the nave was the people's part of the church, it was inevitable that if this direction were to be obeyed most of the new money would go there, although the greater sanctity of the chancel would continue to attract the richer landed patrons to aspire to the great honour of being buried in an altar tomb.

The new money that came in as a result of the Statute of Mortmain explains how the period from 1280 to 1340 became the golden age of church building in England, so tragically ended by the ravages of the Black Death. Much of the new money went to raising the level of roofs. The widening of aisles to accommodate guild altars had made many churches dark and gloomy, especially those with single-span roofs coming down to within a few feet of the ground. Most of these had been steeply pitched to avoid collapse under the weight of snow. A large proportion were thatched until, towards the end of the thirteenth century, the use of lead for roofing came into vogue and during the following century revolutionised roofing styles. The reason why this did not happen more quickly is that at first lead appeared to have the insuperable defect of being liable to 'creep'. Eventually, however, it was realized that lead roofs did not require steep pitch. They could even be flat. Everyone who looks round churches with a perceptive eye must have noticed the lines left by the old roof on the tower wall above the new roof, and by extending those lines must have seen how small the original windows must have been. A light lead roof enabled the interior to be treated with greater freedom, and the outer walls to be heightened to take large windows. Clerestories could be built, and windows inserted in them. The windows in the original clerestories were circular. Soon, however, clerestory windows were designed to match those in the aisles below them. This development can be studied most fully in Northamptonshire, Lincolnshire, and East Anglia where the feeling for light has always been strongest. It was, in fact, in Lincolnshire and

neighbouring districts that the old round clerestory windows were most rapidly superseded by large two-light windows. Boston has two in each bay.

With the decline of monastic control and the arrival of a new type of lay benefactor a different style of motif came into favour. The Englishman was already distinguished by his love of nature, and this found expression in the greater number of naturalistic designs that appeared on pier capitals instead of the geometric designs that had previously been favoured. Nor did this freedom restrict itself to flora and fauna. Seven churches in north Buckinghamshire have carvings of human busts with interlaced arms on their pier capitals. There are similar carvings at Stoke Golding in south-west Leicestershire and at Bloxham and Hanwell in Oxfordshire. But the chief feature of the new style as it matured fully in the fourteenth century was its beautifully designed and structurally balanced windows, each with several lights, culminating in an arch of interlaced tracery shaped to patterns that never cease to surprise and delight. The motifs may be centred in a circle, petalled like a flower, or fashioned in curvilinear designs to form trefoils or quatrefoils either in diminishing tiers or flowing in loops and coils like those at Chipping Norton.

Most of these innovations were designed to contribute directly to both the atmosphere of worship and the convenience of worshippers. The other major advance in church architecture in the fourteenth century, the enlargement and adornment of towers, was practically entirely for kudos. Bells had been used by the Anglo-Saxons. Bede has an account of them at the church of St Hilda, Whitby; but the main purpose of most of the early towers was watch and ward. A simple bell-cote on the roof of a church was usually sufficient to carry the bell. Where not for defence, towers were landmarks to guide pilgrims across desolate marshes with few natural features. In such regions they often carried beacon lights that could be flashed from one to another across great distances. A light flashed from the tower

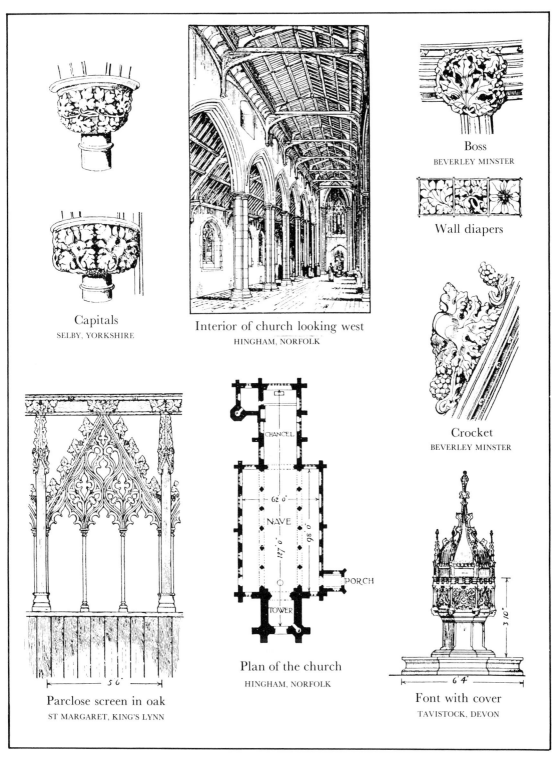

Capitals
SELBY, YORKSHIRE

Interior of church looking west
HINGHAM, NORFOLK

Boss
BEVERLEY MINSTER

Wall diapers

Crocket
BEVERLEY MINSTER

Parclose screen in oak
ST MARGARET, KING'S LYNN

Plan of the church
HINGHAM, NORFOLK

Font with cover
TAVISTOCK, DEVON

6 Decorated architecture – fourteenth century

of Nazeing church above the Lea Valley in Essex, could be picked up at St Albans.

From the reign of Edward II every parish was required to provide fully equipped soldiers for military service – the original Home Guard! – and church towers were used as safe places for the store of arms where an upper chamber of the porch was not available for the purpose, as it often was from the later years of the fifteenth century. The practice of storing arms in the church was officially discontinued after the Civil War, but it continued in many rural parishes until the nineteenth century. The tower at Baldock in Hertfordshire, for example, was stocked with helmets, pikes, and other weapons until the Victorian restoration.

But this does not mean that the tall west towers built onto so many of the old minster churches before the fourteenth century were solely for secular purposes. Many of them were built by bishops as signs that in that particular area the bishop and not the abbot ruled. There is far more significance in the local character of towers than is immediately apparant. To take two contrasting styles, it is only in relation to local history that it can be understood why simple turrets are characteristic of churches in the old Saxon kingdoms of Essex and Sussex, while towers figure so prominently along the Welsh border, where they are clearly related to the castles and fortified manor houses built near them. In fact, the word 'tower' was used only for military structures during the Middle Ages. Church towers were then called steeples, which might carry spires but not necessarily.

Away from regions constantly threatened by invaders steeples with spires became common in mountainous districts, square-topped towers in flat or gently undulating country. No doubt experience with wind pressure contributed to this distribution. We certainly know that in regions where winds gain great velocity because there is no hill to break their force spires were found so costly to maintain that any that were blown down were not rebuilt.

Spires are a separate study in their own right. The distinctively English spire is the 'broach': an octagonal spire supported by frames splayed out from the foot of the spire proper to form a square base overlapping the top of the tower. Good early styles are seen at such places as Old Romney and Bapchild in Kent, and most impressively at Shere and Merstham in Surrey. Most of them are thirteenth-century; but in the north-east Midlands towers and spires were harmonised to form a perfect unity in which the tower is just tall enough to form an impressive base to a spire that soars from its four angles, its height emphasised rather than reduced by the tiers of lights inserted to provide ventilation and allow the sound of the bells to ring out at higher levels. The presence of stone, of course, explains why this particular region got them so early.

In general, early fourteenth-century building testifies to the playing down of the liturgical purposes of the church and the expansion of social amenities in new forms of secular graciousness associated with worship. The nation was becoming 'at ease in Zion'. Alas! the mood was short lived. In the middle of the fourteenth century the Black Death put an end to this expanding movement in church architecture. In 1359 William of Wykeham impressed every good craftsman he could find into the king's service. Three years later proclamations were sent out in London and 24 counties forbidding the employment of masons by private individuals without the king's leave. On the other hand, the scourge of the Black Death turned the minds of the people to God.

As the abbots were no longer able to employ the number of masons and carpenters they had trained in an earlier, and for them more affluent age, a simpler style of architecture, the Perpendicular, was evolved. Although born of necessity it was to develop into England's major contribution to ecclesiastical building. Its distinctive style of window was introduced into the south transept of Gloucester Cathedral in the middle of the fourteenth

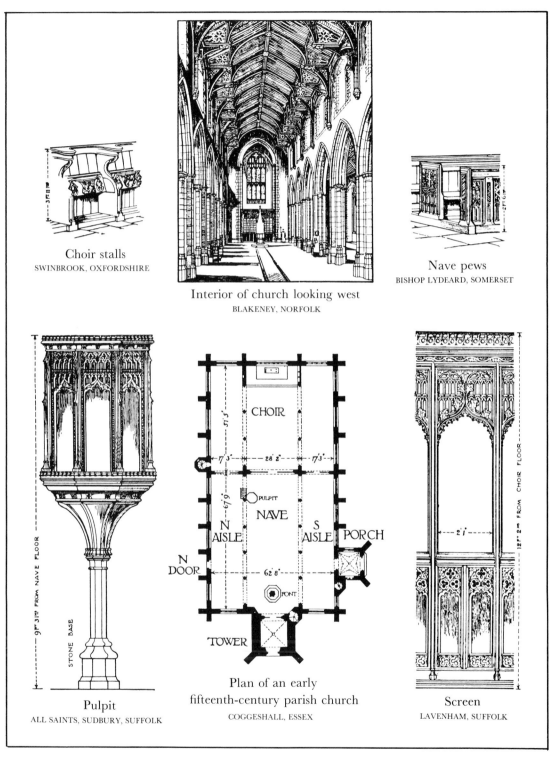

Choir stalls
SWINBROOK, OXFORDSHIRE

Interior of church looking west
BLAKENEY, NORFOLK

Nave pews
BISHOP LYDEARD, SOMERSET

Pulpit
ALL SAINTS, SUDBURY, SUFFOLK

Plan of an early
fifteenth-century parish church
COGGESHALL, ESSEX

Screen
LAVENHAM, SUFFOLK

7 Perpendicular architecture – fifteenth century

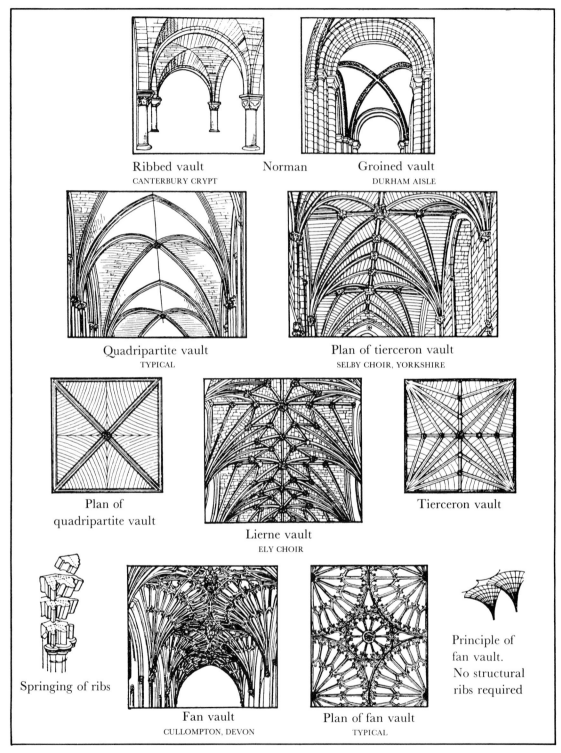

Ribbed vault
CANTERBURY CRYPT

Norman

Groined vault
DURHAM AISLE

Quadripartite vault
TYPICAL

Plan of tierceron vault
SELBY CHOIR, YORKSHIRE

Plan of
quadripartite vault

Lierne vault
ELY CHOIR

Tierceron vault

Springing of ribs

Fan vault
CULLOMPTON, DEVON

Plan of fan vault
TYPICAL

Principle of
fan vault.
No structural
ribs required

8 Medieval Vaulting – Twelfth to Fourteenth Century

century by a master mason whose name has not come down to us, simply as a contrivance for bringing in more light. But as light was already seen as the most urgent need of the congregations that now assembled in churches, not only for the purpose of following the sacred offices intoned by the priests, but to sit and listen in comfort to the messages of the new preachers who were coming into the parishes, larger windows rapidly spread throughout the South of England where the wealth of the clothiers was making rebuilding possible. The masons who could no longer be employed by the impoverished abbots, most of whose affairs were already in a muddle, found new masters in the clothiers, who could pay them well and were willing to be guided by them in making plans for churches that would not only glorify God, but be lasting monuments to themselves. And because these new employers had the ready money to complete a building in a single contract the new churches of the Perpendicular period were to become architectural show-pieces because they had a uniformity of style that had seldom been possible earlier.

With the dissolution of the monasteries the 300-year rule of the abbots ended. The Sovereign became the head of the Church in England and landowners became lay rectors, with rights in the chancel that had hitherto been reserved for the clergy. At Dunster in Somerset the whole of the chancel was reserved for the use of the Luttrell family at the Castle, which, considerations of privilege apart, was better than allowing it to fall into decay as so many chancels did when no-one could decide who was now responsible for their maintenance. These disputes about maintenance were by no means always irrational. The chancels in collegiate churches were often too large for any use the parishioners could put them to. In these circumstances it might appear sensible to demolish them, as was done at Waltham Abbey in Essex. In other places, as at Abbey Dore in Herefordshire and Boxgrove in Sussex only the chancel was retained, while in a few

places, of which Tewkesbury is the best known, the parishioners took over both nave and chancel and in doing so set problems for their successors which have been valiantly shouldered in each generation.

Church furnishings had to be readapted to meet the altered needs of worshippers and the enhanced status of the laity. So pews, which had been installed in many churches towards the end of the fourteenth century, became universal in the fifteenth and sixteenth. Although very few churches indeed were built during the reign of Elizabeth I, with the 'Elizabethan Settlement' lay status was stabilised in the custom of having the lord of the manor, as rector's warden, undertaking to be regular in attendance at Matins himself, and to see that his tenants were equally so. This secularisation was further strengthened by the custom of appointing clergymen to the Commission of the Peace, a practice that was of great value in rural areas, where the parson might be the only educated person resident in the parish.

At the time when this practice was discontinued by a Liberal Lord Chancellor, except for clergymen 'without a cure of souls', one in four of all active J.P.s in England was in Holy Orders, and some were chairmen of Quarter Sessions. The attitude of the clergy to this limitation of their civil authority was well illustrated in letters I once came across from an Essex clergyman who wrote to the Lord Lieutenant to ask why he had not been appointed to the Bench as his predecessors in the living had been. When told the reason, he wrote again asking how he could be expected to preach morality effectively from the pulpit on Sunday if he was denied the authority to enforce it from the Bench on Monday.

Such letters illustrate the typical attitude of the English churchman, whether lay or clerical, as it developed after the Reformation, both to the styling of the parish church and to its furnishings. In 1603 an order was made requiring every parish church to have a 'comely and decent pulpit', and with the pulpit the stage was set for the full impact of Protestantism. The James I Bible followed, and in 1662 the Book of Common Prayer that so many of us are saddened to see discarded. Let us hope that the discarding of hallowed language is not to be followed by the discarding of hallowed buildings!

The Bible reigned supreme throughout the seventeenth century and much of the eighteenth. Texts were painted on walls that had formerly been decorated with figures of St Christopher, or representations of 'Christ in Glory', the 'Harrowing of Hell' or one or other of several superstitious legends. Practically every sermon preached by the new clergy was a practical homily on the rewards that might be expected from the practice of 'true religion and virtue' and the punishment that would surely follow 'wickedness and vice'.

In most churches during these palmy days of Protestantism the parson in the pulpit was on good terms with the squire in the manor pew, to whom he was probably related. If not, when a living came vacant the patron would be as much concerned to find a suitable companion for himself as a faithful priest for the people. The relationship is well illustrated in *Spectator* No. 106, where we are told that Sir Roger de Coverley, in appointing to a living of which he was patron, required a man 'rather of plain sense than much learning, of good aspect, a clear voice, a sociable temper; and, if possible, a man that understood a little of back-gammon'. When this paragon was found Sir Roger 'made him a present of all the good sermons which have been printed in English, and only begged of him that every Sunday he would pronounce one of them in the pulpit'. This reverend gentleman continued to give complete satisfaction for more than 30 years. 'I could heartily wish', comments the *Spectator*, 'that more of our country clergy would follow his example; and instead of wasting their spirits in laborious compositions of their own, would endeavour after a handsome elocution, and all those talents that are proper to enforce what has been penned by greater masters'. This, in fact,

is what most of them did!

In a sense, the link established in Norman times between the lord of the manor and the rector of the parish had come full circle. The intervening monastic dominance had gone. Bishops were drawn from the universities, parish clergy from the minor gentry, and church architecture began to reflect the change in the square-topped windows that displaced the arched and traceried windows of Gothic styles. The furnishings of churches similarly reflected manor house comfort rather than monastic austerity. Beautiful brass candelabra and chandeliers hung from plastered ceilings. The Royal Arms were prominently displayed. Hatchments hung from roof timbers from which angels had been shot down by Cromwell's Ironsides, and by the end of the seventeenth century the churches were ready to adapt themselves fully in classical style to the Age of Reason, with box pews in the nave and a suitably secluded squire's pew, furnished with fireplace, cushions and books of Common Prayer bound in tooled leather. The new churches built in styles derived from those built by Sir Christopher Wren after the Great Fire of London, were stylish to a degree that left little scope for the vernacular or the enterprising use of local material by estate masons. Village churches were built by City architects, and local style became a thing of the past.

Happily the *genius loci* is still preserved for us in thousands of parish churches standing proudly on a knoll to the north of the village, with the largest part of the churchyard between the church and the houses clustered below it. This is the ideal situation, since the sun shines on the south wall most of the day, symbolising a meaning that was understood by the masons who cut a sundial on the wall, usually of the porch, giving the doorway a significance that is both sheltering and welcoming. The path to the door in such churches runs between gravestones carved with the recurring names of local families, many of which have been recorded in the local parish register since parish registers were started by Act of Parliament in 1538. Some of these names go back to Domesday. The name Purkiss must have been at Minstead in the New Forest for 900 years, since it was in a cart belonging to a member of this family that the body of William Rufus was carried to Winchester for burial. The name is still there. Such names give unity to a parish, and where they appear on gravestones that are of the same stone as the church they should never be removed to be ranged in meaningless conformity against the churchyard wall. They are part of the church, and of its life of witness through times of trial by famine, pestilence, war, and oppression from within and without – memorials to 'our fathers that begat us'.

2 South-East England

KENT – SUSSEX – SURREY

Kent is the obvious starting point historically, since it was to Canterbury that St Augustine came as the first Christian missionary to the Anglo-Saxons. It is less obviously the best starting point for a journey in search of local styles, since in addition to the hard, rough-surfaced rag, quarried in the greensand round Maidstone from Norman times, it has a greater variety of building material than most counties, and as the point of arrival of countless waves of immigrants its building styles have been influenced from the Continent more than those in any other part of Britain. In short, the churches of Kent are remarkable for their diversity of styles rather than for their distinctive character.

Most of the county's first churches would be built of timber from the Weald. None remains. Even the log churches built so enthusiastically in the tenth century by St Dunstan, the Saxon Archbishop of Canterbury, have either rotted away or been replaced by stone churches, most of which remain only in such fragments as the double-splayed windows found in at least 34 churches in Kent. Fortunately, sufficient is left of the most important pre-Conquest church in the county, the minster founded in 669 at Reculver, to enable us to identify in it the original plan for the South-East of England, with its apsidal chancel and aisleless nave, while at Dover, in the tenth- or early eleventh-century chapel of St Mary-in-Castro, we have the complete plan of the cruciform church of

the period, with circular windows in the central tower, and double-splayed windows in the body of the church.

As evidence of early rebuilding there is Norman work in a hundred or so Kent churches; but of these only Barfreston and Patrixbourne are 'musts' for the purpose of bringing the building styles of the whole county into focus. Both are of far more than local importance and pages would have to be devoted to them in a fully architectural study of styles. Their importance for our present purpose is that they put us on the scent of what will be the most useful clue to the whys and wherefores of local styles everywhere: the influence of a cathedral. In the case of these two it was obviously Rochester, where work round the cathedral's west door leaves little doubt that the same masons were employed in all three. Their distinguishing feature is the quality of the carving, which is in Caen stone and much finer than anything that could be accomplished by local masons in Kentish rag.

The motifs at Barfreston and Patrixbourne have often been compared with those on the famous Norman church at Kilpeck in Herefordshire; but they are less grotesque. In any case the comparison is unfair since Caen limestone was much more workable for this kind of carving than the hard red sandstone of Herefordshire. From the local point of view, the most important feature is the cornice of carved heads below the eaves: important because it is found in so many Kent churches of the mid-thirteenth century. There is so much fun in these carvings that we cannot help seeing them not so much as expressions of skill, which of course they are, as of medieval zest for life.

The proximity of London and the primacy of Canterbury brought into Kent in the late thirteenth and early fourteenth centuries craftsmen capable of work far beyond the scope of local masons and carpenters. Their best craftsmanship is in the nave arcades at Stone, near Dartford, where the carving is attributed to the master sculptors employed by Henry III at Westminster Abbey. G. H. Cook in *The English Mediaeval Parish Church* says: 'The Geometrical tracery of the windows bears a strong resemblance to that at Westminster, and the wall arcading, carried by detached shafts of Purbeck marble, is the same as that in the choir chapels of the abbey. In no other church is there such graceful and refined Early English foliage as in the spandrels of the wall arcading at Stone.'

Kent was later to give its own name to a style of curvilinear tracery that seems to have originated with master masons working at Canterbury Cathedral during the thirteenth century. This so-called 'Kent tracery' spread as far north as Cartmel and Whitby, as far west as Beaulieu, and as far across the Midlands as Solihull and Chaddesley Corbett. Its characteristic is the free use of such geometric devices as downward-pointing cusps to form stars, trefoils, and designs resembling naturally dentated leaves. Good work in these designs is to be seen in Kent at Herne, Cliffe-at-Hoo, Ightham, and Penshurst. The best is at Penshurst and over the Sussex border at Battle and Winchelsea.

Kent is unusually rich in the variety of its sandstones, including an interesting conglomerate formed of particles of sand or quartz held together by a kind of silica, or oxide of iron and clay, found in the greensand that lies between the Weald and the Downs. But the most localised stone in the county, also found near Petworth in Sussex, is what is called 'Kent marble' and comes from quarries at Bethersden. Barham refers to it in the *Ingoldsby Legends* in the lines:

His tomb in the chancel stands there to this day,
Built of Bethersden marble–a darkish blue-grey.

The correct name for this 'marble', which is formed of the fossilised shells of snails trapped when lakes in the Weald silted up millions of years ago, and can now be polished to brilliant blues and browns, is winkle-stone. We see it in the cathedrals of Canterbury and Rochester, and in any number of parish churches where fonts and altars are carved from it. At Biddenden slabs of winkle-stone even form the pavements of the village street, and a church path at Tenterden was restored with it in 1975 as a fitting local contribution to European Architectural Year.

In sorting out the rich variety of building styles in Kent in search of what is distinctively local, the difficulty arises from the county having scores of outstandingly well-built churches of medium size with little that is distinctive about them except their towers. Despite the dispersed wealth of the county there are few churches in Kent built by rich industrialists like the woolmen of East Anglia and the Cotswolds, and there are only two important churches in Kent built in the best Perpendicular style: All Saints, Maidstone, a collegiate church of secular canons started by Archbishop Courtenay in 1395, and the late-Perpendicular 'cathedral of the Weald' at Cranbrook, where the cloth-weaving industry flourished longer than anywhere else in the county. The other tower that immediately comes to mind when Cranbrook's is mentioned is Tenterden's, the lower stages of which are of Bethersden 'marble'. Tenterden was not only the other important centre of the wool trade in Kent but was united to the ancient town of Rye and had all its port privileges. So if we think exclusively in terms of the wool trade we must regard Cranbrook as being the only great 'wool church' in Kent. But this is not surprising. Neither Sussex nor Surrey has even one.

The most active period for church building in Kent was the thirteenth century, and monastic influence is everywhere apparent in what it produced. This is seen particularly in the number of chancels that are larger than would be required by the parish clergy, and in the provision made for the medieval Sunday processions, which were not allowed to leave consecrated ground. To accommodate these processions Kent has four vaulted chancels, nine towers with vaults over the bottom stage, and at Wrotham a west tower with a vaulted passage underneath it, built there because the tower abuts on the highway. At St Leonard's, Hythe, which claims to have the finest chancel in any English parish church, a vaulted passage constructed for processions runs round the east end.

After the thirteenth century most of the money for church building in Kent came from the gentry and well-to-do-yeomen. Once substantial clearings had been made in the Weald the soil was found to be much more productive than that of either Sussex or Surrey, and gavelkind inheritance, whereby estates descended to all the sons in equal shares, enabled the vigorous men who cultivated it to accumulate means to maintain their churches as well as their estates. There was much rivalry between them as public benefactors. Many wills contain clauses that make it clear that in leaving money for the maintenance of the parish church, the testator's object was to bring his own parish church into line with one in a neighbouring parish that had benefitted by a similar bequest. This, in fact, puts us on to a clue to local styles that will be found useful in every part of the kingdom: while churches built by religious Orders can often be recognised by distinctive styles originating from the Continent, those built by local benefactors are usually found to be copies of churches in neighbouring parishes. This must go a long way towards explaining the practical, dignified, and serviceable style that developed for church towers in the Kentish Weald, particularly in the older villages, with names

ending in -den, where the Kentish swine-pastures were.

Practically all these typically local towers are built of ragstone, often mingled with the attractive firestone that came from quarries near Reigate in Surrey. In fact, the variety of colour found in churches of this period is a constant delight, and nowhere can this be seen more attractively than in the porch of Igtham church, where the colours go through the entire range of sandstones from that of bleached sea-shore sand to the dark brown stone quarried in the Folkestone beds.

The most prominent architectural feature of Kentish towers is that they have octagonal stair-turrets built on to either the south-east or the north-east angle, which rise above a plain battlemented parapet. These sturdy towers, usually with square-headed windows in the top stage, are found at the west end of one quarter of the county's churches, and the consistency in their design suggests that money was usually available to pay for them from the day they were started, while their plainness shows that these solid Kentish folk were not given to over-reaching themselves or showing-off. They also demonstrate that local masons were too fully conscious of the limitations of local rag to try to imitate what could be done with a chisel in Caen limestone. So mouldings tend to be bold and rough, and there are few niches for images. But for simple dignity, and often for the rugged beauty of local stone they represent country-style building at its best.

Another characteristic of the churches of Kent, and to a lesser extent of Sussex, is the lateral placing of so many towers. T. D. Atkinson, in *Local Style in English Architecture*, records finding 'one lateral steeple to every four or five placed at one end or other of the nave' in Kent. This positioning is not unknown elsewhere, but to have so large a proportion laterally placed does make it a local characteristic, which is probably explained by one builder copying another.

From these churches in the heart of the county, reflecting so strongly the prosperity of

9 New Romney, Kent: massive Norman tower, with pinnacled top stage added to serve as a landmark for mariners

the land, the reference to Folkestone immediately conjures up a vision of that other ancient face of Kent: Romney Marsh. As the churches of the Marsh do not, in fact, resemble each other, the term 'local atmosphere' is more appropriate than 'local style' in describing them. No matter how different from each other they may be, they all 'belong'. The pride of the Marsh is, of course, St Nicholas at New Romney, the chief of the Cinque Ports. Its great tower, rising in five stages – four of which are Norman – to a height of 100 feet, has served as a landmark for mariners for 800 years, although New Romney ceased to be a port in the reign of Edward I when a violent storm deflected the River Rother away from it.

Old Romney introduces us to another typical type of Kentish tower: a simple squat structure with a shingled broach spire sitting like a dunce's cap on the top of it. Lydd, called

'the cathedral of the Marsh' in this cathedral-conscious county, was heavily bombed during the Second World War but has been carefully restored. Like New Romney it has a wealth of brass memorials, a feature for which Kent is pre-eminent among English counties – as it is incidentally for lych-gates. At St Mary-in-the-Marsh we have a fourth thirteenth-century church in the sheep pastures, with a shingled spire like those of so many other churches in the South-East, but one that should be visited to see box pews of a type that was once characteristic of old marshland churches.

The other church to be visited to get the feel of this lonely marshland and the life it sustained is at Brookland on the road to Rye, if only to see the most important of the county's many lead fonts and the detached bell-tower. This remarkable thirteenth-century font has two tiers of round-headed arcading round the bowl, the upper tier decorated with the Signs of the Zodiac, the lower with the Occupations of the Months, another favourite subject. The belfry is shingled and octagonal, so conforms basically to the usual plan for broach spires;

31

10   Sandwich, Kent: late Norman tower
with external wall-arcades

but is in three diminishing stages, the whole
locked together by massive timbers arranged
satirewise, which are said to have been
salvaged from wrecks.

It would be confusing to follow up all the
stylistic links between the churches of Kent
and those of other counties; but the links that
cannot be left out are those with the churches
of the extreme South-West of England. Both
regions have tall towers, their height accen-
tuated by the lack of clerestories to the naves.
This similarity is not surprising since in both
regions towers were built for watch and ward.
Nor is their plainness significant except as a
reminder that both Cornish granite and
Kentish rag are intractable stones for carving.
But how does one explain the way both Kent
and Cornwall came to adopt the custom of
building aisles under separate roofs, running
without break alongside both chancel and
nave to terminate in three gables of equal

height at the east end? Most visitors must have
noticed them, if only at New Romney in the
south of Kent and Westerham in the north
near the Surrey border. Some of these aisles
seem to have been added as early as the
thirteenth century, and as they appear to be
wider than would be needed for processional
purposes they may have been built either by
one of the great preaching Orders to
accommodate large congregations, or by
guilds for altars, many of which would be
enclosed with screens.

As we move towards the border with Sussex
we become increasingly aware that besides
the yeomen and the landed gentry as church
benefactors in Kent there were the ironmasters. They can be discussed more usefully in
connection with the Sussex churches, but
before leaving Kent we should visit Staple-
hurst, between Cranbrook and Maidstone, to
see the most remarkable display of twelfth-
century hammered ironwork to be found
anywhere.

Among the great ironmasters of the
Kentish Weald were the Streatfeilds of

11　Westerham, Kent: local style of triple roofs extending to gables at east end (common also in Cornwall)

Chiddingstone, many of whom lie under ironstone grave slabs in the churchyard: the oldest to the memory of Richard Streatfeild who died 'greene in yeres but ripe in faith and frutes' in 1601. There are many of these iron slabs in west Kent and east Sussex, where the oldest is at Kipling's Burwash. Wadhurst has 30 of them, dating from 1614 to 1790. But despite the long period in which it was worked in the Weald, and ironmasters' houses like Kipling's 'Batemans', iron can never have yielded wealth comparable with that produced elsewhere during the fourteenth and fifteenth centuries from wool.

In fact, the Sussex Weald was worked for iron from pre-historic times. In some of the east Sussex parishes with names ending in -field or -hurst there is hardly a field in which rough hummocky surfaces do not appear as evidence that the land has been gone over for iron, while in coppiced woodland round Mayfield and Heathfield small water-filled hollows show where the bell-shaped pits associated with iron-digging have been less carefully filled in than those in the fields.

It is in these places with -field as the last syllable of their names that we find the larger churches in which to look for local styles that can be compared with those of Kent. The best churches in east Sussex are the group in which the great Pelham family left their mark in a carved buckle, the badge granted to them after the Battle of Poitiers. It is not only found in 11 of the county's best churches but also on innumerable fire-back plates in Sussex farmhouses.

The most marked difference between the general run of towers in the two counties is that those in Sussex tend to have been built over a much longer period, suggesting that the need for repair or replacement rather than prestige explains their growth. This is an acceptable explanation if we bear in mind that iron-smelting depended on the availability of timber, and that the clearing of woodland was a slow and sporadic process achieved from dispersed settlements which, for the purposes of church organisation, were administered from a minster. As the plan for these was introduced by St Dunstan, as Archbishop of Canterbury, the South-East of England might be expected to have pioneered the system, as indeed it did.

The churches at Mayfield, Rotherfield, and Heathfield in particular reflect the characteristic evolution of parish church styling in this kind of country. Much of the enlargement of all three dates from the fourteenth century. Mayfield, the most fascinating of the churches of the Sussex Weald, and one that we must return to in a moment, was the mother church of Hadlow Down, Tidebrook, Burwash Weald and other smaller hamlets; Heathfield, 'the capital of the Sussex highlands', where guns were made until 1755 and the furnaces continued to glow until 1787, served a parish extending over 8,000 acres including Broadoak, Paine's Cross, Pummetts Town, Vines Cross, and Cade Street; Rotherfield nurtured to independence part of Mark Cross and the present parishes of Jarvis Brook and Crowborough. The effect of this slow growth from the social point of view is that the churches of Rotherfield and Heathfield have folk interest rather than architectural unity.

Rotherfield's social development is reflected in a Custumal of 1346 which shows that each of the farmers in the parish had originally cultivated a *ferling* of land extending from 100 to 150 acres; but by 1346 each of these holdings was supporting several families in small hamlets into which the parish had been subdivided. This growth is reflected in the church, which began as a building of modest proportions in the thirteenth century, acquired a fine tower in the fifteenth, and in the sixteenth got the imposing block of private pews which still rise like a Grand Stand at the west end of the church. They were installed at their own expense in 1532 by prosperous parishioners, who maintained them for the exclusive use of their own families, exercising

even the right, real or presumed, to sell or bequeath them. They may now be in modified form, since accounts have survived describing the partitions being so high that an average-sized man's chin would only reach the top when he stood for the singing of hymns.

At Warbleton, another ironmaster's church, there is none of this nonsense, as the lords of the manors would regard it, of multiple dominance. There the lord of the manor in 1722 showed the parishioners who ruled the parish by erecting for the use of himself and his household an extraordinary galleried pew which is still in use. Here the tall tower, visible from a great distance and used as a signalling post and place of refuge from persecution during Mary I's reign, is entered from the nave through an iron-clad door fitted with an elaborate locking mechanism believed to be the work of a local ironmaster named Richard Woodman, who despite his skill in inventing defensive devices suffered martyrdom at Lewes in 1557.

Heathfield's tower is built of chalk and only faced with sandstone. There is nothing outstanding about the church as a building; but scratched in the chalk of the east inside wall of the main chamber of the tower is the date 1445 in arabic numerals. This is claimed to be the earliest use of them in England. It would be interesting to know how valid the claim is. What is not in dispute is that the tablet with a figurehead in terra-cotta in the north-east corner of the tower, along with several headstones in the churchyard, preserve the memory of a pottery that flourished in Heathfield for a time as well as the memories of the deceased they commemorate.

Mayfield is the most attractive of the villages of the Sussex highlands, even if the village sign, which derives the 'May' in the name from 'Maid', may be of doubtful authenticity. Surely the more likely derivation is from the aromatic plant which the Saxons called by a name that might be modernised as 'mayweed', and we call camomile. However that may be, the derivation of the church's dedication to St

Dunstan is not in doubt. It could have no other. St Dunstan, the founder, had a forge and palace nearby, and Eadmer, the Canterbury chronicler, has an engaging legend that when the saint went round the original log church in the dedication procession he observed that it was 'out of the line of sanctity', which means that it was not accurately orientated. To correct this he applied the weight of his body to it and pressed it into shape. The legend is interesting because it is so well worth bearing in mind in connection with the legend that leaning chancels were constructed out of line in order to represent the inclination of Our Lord's head on the Cross. In fact, they are usually survivals from an earlier church which, like St Dunstan's, was 'out of the line of sanctity'.

Parts of the church which succeeded the original log church at Mayfield survive in the tower and round the lancet window in the west wall of the north aisle. But the most interesting feature from the point of view of local style is that the present nave dates from the first quarter of the fifteenth century and represents early Perpendicular style in Sussex at its best, while the unusually large fourteenth-century chancel is striking evidence of the parish retaining independent clerical control after this had declined in Heathfield, Rotherfield, and Warbleton. The parish is now in the Chichester diocese; but it was an ecclesiastical 'peculiar' for a thousand years.

The stone at Mayfield is from a local quarry, and like so much local stone in the South-East is one of the church's main attractions. From the point of view of colour, the sandstone quarried in the vicinity of East Grinstead would probably be voted the most characteristic; but Tilegate stone has weathered better and has proved the most workable for decorative carving. We see it in the towers of Brightling, Fletching, Lenhurst, and Lindfield – one of the few churches in Sussex that became fully Gothic.

Because it splits into thin slabs for roofing, the best-known Sussex stone comes from Horsham. The characteristic of Horsham roofs is that they are carried in a single span over nave and aisles, descending in some cases to within a few feet of the ground, so are in sharp contrast to the triple-gabled roofs of Kent. Their disadvantage is that the weight of the slabs is so great that the pitch has to be low and rest on a massive oak frame, which tends to make the larger churches dark and even gloomy in daylight. It would be to gain more light that Mayfield's roof, originally of this 'catslide' variety, was raised during the reign of Henry VIII.

These churches with single-span roofs usually – perhaps invariably in Sussex – have the broach spires on low towers that are so characteristic of churches in the South-East. Although architecturally less impressive than the stone broach spires of the East Midlands, they have a home-made friendly air that harmonises well with the gentler landscape of the Weald. The shingles that roof them were traditionally of split oak. Now they are being replaced with Canadian cedar, which although not local is thinner, smoother, and weathers to a pleasant silver-grey. A peculiarly local aspect of the Sussex broach spire – many of which on the smaller churches surmount tiny weather-boarded bell-turrets – is that they are often built between the chancel and the nave, indicating that the Roman plan remained in favour in Sussex after it had been superseded in other counties.

The interest in this last feature is that it is yet one more instance of the continuity of style for which Sussex is so remarkable. The explanation must be derived from the kingdom of the South Saxons having such a self-sufficient economy and having been evangelised early. When St Wilfrid landed at Bosham (Bozzam) in 681, after being expelled from his native Northumberland, he found a colony of Benedictine monks already there. Bosham's present church was built after the manor had been annexed to the See of Canterbury in 1035, and although it is the best known of the pre-Conquest churches in West Sussex there are so many of eleventh-

12 Findon, Sussex: downland flint church, twelfth century

that there was vigorous building by local masons during Edward the Confessor's reign – and Edward, it may be remembered, was 'all Frenchified' – so these Saxon masons were able both to benefit from the supervision of those brought over from Normandy for the building of Chichester Cathedral at the end of the eleventh century, and to contribute their own skill in the use of flint, the commonest building material throughout the South-East.

But while this, no doubt, explains how Sussex came to be so rich in eleventh-century churches, it does not fully explain the conservatism that continued to be so characteristic of the county's building styles. An important factor in this is that many Norman lords of Sussex manors, instead of building churches themselves, as lords of manors did in most other counties, were grateful for what were there already, and gave of their wealth to the founding of small local priories, which began as dependencies of French abbeys and never achieved independence. Parts of these ancient priories can still be identified in the walls of farmhouses and farm-buildings all over West Sussex. Some can only be reached today through farmyards, as at North Marden, or across fields as below the Downs at Didling.

The only two influential religious houses in East Sussex were the Benedictine abbey at Battle, and the Cluniac priory at Lewes, which left no major church in the town as a memorial to its wealth, although Cluniac influence is seen in some of the village churches as well as at Ashford and Tenterden in Kent. With both, the characteristics of their architecture are not those we should normally associate with Sussex. After the Dissolution the whole of Sussex became a county of great landowners like the Dukes of Norfolk and Richmond and the Lords Leconfield, who by restricting industrial development contributed so much to the conservation of its natural beauty.

century date in this part of the county that they must all be viewed as a local style inviting explanation. Of these, St Rumbold's in the southern suburb of Chichester, and the churches at West Hampnett and Ovingdean – all mid-eleventh-century – resemble each other to the extent of having chancels that must originally have been almost identical in their measurements. Worth has an apsidal sanctuary – a rare feature in a pre-Conquest church.

Whereas in most parts of England there was little church building done either immediately before or immediately after the Conquest, the amount done in Sussex makes the region south of the Downs, and in particular the fascinating district on the Hampshire border, an incomparable field for studying the overlap of Saxon and Norman styles. The combination of the two suggests

13 Sompting, Sussex: downland church with 'Rhenish helm' spire on Saxon tower

The villages under the foothills of the Downs are so closely linked with the 'hill', as local people call the Downs, that in practically all of them the main street leads directly up to it, showing that they were shepherds' villages, with shepherds' churches, as distinct from the ironmasters' churches of the Weald. We see this, for example, at Findon behind Worthing, anciently the scene of a great sheep fair, where the flint church dates from 1150. This is a very different link between parish churches and wealth-producing sheep from that in the great abbey towns, ruled by abbots whose flocks grazed on the marshes of East Anglia or the Wolds of the West Midlands. These downland churches served the kind of shepherds W. H. Hudson wrote about in *Nature in Downland*. There are none of them left now; but in a forge at Pyecombe where shepherd's crooks were made in the sixteenth-century the same crooks are now made for bishops.

Sussex folk continue to love their homely flint churches. Although Up Marden's thirteenth-century gem, found behind a barn on the western slopes, is no longer used, its brick floor, plastered walls and box pews are as well cared for as they could be if services were held there regularly. The churches at Patching and Clapham, the one plain and barnlike, the other near a derelict brick-and-tile farmhouse, are in villages included in the old estate of the Shelley family, which extended from Poling to Shoreham. Woolbeding, west of Midhurst, is in an entirely rural setting, and Lyminster, north of Littlehampton, clearly began with an exceptionally tall aisleless nave and chancel of the same type as Woolbeding's. Commenting on it Pevsner says: 'It suggests rather amusingly that the Normans were quite nonplussed with the strange proportions they found.'

While in the Littlehampton district Yapton, in the cornfields north-west of the resort, might be visited as a typically Sussex-style church of the 1180 to 1220 period, and particularly to see the influence of Chichester Cathedral in the carving in hard chalk of the scalloped, or fluted, pier capitals.

On the lower slopes of the Downs to the east of Worthing is Sompting, with the famous 'Rhenish helm' tower – rare but not unique – that looks so un-English that a rumour got about that it was not original. To establish the truth, Cecil Hewett climbed inside it and fully satisfied himself that the timbers were nearly 1,000 years old, and were built into the tower.

Over the Downs lie Bramber, Upper Beeding, and Steyning, with a fine collegiate church in which Norman influence remains strong. The arcades have late-Norman chevron mouldings; the nave is lofty and spacious, with a clerestory and a chancel arch 38 feet high. About 1600 the original central tower was replaced by one in flint and stone chequer work. Today the whole fabric is of great dignity, while at the same time restrained and unostentatious in true Sussex style.

Many of the churches on this side of the Downs were remodelled from existing material in the thirteenth century and are notable for having more personal and manorial features in both their names and their furnishings than are found in churches south of the Downs. Edburton was founded by Edburgh, King Alfred's daughter, about 950; Poynings derives its name from the Poynings lords of the manor, two of whom left money for its rebuilding in 1368–9, which places it in the same decade as St Andrew's, Alfriston, which has changed little since it was built in the form of a Greek cross about 1360. These churches are especially to be noted because they represent the final development of Gothic architecture in downland Sussex.

The reason why the fourteenth- and fifteenth-century churches in Sussex are confined to small areas is because the county suffered more than most from the ravages of the Black Death in the middle of the fourteenth century, and the charm of both Poynings and Alfriston is that they retain so closely their connection with the Downs behind them. When a shepherd was buried at Alfriston in 1932 the ancient custom of placing a tuft of sheep's wool in his fingers was

14 Steyning, Sussex: twelfth-century nave with clerestory, tower with flint and stone chequer-work, *c.* 1600

observed. The modern churchyard gates were made by local blacksmiths; the lectern and oak doors in the church were made locally in 1958. Alfriston, too, has its local style of font – seen also at Eastbourne, Willingdon, and Westdean – with a plain square bowl mounted on a pedestal with octagonal shafts.

From Alfriston we may drive or walk through the lovely Cuckmere valley to East-dean, calling on the way at Lullington – so small that it cannot seat more than 20 in comfort,* Westdean and Friston (where the font is of winkle-stone) before finally reaching the church at Eastdean that has been so tastefully restored and enlarged. Here we see the style of churchyard gate peculiar to Sussex called a tapsell from the name of the Wadhurst blacksmith who made them. Their unique feature is that they are pivoted in the middle.

Every ancient church on the Downs round Eastbourne and in the Cuckmere Valley has a north as well as a south door. Most of the north doors are now bricked up. In Sussex they were called 'Devil's doors' from the belief that the Devil used them to escape from the church after being exorcised and expelled by the regenerative power of baptism.

This, then, is the Sussex that Kipling knew so well and celebrated with such historical accuracy as well as poetical perception in the lines:

Here, through the strong and shadeless days
The tinkling silence thrills;
Or little, lost, Down churches praise
The Lord who made the hills:
But here the Old Gods guard their round,
And, in her secret heart,
The heathen kingdom Wilfrid found
Dreams, as she dwells apart.

* Lullington is only the chancel of the original church.

39

When we move into Surrey we may see much less that is different from what we saw in Sussex than we saw in Sussex when we moved out of Kent. Both Surrey and Sussex were poor relations of Kent when their churches were acquiring their distinctive styles. Flint predominates in Surrey as in Sussex, and outside the Greater London area we may feel that there is little in their building styles to distinguish them. If we run into Surrey from Westerham, the first village we reach is Limpsfield, where St Peter's has a late twelfth-century squat tower, pyramid capped like those in Sussex, a 'catslide' roof, a fourteenth-century lych-gate, while the rest of the building is true to the prevailing thirteenth-century style common to both counties.

Tandridge has a typical late-Norman and thirteenth-century church, with a belfry supported by massive cross-braced timbers splendidly in harmony with the Wealden farmhouses found in the woodland belts of both counties. Here we may look again for ironmasters' churches, and when we reach Crowhurst, which is in the same part of the Weald, but has walls of sandstone and a late fifteenth-century belfry carrying one of Surrey's tallest spires, we may think we have

found one on spotting an iron grave slab. Alas! it is the only one in the county.

By this time we may begin to sense individual character in Surrey, although it is not until we reach Godstone and Merstham, built of the beautiful firestone – a calcareous fine-grained sandstone – quarried in both parishes – that we become conscious of being well and truly in a different county. From here we run into heathland that is as quintessentially Surrey as downland is Sussex. The scale and geology of the landscape too become noticeably different. Instead of Kipling's bare-backed downs with lonely and apparently deserted churches in or near farmsteads we have greensand hills as the setting for small friendly churches on furze-covered knolls, reached through lych-gates along a flagged path leading between ancient yews to a low-roofed building with a white, weather-boarded bell-turret. However similar individual features may be to those in churches elsewhere, we know that collectively they represent Surrey.

Away from the heaths there is the Surrey that can most easily be identified as the 'fold' country: Chiddingfold, Dunsfold, Alfold (pronounced Arfold), with Chiddingfold as their parent settlement – villages that have an air of well-being which clearly predates stockbroker infiltration. They are linked by ancient lanes winding through oak woods and coppices

15 Merstham, Surrey: thirteenth-century tower of local firestone with shingled broach spire

16 Compton, Surrey: commandingly arched nave arcades and double chancel arches, *c.* 1170, in Surrey's finest eleventh- to twelfth-century church

where trees were felled, as in the Sussex Weald, to provide timber for village industries. Place-names with descriptive terminals are always late and indicate that the land had to be cleared before it could be settled and cultivated. Dunsfold's church is the most impressive late thirteenth-century church in the county. Its shingled spire was added in the fifteenth century, and the main door is reinforced with locally forged ironwork. But the clue to local prosperity in this part of Surrey is more likely to be found in records of its short-lived prosperity from the making of glass than of iron. Money produced from glass gave Chiddingfold its great west tower, tall fifteenth-century arcades, and fragments of local glass in the west window.

It is in this part of the Surrey Weald that we find the fine carpentry that puts the county in a higher class than its neighbours for church craftsmanship. The best fourteenth-century Surrey porches are comparable with those of Essex rather than with those of Sussex or Kent. We see them at Bisley, Elstead, Ewhurst, Merrow, Pyrford, Seale, and Wisley. There is also a similarity with Essex in the way some of the wooden turrets are supported by massive balks of timber (although many more are supported by tie-beams) as at Dunsfold, Alford, and Tandridge. These usually carry slender spires, called flèches, from the French word for arrow, which gave us the surname Fletcher for an arrow-maker. They are more closely associated with the Home Counties north of the Thames – Hertfordshire especially. Like the taller spires they are usually shingled in Surrey, leaded in Hertfordshire.

Curiously in so sophisticated a county, simplicity is the word that comes first to mind in thinking of Surrey churches, even if it is a well-heeled simplicity. Many of them are unspoilt survivals of unaisled Norman churches with chancels rebuilt in the thirteenth century. Even in the enlarged churches at Betchworth, Chobham, and Shere we can still trace the original plan, while at Godalming the basic Norman plan incorporates the remains of an earlier Saxon church. This respect for the past and for local tradition is best seen at Shere, Surrey's favourite village, where traditional treatment is brought forward into the present century in the lych-gate designed by Sir Edwin Lutyens. The church is now so large that it is a complex of roofs and gables built, patched and rebuilt in any material available as an elderly nobleman who clings to the familiar comfort of old clothes might have a favourite suit made and remade. And all is accomplished with no loss of dignity, since pedigree is established in the centre of the church in the great thirteenth-century broach spire with one of the finest timber frames in England, and throughout the building there is the same local integrity that we found at Mayfield, Steyning, and Alfriston in Sussex, which is so typical of the village architecture of these two counties, in which affluence has never been allowed to become ostentatious.

3 Southern England

HAMPSHIRE – BERKSHIRE – WILTSHIRE – DORSET

The landscape of Hampshire is similar to that of Sussex and Surrey but in minor key. Weald continues across the Hampshire border to die out beyond Petersfield. South of it a band of alternating clays and gravels extends across the entire width of the county, to take in the New Forest as it spreads out beyond Southampton. The downland that crosses Surrey broadens out in Hampshire to form the rolling tableland 25 miles wide that brought the great prehistoric ridgeway from Stonehenge out of Wiltshire to split on the Berkshire Downs, one limb to reach Surrey by way of the Hog's Back, the other to cross the Thames at Streatley and continue through the Chilterns.

From this tableland flow the streams so much favoured by anglers: the Avon, the Test, the Itchen and the Meon, and it is in the valleys of these rivers that Hampshire's oldest and most characteristic churches are found. Along some they appear every mile or two, bearing witness to the strength of settlement by the Jutes in the Meon valley, the Saxons in those of the Test and the Itchen, and to the evangelisation of the county by St Birinus in 634, preparing the way for the consecration of Lothere as Bishop of Winchester in 670. Like the ancient churches of West Sussex, most of those of Hampshire are shepherds' churches, with flint predominating in their fabrics. The same type of white-painted, weather-boarded bell-turrets cap the roofs, and many of the interiors have the same rural simplicity.

Although ancient, fewer churches in Hampshire than in Surrey retain Saxon work; but what is lacking in quantity is compensated for in three gems: Corhampton near the Meon, of which the dedication is unknown, St Swithin's at Headbourne Worthy near the Itchen, and St Mary's, Breamore, in parkland three miles north of Fordingbridge, at the place where 5,000 Britons are traditionally believed to have been slain by the Saxons in 519, giving meaning to the inscription in Saxon lettering over the narrow arch of the south transept, which may be Anglicised 'Here the Covenant becomes manifest to thee'. Breamore's St Mary is attributed to c. 980 on the strength of this lettering; but it has been restored to an extent that makes the original plan uncertain. In view of its early date it may never have been completely cruciform. Many of the windows have been altered, but seven are the original double-splayed Saxon.

Both Breamore and Headbourne Worthy have defaced Saxon roods, a feature which Pevsner examined along with other stone carving in the county and finally pronounced Hampshire pre-eminent for pre-Conquest sculpture. The finest of the Hampshire roods is the one with the arms of Christ outstretched and the 'Hand of God' coming down from above on the outside wall of the south transept of Romsey Abbey. Behind the altar in the south transept is a small Saxon rood of c. 960. Corhampton's church, a quarter of a mile out of Meonstoke, is hidden on the south by an

17 Breamore, Hampshire: traditionally believed to mark the site of the 519 Saxon victory, with early work now attributed to *c*. 980

enormous yew, and further disguised by a brick east-end; but is Saxon of *c*. 1035 and should not be missed. No doubt the work that Pevsner admired so much was done by masons from Winchester, since only in the Test and Itchen valleys do we find anything so outstanding in the quality of the carving.

Winchester's early importance gave Hampshire a large number of Norman churches and four of the finest in England: Winchester Cathedral (completed in the reign of Rufus), the Church of the Holy Cross at Winchester, Christchurch Priory, and Romsey Abbey. What is surprising until the explanation becomes apparent is that the county has few other churches on anything approaching the same scale, although at the height of its power the Church owned two-thirds of the land in Hampshire. The explanation, of course, is the lack of good

stone except near the Sussex border and in the Isle of Wight. The distribution from these two sources was too uneven to be comparable. The Augustinians of Porchester left a large number of recognisable marks of influence on churches in the east of the county, as well as in the south-east corner of the castle. Stone from the Isle of Wight is seldom found in parish churches outside Christchurch and its sphere of influence, most notably at Milford-on-Sea. Stylistically, however, the influence of the great churches probably explains the tendency to build in stolid style, with squat piers, usually round, and only slightly pointed arches to both chancel and nave windows, suggesting 1180–1220 dating. We see them at Milford-on-Sea.

The difficulty in regionalising church styles in Hampshire away from Winchester may be due to the regal and episcopal manors being so widely dispersed. The prestige of these exalted associations occurs sporadically and in unexpected places. The best example is at East Meon, where Bishop Walkelin (1070–98) had a palace and built the finest church in Hampshire that was actually built as a parish

43

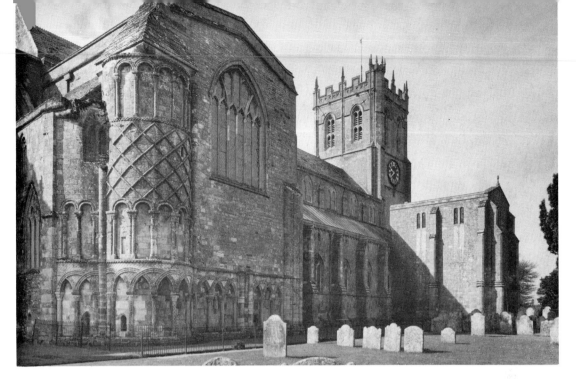

church. Christchurch and Romsey were not. It is a cruciform building of great dignity, with a leaded spire surmounting the tower. The nave and transepts are still largely original. It is, as Pevsner describes it, 'one of the most thrilling village churches in Hampshire'. The Tournai marble font closely resembles one at Winchester. Other churches that bear witness to the zeal of Bishop Walkelin are St Peter's, Petersfield, a 'new town' that took its name from the church, Easton, *c.* 1200, and Stoke Charity, now in the middle of a field. These were all on the episcopal manors and show the influence of East Meon in their styling. Winchester's wealth also contributed to the building of churches at Alton and Kingsclere.

18 Milford-on-Sea, Hampshire: fine 'master mariners' church', with local-style low arcades and thirteenth-century west tower

19 Christchurch Priory, Hampshire: the church of an Augustinian Priory which became a parish church at the Dissolution; strongly local in its association with castle and town

The martial and ecclesiastical traditions of the county are most impressively demonstrated in the siting of the Priory church at Christchurch on a tongue of land between the Avon and the Stour, with the castle close by. Like the great church at Romsey, Christchurch owes its preservation to having been bought by the townspeople at the Dissolution. By contrast, the small but beautifully kept parish church at Beaulieu is merely the refectory of a Cistercian abbey founded by King John. According to legend, the explanation of this unexpected generosity by a parsimonious monarch is that shortly after it came to his knowledge that the Cistercians had heard of his plan to tax them he had a dream in which he was being cruelly flogged by Cistercian abbots. This so terrified him

45

that he built Beaulieu as a penance. The present pulpit, now built into the thickness of the west wall, is the monastic reader's *pulpitum*.

Such foundations as these would ensure the presence of skilled masons on the fringe of the Royal Forest; but they had little effect within its bounds. The two finest New Forest churches, those at Lymington and Milford, both reflect post-Royal importance. The chancel of Lymington's church is thirteenth-century, the nave Georgian, with galleries that contribute much to its character. At Milford the core is Norman, and both this and the tracery, as already suggested, are clearly derived from Christchurch; but like Lymington's, the church at Milford today reflects the lost prosperity of the decayed ports of the New Forest rather than royal patronage. The 54 carved oak bosses on the ceiling, which date from the seventeenth century, were probably the work of craftsmen employed in the shipyards of the Solent. On the outside of the church, however, the vernacular spirit of an earlier age is delightfully represented in two bosses on the dripstone of the tower, one depicting a man playing a bagpipe, the other wearing ear-pads to deaden the sound.

Few New Forest churches have either unity or distinction. By far the most appealing is All Saints, Minstead, in which everything seems to have come about as naturally as in those long low houses that have grown out of modest family homes to meet expanding needs without losing any of the charm of their original character. It has two 'squire's pews' complete with fireplaces, a three-decker pulpit for parson and clerk, box-pews for the tenantry, with stout wooden hat pegs on the walls that only need hats on them to bring back the sense of unseen presences of 200 years ago. It is in such intimate features as these that

20 East Meon, Hampshire: the county's finest church actually built as a parish church

Hampshire's churches come nearest to having local style. The most perfect of these squire's churches is at Avington, north-east of Winchester, with all its period furnishings intact, even to the velvet-bound prayer-books in the manor pew.

There are few tall towers or spires in Hampshire that give the landscape the kind of additional dimension that we find in some of the West Midland counties, or those of the south west of England. The most representative are probably the handsome seventeenth- and eighteenth-century brick towers, such as we find at Tichborne and Wolverton. There is good pre-Reformation tower work at Micheldever, Barton Stacey, Fordingbridge, King's Worthy, and Soberton; but the truth is that Hampshire has fewer fine parish churches than might be expected in so socially favoured a county. The only outstanding fourteenth- or fifteenth-century churches are at Alton, Basingstoke, and Basing.

Much of the undoubted charm of the smaller churches, notwithstanding their lack of architectural distinction, springs from their pastoral setting and such sympathetic personal associations as those with Jane Austen at Chawton, Gilbert White at Selborne, and Izaak Walton at Droxford, which he made his home-from-home after his daughter married the rector. Nowhere is this pastoral serenity more complete than at Ellingham, the most rewarding from the local historian's point of view of the five churches in the water meadows between Ringwood and Fordingbridge. In both its fabric and its furnishings we can read the folk record of every century of its quiet life of witness. The chancel, 35 feet long, is a reminder that it was a collegiate church. The porch, with a brightly painted sundial in the gable, is of mixed stone and brick and bears the date 1720 along with the initials J.M., which were those of James Mist, churchwarden. Both north and south walls of the church are pleasingly dappled with ironstone, and in the north wall of the chancel there is rough thirteenth-century rubble and brickwork from an earlier church on the site, fragments from which can be discovered in unexpected places. The last time I was at Ellingham, while pausing to admire a peacock sunning himself on the churchyard wall, I noticed a piece of ball-flower stone carving in the rough masonry which must have come from the church in one of its restorations.

Inside the church, the rudeness of the fifteenth-century screen might appear to lack interest until we notice slanting grooves on the south of the opening, which were obviously cut to support a sloping reading-desk, and we are grateful that the screen was not thought due for removal when three beautiful brass chandeliers were hung in the nave. Unfortunately, the three-decker pulpit has gone; but the hour-glass, one of only 11 surviving in English churches remains, and the tympanum above the screen, inscribed with the Lord's Prayer, the Decalogue, and the Creed in black lettering and quaint spelling, framed in Renaissance borders, silently continues to proclaim the Protestant cause.

Berkshire's downland churches have the same general character as Hampshire's, even to their minor literary associations, like that with Mary Russell Mitford's *Our Village*. Flint is still the commonest building material, and flint buildings have an uncompromising timeless character that makes them fit well into the chalk landscape of all these southern counties. If the small churches of Berkshire's downland have a distinctive character it is that so many of them have tiled roofs with dormer windows.

On looking, however, more closely for local styles in Berkshire, we see that there is far more variety than in Hampshire. There is, for example, the group that includes Binfield, Warfield, Winkfield, and Wokingham, in which use is made of the interesting dark brown conglomerate rock formed of pebbles locked in ironstone similar to the conglomerate found at Byfleet and Chobham in Surrey. In the north of the county we find stone that could not have been locally

21 Avington, Hampshire: late eighteenth-century interior handsomely furnished by Margaret, Marchioness of Caernarvon

quarried coming into use. It would be brought in by water and packhorse, and some of it may have come from places as far away as Bath, Headington, and Portland. In the towns of the Thames Valley a local style of tower becomes identifiable. It starts with Reading St Laurence, which has a tower built of flint rubble with oolite dressings, supported by octagonal buttresses rising to somewhat heavy pepper-pot turrets with plain pinnacles. The one rebuilt at Newbury by the rich clothier, Jack of Newbury, is elaborated by doubling the windows at the top stage, adding an under-parapet of panels with quatrefoils, and introducing a single large window to each face at the middle stage.

These towers spread so far along the Thames Valley that monastic origin becomes obvious. This must have been Reading Abbey, founded by Henry I with monks from Cluny. We see the same style of tower at Henley-on-Thames, but without spirelets to the turrets, and at Theale, Hungerford, and St Peter and St Paul, Marlborough.

The other major monastic influence in the Thames Valley came from the Benedictine abbey at Abingdon, where the abbot's lordship of land included the whole of the town, enabling him to take tolls on all wool and timber landed there, and also on cargoes carried down the river between Oxford and London. Evidence of rapid accession of wealth is shown in that the church of St Nicholas, Abingdon, was built in a single generation and that the one immediately before the Dissolution.

Both Abingdon and Reading had successions of abbots who were continuously in conflict with the wealthy wool merchants and clothiers on their estates. The building of magnificent churches was the most effective way of proclaiming local power in the Middle Ages, and no doubt Jack of Newbury's elaboration of local style in rebuilding his own parish church had that in mind. The history of Abingdon is more closely associated with Oxfordshire than with Berkshire; but it was to Berkshire that it belonged before the recent reorganisation of local government, and it is to Berkshire that it must be related ecclesiastically as well as geographically in the Middle Ages. The most impressive demonstration of early monastic influence in Berkshire was the building in the middle of the thirteenth century of the great church at Uffington, with the crossing tower that was crowned with an octagon in the eighteenth century. The south porch is described by Pevsner as being 'on a cathedral scale'. The buttresses are enriched with carved figures, and the doorways have stiff-leaf capitals. Big medieval churches are a feature of this part of Berkshire. We see them at Blewbury, Wantage, Sparsholt, Warfield and many other places – all built of stone that

must have been brought along the Thames by water or inland by packhorse.

Lambourn in the west of the county is another church with an interesting crossing tower. It is of several periods, with fine late-Norman crossing arches inside and arcades with Norman piers decorated with scalloped capitals and foliage. For another splendidly unique church we should go to Sunningwell, if only to see the west porch built by Bishop Jewel (c. 1560–70) to commemorate his having been rector there before becoming Bishop of Salisbury, where he built the cathedral library.

In the north-west corner of the geographical county of Berkshire – now in Oxfordshire – are some of the county's most fascinating churches: Bessels Leigh, the only church in Berkshire retaining all its box pews, Radley, Wootton, Childrey, and unspoilt East Shefford. Although they have close affinities with Cotswold churches, they belong to Berkshire. At Compton Beauchamp below White Horse Hill the church is built of chalkstone, or clunch, of so brilliant a whiteness that a visitor might imagine himself in the Chilterns. And all round the Vale of the White Horse we look for sarsens, or heath stones, locally called 'grey wethers' because from a distance they look like sheep. They are the local equivalent of the moorstones of the West of England and the sarsens of the East, and served the same purpose of providing foundation stones for church towers.

After touring these counties we may ask why so much of the building in Berkshire generally is later than that in most of the counties so far sketched. The explanation is again historical. North Berkshire was ravaged by invaders fighting for control of the fords and bridges of both the Thames and the Kennet throughout the entire period between the Roman withdrawal and the Norman Conquest.

From Berkshire we turn to Wiltshire, where to archaeologists even pre-Conquest work is modern. Although on the surface much of the landscape is simply a continuation of

Berkshire's in that the Marlborough Downs match the Berkshire Downs, the Vale of Pewsey the Vale of the White Horse, with rivers indistinguishable from those of Berkshire – or of Hampshire for that matter – the difference between Wiltshire and the counties to the south and east becomes dramatic as we approach Salisbury Plain. The valleys become noticeably narrower and the downland ascents more precipitous. We are then struck by the way the lack of space for expansion has meant that communities have been more tightly packed into sheltered hollows in the foothills of the downs, or at points along the streams where an intruding knoll has formed a wind break.

Fortunately, several of these withdrawn villages were bypassed by the nineteenth-century restorers who had rather a 'field day' in Wiltshire, so remain records of local history comparable with those described in Hampshire. Stockton near Wylye is one of the most charming of these; Great Chalfield, north-east of Bradford-on-Avon, has a two-decker pulpit with tester, and wall-paintings depicting the story of St Catherine; Dilton, tucked into the downs near Westbury, keeps its box-pews and three decker pulpit.

Such churches as these are redolent of eighteenth-century social life; but the main point about Wiltshire is that it is a county in which more than half the historical monuments are pre-Christian, and in which every downland settlement can be traced to ancient roots. Salisbury itself, although its cathedral is thirteenth-century, does not forget that it sprang from prehistoric Sarum. As for the flint churches of the villages, there is an earthiness about them that goes back beyond human settlement and seems to relate them to pagan rituals. The timber producing Weald is now far behind us. Stone is dominant. The bell-turrets, which have been weather-boarded on the smaller churches of the south-eastern and southern counties may now be of stone and slightly rounded. Certainly none of the counties to the east would have dared to set up on the west end of their churches the square

stone bell-cote with crocketed spirelet we see at Great Chalfield, reflecting the defiant affluence of the Wiltshire clothiers. Others, set diagonally on the west gable, are seen at Bildestone, Sevington, and Castle Combe, where the church tower is in the Somerset style. Ten Wiltshire churches have stone screens. This is fewer than Devon's 15; but the tracery in the Wiltshire screens is so fine that they give the county pre-eminence for this kind of work. The best is the late fifteenth-century screen at Compton Bassett, where the shafts support cusped arches with figures in richly carved niches.

The complexity of Wiltshire's geological structure has produced more than one local style. The village churches at Great Hinton, Keevil, and Steeple Ashton are on a plateau of Corrallian limestone east of Trowbridge and west of the Vale of Pewsey. South of Devizes, limestones were quarried between Potterne and Great Cheverell, and between East Knoyle and Tisbury. Greensand quarried at Potterne is found in church buildings throughout the Vale of Pewsey, and there are other beds of greensand round Zeals and along the Somerset border, while in the north-west of the county, and along the Dorset border is that best of all building stones, the oolitic limestone that enabled the rich clothiers of the fifteenth and sixteenth centuries to build the 'wool churches' at Malmesbury, Chippenham, Melksham, Westbury, and Trowbridge. Unhappily, many Wiltshire 'wool churches' were damaged by nineteenth-century restorers – most sadly those at Trowbridge and Westbury. However, Steeple Ashton's splendid church suffered least, and is now to Wiltshire what Northleach is to Gloucestershire – the county's monument to the munificence of the clothiers.

The presence of good limestone led here as elsewhere to the building of noble towers, many of them on the crossing of cruciform churches. F. J. Allen, the acknowledged authority on church towers, singles out the group made up of Devizes, Nettleton, Yatton Keynell, and West Kington as constituting a

22 Uffington, Berkshire: noble thirteenth-century cruciform church with octagonal tower and fine south porch

noteworthy local style. These are all of oolitic limestone and have the distinctive feature of hexagonal stair turrets with ogee cupolas. The bell-openings in them are arranged in rows of three lights with a transom. All the lights are blank except the middle lights of the upper stages. Cricklade, Marlborough, and Mere have octagonal buttresses.

Down the western side of the county, where the best stone is found near Corsham and Bradford-on-Avon, whole villages are built of limestone as they are in the Cotswolds. In these districts the influence of masons from Gloucestershire and Somerset is seen in ornate towers with panelled parapets and a particular kind of window tracery. At Colerne, near the meeting point of the three counties of Somerset, Gloucestershire, and Wiltshire the prominent string courses and panels in the

middle stage are distinctively in Gloucestershire style. So Wiltshire church styles, like those of so many counties, are as mixed as its geology. Perhaps it would be fair to say that the tendency to introduce square-headed windows into larger towers, with panelling at the belfry stage is common enough to constitute a local style.

Viewed chronologically, Bradford-on-Avon, Wiltshire, now has the most fascinating Saxon stone church in the South of England. For this we have to thank Victorian restorers who here made amends for what their misguided fellow-enthusiasts did elsewhere. This important church had been virtually destroyed until in 1856 what remained of its chancel was identified in a cottage, with a chimney stack built into the chancel arch. There were house windows in the west front, and the upper part of the nave was used as a school. The rescue came about through the vicar of Bradford at the time, Canon Jones, noting a reference in a book written by William of Malmesbury, *c.* 1125, to a church built at Bradford-on-Avon by St Aldhelm. He identified the building; but its conversion to secular use meant that although there were remains of the eighth-century Saxon church at the core, there was nothing remaining of the Norman church that must have superseded it, and very little Saxon work except two pieces of sculpture high up on the eastern wall of the nave that could have been part of a rood similar to those we found in Hampshire. However, all that can be said of them is that they are flying angels which seem to be related to the famous piece of sculpture at Malmesbury, where an angel is depicted flying over the seated figure of the apostles, who are ducking their heads. There are other pieces of Saxon sculpture in Wiltshire; but they are not significantly local except in relation to those in Hampshire, which are accepted as constituting the first stages of stone carving in the churches of southern England. Of Norman architecture, Wiltshire has Malmesbury, with a south porch enriched with some of the finest Norman work to be found anywhere in England.

That Wiltshire did not get widely dispersed local styles earlier must be largely due to its having had to wait until the thirteenth century for its great cathedral at Salisbury, begun *c.* 1220. This late start meant that in cathedral timing the work was hurried. Unlike other cathedrals in the south it did not grow in stages as Gothic styles evolved, but is of uniform style throughout. Nor was it the work of local architects whose work can be identified elsewhere in the county. The source seems to have been in East Anglia, possibly at either Ely or Dereham. But the stone was local. It came from quarries at Chilmark, and the working of the stone does bring the cathedral into relationship with other churches in the county that got their stone from the same quarries, including that at Chilmark itself. Others built of Chilmark stone were the churches at Heytesbury, Luckington, and Wilcot. Unfortunately, of this group Heytesbury, *c.* 1165, which was collegiate, was so vandalised by the restorers that few traces of

23 Bradford-on-Avon, Wiltshire: Victorian reconstruction of a Saxon church dating from the eighth century

its early magnificence remain, and Luckington and Wilcot suffered at the same hands. Churches on the Bishop of Salisbury's manors, however, fared better. The cruciform collegiate churches at Potterne and Bishops Cannings are examples of this, both in architectural elegance and the style of some of the motifs in their tracery.

Cruciform churches are a Wiltshire feature. There is a group of them in the middle of the county made up of the old churches at Calne, Bishops Cannings, Devizes, Potterne, Edington, Amesbury, and St Martin, Barfoot. The most remarkable in the group are St John,

24 Devizes, Wiltshire: the Beauchamp chapel

Devizes, built within the inner bailey of the bishop's castle, and the priory church of St Mary, St Katharine, and All Saints, Edington, the county's finest collegiate church. As the former is Norman, the latter fourteenth century, they show the continuity of style in Wiltshire, although fourteenth-century style is not prominent in the county. As the fourteenth century was the great age of the wool trade, as distinct from the woven cloth industry which flourished in the fifteenth and sixteenth centuries, and Wiltshire was a great wool producing county, the lack of fourteenth-century churches may be thought surprising. The most probable reason for it is that the building of Salisbury Cathedral in the thirteenth century gave such an impetus to church building in the diocese that little was required in the fourteenth in a region where local stone is so durable.

Edington's splendid church did not originate in a local need, so its survival after the dissolution of the priory for which it was built is something of a marvel. The parish it served can never have justified a church on such a scale, despite its being so strategically placed where the downs come down to the lowlands of the Wiltshire Vale, the one producing wool, the other cloth. It was built near the old Salisbury to Bath road as it runs under the Wiltshire Downs by a native of the village, William of Edington, Bishop of Winchester, Treasurer and Chancellor of England, for the Black Prince, who wanted accommodation for an Order of canons. This achievement of the combination of royal and ecclesiastical patronage was started in 1352 and consecrated in 1361, which means that the work was done only a few years after the Black Death. As there was little work available during those years for the craftsmen who had reached such a high level of skill in the early years of the fourteenth century the finest sculptors in the country had become available for work in this remote place. So we see here Decorated and the first flights of Perpendicular work co-existing in perfect harmony. Pevsner says of the chancel that it is 'an

exquisite composition, not over-decorated, yet of the finest craftsmanship in the manifold but subdued enrichments'.

The first thing that may strike the historian of church architecture about Edington is that it appears to owe so little to other great churches in the south-west Midlands built shortly before it: Bristol Cathedral (1311–40), St Mary Redcliffe (1355–1450), or the tower and spire of Salisbury (1334–80). As the Perpendicular and Decorated styles co-exist so well at Edington, those who remember that the one evolved from the other at Gloucester may suspect that the best work at Edington was done by the same hands. It might even be thought surprising in all the circumstances if it did not, since the Black Prince and the Treasurer of England were able to command the best masons, and there were none better than those trained at Gloucester.

By rare good fortune all that has been done at Edington by way of restoration has been of the highest order, the latest being the restoration of the fourteenth-century east window of the north transept in 1970 by the Glaziers Trust. The influence of Edington is seen in the neighbourhood in the towers at Westbury, Bratton, Keevil, and the oversailing parapet at Dinton.

In travelling westward it has been difficult to decide whether Dorset should be included in the southern or the south-western grouping for the purposes of this book. It is betwixt and between both historically and architecturally. Geologically the county is divided into five elongated strips. Chalk downland continues out of Wiltshire to run transversely across the county from Cranborne Chase before breaking up between Beaminster and Dorchester. South-west of this line is the undulating coastal strip from Lyme Regis to Weymouth, south-east is the Isle of Purbeck. To the north-west of the chalk downs is the Vale of Blackmore, to the south-east is the Heath. Merely to name these divisions is to conjure up scenes from Hardy's poems and novels, and because Hardy was both the most 'churchy' of writers and the one most in tune with the Dorset landscape the scenery he selected as the settings for his most dramatic incidents is the landscape against which we can most rewardingly visualise the churches. It is a nostalgic rather than an exciting landscape, and it is significant that for his own regional purposes he revived the concept of the ancient kingdom of Wessex.

Many of the smaller churches might still look like Hardy museums, even to having old church instruments displayed in them. In fact, church bands continued longer in Wessex than elsewhere. The best remaining musicians' gallery is at Puddletown, five miles north-east of Dorchester. In 1820 the band at Winterborne St Martin had four clarionets, a hautboy, and a 'base viol'. Many of the tunes played by these bands were composed locally. They will tell you at Dorchester that John Brown, the carpenter choir-master of St Peter's, after exercising his privilege of announcing the number of the psalm, would add solemnly: 'to a tune of my own composing'. Such characters were ready-made for Hardy, who must have been saddened to learn that the last of the bands played its final tune in 1895, although it may be doubted whether the church reformers of the day had any regrets at their passing. It is said that at the end, the band at Winterborne St Martin had only two tunes left: 'thick an' t'other'. Winterborne Abbas battled on until even its most loyal supporters felt that the end must come when at a wedding at Steepleton it played out the bride and bridegroom to the strains of Baring Gould's

Onward, Christian soldiers
 Marching as to war.

Local character, sensed most nostalgically at Puddletown, with its box-pews, gallery just mentioned, and canopied pulpit, is found in scores of Dorset churches. At Affpuddle, a thatched village where the lawns of the old vicarage slope down to the Piddle, the church has a mid-sixteenth-century pulpit dating from 'the tyme of Thomas Lyllynton vicar of thys church'.

While Time is a palpable presence in Dorset, it is on a shorter and more friendly scale than in Wiltshire. The true Dorset churches are farmers' churches. There is no arty nonsense about them. They are earthy like those of Wiltshire; but not with the pre-Christian earthiness of the bare bony downs around Stonehenge. The Dorset downs are cultivated. Consequently the settlements in the valleys seem less remote from the hillside farms in Dorset than they do in Wiltshire. The barren landscape in Dorset is the Heath around Wareham: 'untamable, Ishmaelitish', as Hardy described it, 'Civilisation was its enemy; and ever since the beginning of vegetation its soil had worn the same antique brown dress'.

This shortening of the time scale is not fanciful. The Anglo-Saxon Chronicle has little to record about Dorset. Although 80% of its place-names are Saxon they are late. There are only two important memorials of Saxon invasion and settlement in the county, Wareham in the south and Sherborne in the north; but both are of prime importance, and Sherborne, dating from the abbey founded *c.* 705, is not only Dorset's finest ecclesiastical building but summarises in stone its entire church history.

The generally modest character of Dorset's churches is probably explained by their being the offspring of minster churches rather than cathedrals under the patronage of wealthy bishops. These Dorset minsters were large semi-collegiate churches founded by Orders whose members were not subject to monastic rule. In the Middle Ages, large areas covered by light soil of low productive value were administered from religious community centres, many of which became market towns with 'Minster' incorporated in their names: Beaminster, Charminster, Iwerne Minster, Sturminster Marshall, Sturminster Newton, Wimborne Minster. Before these minster parishes were broken up and churches built in them preaching crosses were set up as rallying points. One of these serves as the font at Melbury Bubb, and a cross-head is preserved in the church at Cattistock. This preaching-cross origin is significant because wherever it is found – as in the far-West and the far-North – the Bible rather than the liturgy determines churchmanship and consequently the local style of churches. Here again, the clergy are not so much priests as Minister's of God's Word.

This lack of strict division between priest and people had actually been fostered from St Dunstan's time in one of the county's few abbeys, that at Cerne, by Aelfric, who used English, not Latin, for pastoral letters to the clergy, as well as paraphrases of the Bible and treatises on the Scriptures. This tradition continued under the missionary clergy from the minsters, who would be hospitably received in the homes of the lords of the manors until, in the seventeenth and eighteenth centuries, when Dorset landowners became wealthy, the traditional link between church and manor house was strengthened by the landowners building new churches on their estates, or beautifying old ones, many of which had a son of the manor as rector. Thus Sir Thomas Freke rebuilt the nave, north aisle and south chapel of Iwerne Courtenay church, Robert Browne built Frampton church tower, and the strength of this link between Church and Manor in Dorset was so well maintained that the county remains to a quite exceptional degree one of deeply rooted families with strong stakes in the land, ruling benevolently from medium-sized manor houses built close to sturdy but un-demonstrative churches. A fine example of church and manor house forming a single composition is seen at Chettle in the north-east of the county, where a fine early eighteenth-century Great House has a church in the grounds with a Perpendicular west tower built in local style – that is to say, with horizontal bands of stone and knapped flints alternating, the style seen also at Upcerne and Cranborne.

From this local patriotism emerged in the eighteenth century the Georgian revival of county architecture that is so notable a feature of the small towns of Dorset, and is seen outstandingly at Blandford, where the church was designed and largely built by two local architects, John and William Bastard between 1733 and 1739. Again we have the Dorset flare for pioneering a style. The Bastards were obviously influenced by Wren's London churches, but they introduced a unique local style into Dorset, notably in the large keyed-in windows. The part of Blandford's church that was not theirs is the cupola on the west tower. The Bastards intended it to have a spire. Their influence is also seen at Charlton Marshall (1713), where the nave and chancel combine to form a Georgian auditory church with arched windows.

The imposing pier arcades at Blandford may prompt those who see them to ask why the Portland stone of which they are constructed was not more widely used in Dorset churches. It was, after all, the stone that Sir Christopher Wren chose for St Paul's. The reason may have been that it was a hard stone that was costly to work and came from an inconveniently placed part of the county. An even stronger reason was that Dorset is uncommonly well provided with local stone, and those who built the churches would not see the point of buying expensive stone elsewhere when they had good quarries on their own estates. Even Sherborne was built of locally quarried oolite, and Blandford and Charlton Marshall of greensand.

But there is another church building tradition to be traced in Dorset, and one of far more than local importance. The abbots of the Benedictine abbeys at Shaftesbury, Sherborne, and Cerne in the north of the county, and Abbotsbury in the south, could afford to buy stone at Portland and in the Isle of Purbeck, and evolve new styles in its decorative use which were to be fully developed in Somerset. This became convenient, even where local stone was available, because the Purbeck and Portland masons were pioneers in producing the finished object in their quarries when in other

25 Blandford, Dorset: Georgian classical interior

parts of England the stone was merely broken up into pieces of convenient size to be finally cut and worked on the building sites. No doubt this employment of masons and sculptors at the quarries, or in lodges near them, came with the popularity of Purbeck stone for fonts. Only as finished articles could the shafts and bowls have been carried such long distances to adorn churches in every part of England where local 'marble' could not be quarried. From Purbeck the practice spread to other quarries in the south-west of the region. Windows and pier arcades made from Ham Hill stone can be found in South Wales, which was a considerable distance for transport in the fourteenth century, and some may be even earlier. Later this commercialisation of masonry spread to the quarries at Beer in South Devon.

Masons trained at Purbeck may well have been responsible for such a gem as the twelfth-century church at Studland, with its rib-vaulted central tower, which ranks as one of the most perfect village churches in England. There is another remarkably complete Norman village church at Winterborne Tomson in the same part of the county, while the magnificent thirteenth-century cruciform church at Church Knowle is evidence of the prosperity which by that date the quarries had brought to the Isle of Purbeck.

Elsewhere in Dorset distinctive styles are found in such features as the twelfth-century crossings and blank arches in the tower at Wimborne Minster being similar to those at Sherborne; but mainly in the towers of the large number of parish churches that were rebuilt when the wool trade was at its peak. Where a church was not in need of rebuilding or major restoration it was given a new west tower. Certainly it is in the towers that we have the most clearly identifiable local feature in Dorset's village churches, so many of which conform to a standard pattern that we must again feel that they were furnished with features produced in bulk at the quarries and only assembled on the site. I am told that the various stones used are readily identifiable by those familiar with West Country quarries. Where good stone was not available use was made of 'cob' for the body of the church. This 'cob', which Dorset claims to have invented before passing it on to South Devon, is simply clay reinforced with straw. Cob churches with thatched roofs are particularly associated with the Vale of Blackmore.

The finest stone used in Dorset, apart from the nationally famous Portland and Purbeck, is the golden brown limestone quarried at Ham Hill, near Yeovil. Many of the most attractive villages on the Dorset–Somerset boundary are entirely built of it. For towers it was superb. Of the best, the one at Beaminster is the most elaborate, the one at Milton Abbas the most interesting from the point of view of the historical development of styles. It is usually described as 'very early Perpendicular', and was copied at Cerne Abbas more than a hundred years after being built. The outstanding feature, of which no earlier parallel is known, is the octagonal buttresses, diminishing at each string course to finish up as octagonal pinnacles. The stair turret ends in a spirelet, and beautifully sculptured niches enrich the tower: eight in the lower stage, three on the west side of the middle stage, with two original statues surviving in the upper niches. Although situated close to the Somerset border, this remarkable tower is not derived from a Somerset model. It is difficult to see where some of the more sophisticated features were inspired. It is not unlikely that the paired windows found in most of the larger towers of Dorset were introduced from Christchurch Priory; but the feature of a small flying pinnacle corbelled out of each corner of the tower parapet at Sherborne, Cerne Abbas, and Norton-under-Hamdon, may have originated in Dorset.

Professor Allen examined in detail several features in Dorset towers that appeared to anticipate those that were to be developed to perfection in Somerset, and found it difficult to decide in which they appeared first, particularly where the stone came from the same quarries and was worked there to a standard pattern. There is great similarity in the tracery found in the tower bell-openings of the two counties. A feature that intrigued me personally when I first encountered it, because I had hitherto associated it distinctively with Kent and Sussex, is that at least half a dozen Dorset churches have towers built on the south side, not the west end, while at Canford Magna, a fascinating church in which the chancel is the nave of a late Saxon church, the Norman nave has a tower of the same period on the north side.

The most advanced style of tower in Dorset is found at Sherborne and in a group round Dorchester. In these, rectangular buttresses are usually placed a few inches from the corners and built up to within a few feet of the parapet. From the top of each a triangular pilaster runs up through the battlemented parapet to terminate in pinnacles, which means that the pinnacles are not at the corners

26 Wimborne Minster, Dorset: Norman work in the nave

27 Puddletown, Dorset: typical Dorset roof and unaltered seventeenth-century furnishing

of the parapets but a few inches from them. The design is then further advanced by having another pinnacle in the middle of each side.

4 South-West England

SOMERSET – DEVON – CORNWALL

In Somerset the austerity of the Downs is finally left behind. Warm welcoming stone breaks through the green landscape in prosperous farmsteads and hamlets. Noble church towers, unsurpassed elsewhere in England, rise above the cottage roofs of scores of villages. The reason for this wealth of architecture is two-fold. The first is that as the freestone from the local quarries was easily worked, lodges of highly skilled masons were established at Wells in the heart of the county, Glastonbury in the south, and Bristol in the north. The second is that when the great towers were being built Somerset had the means to pay for them.

Somerset towers have been classified and reclassified by experts. The tourist, after admiring and feeling at home among the forthright towers of Dorset, finds himself confronted in Somerset by elaborately pinnacled coronals and traceried panels of such cathedral-like perfection that they look almost excessively ornate in so rural a setting, and he wants a simple explanation of this sudden proliferation of splendour. Basically it is to be found in the influence of the cathedral from which the particular local style was derived. In the Mendips, although the arrangement of belfry windows, buttresses, and parapets may vary, the inspiration of nearly all the tower designers was the central tower of Wells Cathedral.

The first of the Mendip towers to be built was Shepton Mallet's, begun in 1375 and clearly designed to carry a spire instead of the lead pinnacle that now caps it. In travelling across the southern counties we may have noticed that tall spires in parish churches are not numerous; but this early abandonment of the plan to build one at Shepton Mallet becomes more than locally significant if we see it in relation to the number of spires in other counties of the South West. East to west, Dorset has only two ancient spires, Devon has seven, Cornwall three, while Somerset situated between Dorset and Devon has 16. This surely suggests that spires were intended to be a feature of these ambitiously designed Somerset towers – which would then be called steeples – but were abandoned in favour of concentrating every device of art and skill on the towers themselves. We can imagine that when plans were being drawn to introduce into the faces of towers such features as panels decorated with intricate tracery, and to surmount them with no less intricately designed pierced parapets broken by elaborately carved pinnacles, someone would suggest that to add a spire to the composition could only detract from the total effect by directing the eye away from what had been designed to be the main attraction.

The symbolism of architecture must have been discussed in Somerset with more learning and insight than in most parts of England. At all events, it was in Somerset that the conflict between the symbolism of the spire and the noble stability of the tower seems

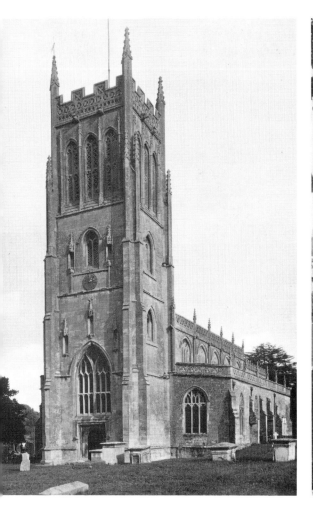

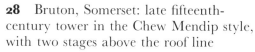

28 Bruton, Somerset: late fifteenth-century tower in the Chew Mendip style, with two stages above the roof line

29 Wrington, Somerset: elaborately traceried parapet with pinnacles; tower, with only one tall stage above the roof line

to have been most resourcefully resolved. This was done, as in other places, by constructing the tower in narrowing stages, often with blind panels emphasising the length of the dividing vertical lines – features that are especially characteristic of Mendip towers. But in Somerset the symbolism of the spire was most effectively expressed by erecting pinnacles at the heads of the buttresses, which terminated one stage short of the parapet.

All the Mendip towers have straight moulded-parapets pierced with trefoil or quatrefoil motifs, and all except South Brent have Shepton Mallet-type tracery of a design copied not only for other towers in Somerset but also in Gloucestershire. Most of them have triple windows abreast in the top stage with only the middle one open.

Part of the difficulty in classifying Somerset towers, even those in which Wells was the dominant influence, is that they were built when ecclesiastical architecture was at its peak in the West of England, so there were cross-currents of influence from Glastonbury,

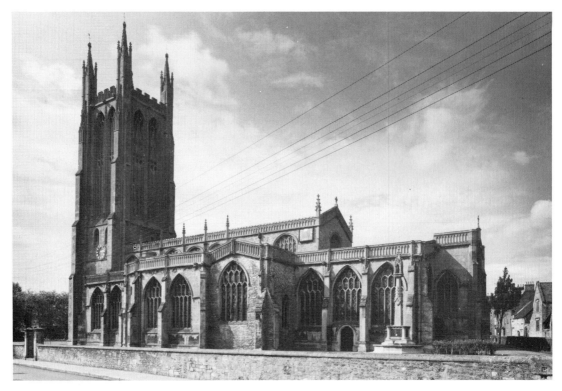

30 Wells, Somerset: the stately and spacious church of St Cuthbert

Gloucester, and Bristol, and within these major influences changes were rung according to the relative values placed by the builders on such features as niches for statues, buttresses, pinnacles, and so forth. In particular, there must have been endless discussions on devices that might be used to enhance the impression of height in such places as Ilminster, Mells, and above all Glastonbury, for which the inspiration was Gloucester Cathedral.

One fairly clear-cut division of Somerset towers is that between those in which the whole of the height above the roof line is in one tall stage, as at Wrington, and the Chew Mendip type with two stages above the roof line, as at Shepton Beauchamp, where the two stages have a string course between them. This latter style is seen to perfection at Bruton, a late fifteenth-century tower built of

Doulting oolite, with string courses between each of the four stages, single windows in the second and third stages, and tall triple windows in the top stage. An early tower that draws inspiration from outside the county is Chew Magna's, which was built in 1380, only five years after Shepton Mallet's, yet with a different source of inspiration, in this case Gloucester.

Somerset is a large county, and one in which each student of its churches will have his own system of classification. The simplest division for anyone merely touring the county is between the two hill groups of the Mendips and the Quantocks, which must obviously differ if only because when we reach the Quantocks the limestones have petered out and the red Keuper sandstone that provides a preview of Devon has come into use. The masons who became so expert in the use of this stone worked from Taunton. The earliest and plainest of their towers are at Bishops Lydeard and Lyng, the finest at St Mary Magdalene, Taunton, rebuilt in 1862.

31 Weston Zoyland, Somerset: the great fifteenth-century tower that dominates the Sedgemoor marshes

If we are looking for a tower that can be used as a student's text book in styles we should go to Weston Zoyland, which because it was so well situated geographically was able to derive the maximum benefit from both Mendip and Quantock skills, while for sheer piracy – and there is no copyright in building styles – the prize must go to Batcombe, built in 1540 of Doulting oolite, with a straight parapet of the West Mendip type, triple windows of the East Mendip type, tracery derived from the Quantock group in the top windows, and long panels with vertical lines continued down through the stage below as at Wrington and Evercreech, to form a fine composition that is centred in carvings of Christ in Glory attended by three pairs of angels!

In looking at these towers architecturally we need to keep in mind that ornate towers were built for the ringing of bells, and that the richest counties for old bells are Somerset and Devon, which still have not only the strongest towers in England but by far the largest number of rings of five bells or more.

After towers we look at roofs, which in the West Country are almost invariably of the waggon type – so called because the principle of supporting a roof with a series of closely-set arched trussed-rafters is the same as that of supporting the awning of a waggon with a frame like an inverted cradle, the alternative name for this kind of roof. The practical advantage of the waggon roof is that it distributes the weight evenly along the walls. When these roofs are boarded on the inside they are usually called barrel-roofs. in the larger churches this semi-cylindrical ceiling is divided into square or rectangular panels with carved and often brilliantly coloured bosses at the corners, a device that was adopted by Bodley in the nineteenth century to achieve the maximum effect of interior height in churches. In the fourteenth century this type of roof reached its peak of perfection, or at all events of virtuosity, at Shepton Mallet, where the ceiling has 350 carved panels, 306 bosses, 90 half-bosses, and 1,400 leaves, yet in only one of the panels is a design duplicated. Few roofs reached anything approaching this standard. One however surpassed it from an artistic point of view in the fifteenth century at Cullompton in Devon.

The squared effect favoured for both towers and roofs in the West of England was also adopted for furnishings. Square-headed bench-ends are almost universal in Devon. The best are in the Quantocks, with the most remarkable set at Bishops Lydeard, a church which is to me supremely typical of the West Country aptitude for reconciling the secular with the sacred in parish church symbolism. One of the Bishops Lydeard bench-ends has a representation of a windmill with three birds between the sails, and a miller with his horse at the base. Having noted the professionally skilled architecture of Somerset it is good to

(a)

(b)

the tools used in them. At Spaxton below the eastern slope of the Quantocks for example, a tucker is depicted standing in his shop pounding a piece of cloth with a two-headed mallet. Shears, a knife, a comb, and a three-pronged teasle-holder are also shown along with a length of cloth hanging from a weaver's beam.

Documentary evidence of the strength of communal enterprise in the region is found in the records of Dunster, where a contract for the building of the present central tower was drawn up in 1443 between John Marys, a mason of Stogursey, and the parishioners of Dunster to a design supplied by a freemason named Richard Pope, in which 'the parishioners undertook to provide all the ropes, pulleys, winches and other necessary implements, and to deliver the building materials in the transept of the church as they were required'. As the central tower at Dunster is 100 feet high this was no mean undertaking.

Dunster's cruciform church is the finest within the Exmoor National Park. Its magnificent screen, extending in the West Country manner across the entire width of the church, was set up in 1498 to divide the interior between the monks of the local Benedictine priory and the parishioners. As we are now on the borders of Devon, the county pre-eminent for carved rood-screens, we might take the opportunity to bring the distribution of screens into focus. The two regions that excel in them are East Anglia and the West Country. The differences between the two could not be greater. In the lofty churches of East Anglia vertical lines are dominant, with restrained geometric tracery between the shafts to harmonise with the Perpendicular architecture. In the low-roofed, wide-aisled churches of the West the dominant lines are

find vernacular art represented in so many of the county's churches.

The most remarkable examples of this local expression are the bench-ends in the Taunton area carved by a sixteenth-century craftsman named Simon Werman and others who came under his influence. They are particularly interesting when they depict local trades and

33 Culbone, Somerset: the interior of the smallest medieval parish church in England, now smothered in an Exmoor combe above Porlock Weir

horizontal, with fan vaulting supporting the cornices of broad lofts festooned with a profusion of naturalistic carving entirely unlike anything in East Anglia, where motifs derived from nature are represented in stylised forms.

In Devonshire oak leaves, acorns, vine leaves and tendrils loaded with bunches of grapes are clustered together with such exuberance that the broad pillars of the screens look like recreations of orchard trees and the thin stems of intertwining tracery like vines restored to life with all their fallen leaves and fruits returned to them. These village carpenters were paying tribute to the God of Harvest, the god they understood best. After seeing their work no-one could be surprised that it was a West Country parson, R. S. Hawker of Morwenstow, who in 1843 introduced harvest festivals into the modern English church, or that Parson Herrick of Dean Prior should have celebrated in the 'Hock Cart, or Harvest Home', the bringing in of the corn and the crowning of the Lord of Harvest in such lines as:

Some bless that cart, some kiss the sheaves;
Some prank them up with oaken leaves:
Some cross the fill-horse; some with great
Devotion, stroke the home-borne wheat.

Unquestionably the spontaneity of these West Country screens, and their vernacular eloquence is explained by most of them being the work of local carpenters, not of itinerant craftsmen sent in by the heads of remote abbeys. The number of place-names ending in 'Episcopi', or beginning in 'Bishops', reflects how much closer the relationship between Church and people was in the West Country than in regions dominated to a greater degree by wealthy Benedictine abbots. Francis Bond, in *Screens and Galleries in English Churches*, quotes from Bishop Hobhouse's *Somerset Records* evidence that the screen at Yatton, erected *c.* 1454, was made on the spot by J. Crosse, a carpenter who lived in the parish, 'the oak being bought by the churchwardens in standing trees, which they selected, felled, and seasoned'.

When we travel westward the relationship

between Church and landscape changes dramatically. The sea becomes the dominant factor. Trees become progressively fewer, so that when we get into Cornwall the only mature trees are found sheltering the parish church in scores of parishes like Braddock, Davidstow, St Clement, St Enoder, St Just-in-Roseland, Lewannick, Linkinhorne, Mawgan, Michaelstow, St Mellion, Penzance, and Wadebridge. We first sense the change from the lush to the austere as we leave the Quantocks and drive across Exmoor into north Devon. In the first few miles of the journey the traditional scene has been masked by the public-spirited generosity of the Acland family in planting hundreds of thousands of trees. Few visitors to Exmoor appreciate how much of the landscape they admire today was created by the Acland and Knight families in the nineteenth century.

At Selworthy, the most photogenic of the Exmoor villages, the severity of the winter storms is still acknowledged by the church council in continuing to coat the fabric with a mixture of lime and tallow for protection against the driving rain. Today Selworthy is the only church on Exmoor protected in this way, whereas plastered and slated roofs remain an important aspect of local style on Dartmoor.

The moorland style for smaller churches is first found along this westward journey in the Brendon Valley at Oare, in the 'Lorna Doone' church which stands close to one of the manor houses that are a feature of this hunting country. Oare has box-pews, a squire's pew with seating on three sides, and slate memorial tablets. Although the tower was rebuilt in the nineteenth century it is of the same simple embattled style typical of moorland churches in most parts of England. From Oare we may go to Parracombe's St Petroc, which was saved from demolition in the nineteenth century when a second church was built in the parish, and has now been restored by the Redundant Churches Fund. It has a low west tower, thirteenth-century chancel, with two-light window, fifteenth-

century nave, sixteenth-century porch and south aisle, with square-headed windows, each feature showing how a moorland church grew out of its own hillside as inevitably as the churches in the deep combes of the south grew out of their mellower landscape. In Devon there is frequently the contrast between lush meadowland, producing a way of life subject only to the vagaries of the seasons, and bleak, coastal moorland subject to all the cruel and unpredictable moods of the sea within two or three miles of each other.

Evangelical churchmanship of the kind that was to prove congenial to conversion into Methodism flourished early in the fishermen's villages of Devon and Cornwall, where the ruggedness of the coast and the treachery of the sea meant that sudden death was always in mind. So it is not surprising to find in the records of Parracombe that when in 1779 Bishop Ross confirmed more than 4,000 candidates drawn from 39 parishes, 86 were from Parracombe, which although supporting a larger population than now was still remote and uninviting.

The name Parracombe is a corruption of 'Petroc's Cove', perpetuating the fame of the greatest of the Celtic missionaries who landed on the north coasts of Devon and Cornwall from Ireland and Wales at the end of the fifth and the beginning of the sixth centuries to give their names to scores of places – in Cornwall especially. Most of these Cornish saints bear names never heard of in the rest of England. St Petroc was the most popular dedication, showing that the mission he conducted from a hermit's cell at Bodmin established a Celtic tradition that has coloured the whole of the church history of Devon and Cornwall. Devon got its first minster church in 739 at Crediton, later the head of a See in communion with Rome. But Crediton was no more successful in subduing the Celtic spirit

34 Ottery St Mary, Devon: the vaulted nave with curled ribs rebuilt by Bishop Grandisson of Exeter

than Augustine had been when he convened a conference near the Severn with the object of bringing the Celtic bishops into conformity with Canterbury.

This fierce religious independence of the West flared up most violently 800 years later in armed rebellion against an Order for the adoption of Cranmer's 1549 Prayer Book, requiring services to be conducted in English, which was only put down by the savage intervention of an army under the command of Lord John Russell. It is evidence of the emotional element continuing to empower the religion of the West, that after defying Canterbury in the eighth century and Parliament in the sixteenth the response to the preaching of John Wesley in the eighteenth century was more immediate and lasting than that to any other missionary since Petroc preached from wayside crosses a thousand years earlier.

This religious fervour was reflected in church furniture, but not noticeably in plans. The original minster church at Crediton was cruciform, and despite the extent of the medieval rebuilding there are still many churches in Devon that remain cruciform at the core. Few bear testimony to the monastic influence that affected local style in so many counties during the thirteenth century. The great age of rebuilding in Devon was the fourteenth century, and of churches of that period which remain cruciform we may think of Mortehoe, where fishermen's nets are hung out at harvest festivals. Tawstock, West Putford, and Widecombe-in-the-Moor in the north of the county, and Ottery St Mary, Paignton, Poltimore, West Ogwell among others in the south.

The low towers round Exeter, which are so different from the tall towers of Dartmoor and Cornwall, probably derive their style from the squat towers normal in the older cruciform churches. Many Devon towers are in fact Norman. The tower at Colyton is one of many that were built up to stately proportions from a Norman base. Some idea of the original spread of Norman churches may be gauged from the distribution of Norman fonts, only 15 of which, incidentally, are circular. Perhaps, generally speaking, Branscombe's fascinating church, overlooking Lyme Bay, might be said to be representative of Norman style in Devon at its most typical. It has a Norman nave as well as a Norman crossing tower with narrow windows in the north face, and the inner wall of the tower may well be Saxon – a rare feature in Devon.

The wave of rebuilding that finally encompassed the whole of Devon and much of Cornwall started under the influence of Bishop Grandisson of Exeter (1327–69), who built the splendid nave of his own cathedral and the church at Ottery St Mary, where he founded a college. We see his hand at Bere Ferrers, built by the Ferrers family, at West Ogwell, and at Tawstock in the park of the former earls of Bath. But although this was so great an age of church building in England generally, it failed to produce in Devon the beautiful tracery associated with the fourteenth century in other counties. Consequently the rebuilding done in the fourteenth and fifteenth centuries in Devon tends to merge into what appears to be a single architectural style into which, with minor variations, nine out of ten of the county's churches can be placed.

In most, the alterations did not run to complete or even nearly complete rebuilding, but were restricted to the addition of aisles to the existing buildings to accommodate the larger congregations brought into the county by the clothing industry. From this expansion we got the three-hall type of church, with aisles under separate roofs extending along both sides of the original nave and chancel that we noted in Kent at Westerham and New Romney. In some, however, the aisles stop short of the final eastern bay. Where this occurs it is worth while looking to see whether the aisles took in existing transepts and stopped short of the chancel in order to retain the existing east wall – in other words, to see if the church was originally cruciform. Ashcombe's St Necton at the head of Dawlish

Water is an example of a small cruciform church that lost its north transept in this way. It is to be noted, however, that partial abandonment of the cruciform style did not continue into Cornwall.

Although the building of clerestories rarely accompanied this enlargement of existing churches in Devon, ample light was provided for by giving the aisles large windows, either low-arched or square-headed. Unfortunately in many the light that came through these new windows in the pre-Reformation period failed to reach the nave because the aisles got cluttered up with guild altars encased in tall screens. At Tavistock, for example, there were nine of them. Besides the one to the church's own patron saint, St Eustace, there were altars to Our Lady, the Holy Trinity, St Saviour, St John Baptist, St Stephen, St Blaise (the patron saint of woolcombers), St Katherine, and St George. With altars erected side by side, like booths or stalls in a market place, the architectural dignity of a church must have been sadly diminished, and any impulse to introduce beautiful tracery into the windows may have been checked for that reason. Happily, this did not apply to all churches with guild altars along the aisles. The outstanding exception is the Lane aisle at Cullompton, one of the most beautiful aisles in England, where fan tracery vaulting is seen at its best. This magnificent aisle was built of Beer stone in 1529 as an outer south aisle to serve as a chantry chapel to John Lane, who is described in an inscription as 'Woolwarden of the Wapentake', *Wanpat custos launarii*.

In these long, low churches chancel arches tend to become less common as the Tamar is approached. In Cornwall they are entirely absent from churches rebuilt in the fifteenth century. The result of adopting this open-plan style would have been bare in the extreme after the guild altars had been cleared away at the Dissolution of the monasteries, if beauty had not been introduced by adorning the three parallel barrel roofs with decorative bosses, and constructing elaborately carved screens across the entire width of the church.

Some of these screens were of stone, and as stone is so plentiful in the West we may wonder why there are not more of them, although, in fact, screens that are not of oak are rare in any part of England. No doubt the greater ease of working in wood explains this. Nevertheless, the stone screens of Devon are to be noted as an important contribution to local style. They include in particular those at Ottery St Mary, Paignton, Awliscombe, Poltimore, Totnes, and the Hurdwick screen at Tavistock.

At Hartland, which has a church as famous in the north of Devon as that at Ottery St Mary is in the south, we find the highest tower (128 ft) and the largest and in some respects most magnificent rood screen; but the two screens that would probably be voted the finest in this county that is so rich in them are both in the south. They are the ones at Kenton, which is believed to be the work of Flemish woodcarvers, and at Totnes, which was commissioned by the Corporation of the Borough with the stipulation that it should be of freestone like the one in Exeter Cathedral. In style it is a typical Devonshire screen. Many of the best of them have panels painted in delicate colours portraying the saints, curiously arranged with the men to the north of the opening, the women to the south.

If we go into the villages of what might be called deepest Devon – and no other county has villages so hidden and secluded – we find some of the best churches in the villages between Dartmoor and Exmoor. The best bench-ends, for example, are at High Bickington, on a hill above the River Taw ten miles or so out of Barnstaple. There are 70 of them in two sets, one Gothic, the other Renaissance in design. Some of Devon's best church screens are found in the same district. At Chulmleigh, where the waggon roof of the church is adorned with carvings of angels, there is a screen longer than Hartland's, while Brushford in the Taw valley has a tiny Norman church perched on a hilltop, which surprises with a shingled spire, and has most delicately carved tracery in its chancel screen, which appears to have been designed for the private chapel of John Evans of Coldridge, where there is a similarly designed screen. Both suggest Breton influence.

Tracing origins of local features, even in response to such simple questions as why a screen like Brushford's is there and not at Coldridge, is great fun in Devon, where there seems to have been extraordinary enthusiasm for the 'make do and mend' principle in church restoration. At Hatherleigh, south-west of Brushford – another church with a shingled spire – the pulpit and reader's desk are obviously made up of bits of an old screen, and a pew near the south door has Jacobean panelling which looks as if it came from somewhere else. The church at Hatherleigh has a medley of treasures, including two fonts, one Norman, the other reputed to be Saxon, with Barnstaple tiles set round them, and roundels of old Flemish glass in the windows, while at Dolton the ultimate was achieved in 'make do and mend' by cutting a Saxon cross into two parts: the lower half, which is carved with sharply cut strapwork, to serve as the pedestal, the fantastically carved upper part as the bowl of a magnificent font. But the thrill in this little-visited church is in the discovery of four exquisite wall tablets, one to Barbara Lister, who died in 1969, three in the south aisle modern work by Laurence Whistler, whose brother, Rex, designed a stone in the churchyard.

From Hatherleigh we might make our way to Dartmoor; but the curious traveller should take in Sampford Courtenay on the way in order to see both a good Norman font and the kind of country-style woodwork found in so many small Devon churches, and most delightfully at Honeychurch, where a small twelfth-century church must be as typical of Norman style in the north of the county as Branscombe's is in the south. Here again is a Norman font decorated with cable and zig-zag work.

Before reaching Chagford as the gateway to Dartmoor from this side, we should look in at Throwleigh for another exercise in detecting sources of furnishings. Here a section of a 1544 screen was used to make the pulpit. Although its church is over-restored, Chagford has all the character of a true Dartmoor town, in so many of which the church towers stand four-square and stalwart to defy all the fury of Dartmoor weather. Many are unbuttressed; but are firmly grounded in massive blocks of moorstone. Where they do have buttresses these are usually found to be built in pairs a short distance from the angles in the Dorset style. Their other prominent feature is the stair turrets, which may be either at one of the angles or in the middle of one side, in positions suggesting that they were built primarily for defence and as look-out stations. This feature, which we first encountered in Kent, turns out to be common in most coastal counties, which makes its look-out purpose indisputable.

An exceptionally large proportion of Devon churches have crosses in their churchyards. Unlike those in Cornwall, they are not as a rule ancient. Most of them date only from the fourteenth or fifteenth century; but the men who set them up were acting on a deeply rooted West Country instinct which also led to many old churchyards being found remote from churches, a local feature Baring Gould believed had its origin in fear of the dead. If this is so, it suggests that the erection of these churchyard crosses was to proclaim the sanctity of the enclosure and to propitiate the spirits of dead ancestors. Many are known as Palm Crosses, a reminder that in the pre-Reformation Spring processions of witness a ceremony would be performed before them in preparation for moving into church. In some parishes – Manaton was one – a coffin was carried three times round the cross before burial.

Many of the granite towers on Dartmoor

35 Cullompton, Devon: stylistic perfection, with West Country romanticism in the superb rood screen and the richly embossed roof extending along the entire length of the church

disdain ornament entirely. In some the only window is a small one to light the ringing chamber, and there it may be no more than a slit in the wall. But in the old tin-mining settlements the towers have well carved pinnacles at the corners of their parapets which we may marvel to see in moorland granite. Probably they were not. They may be of stone turned or carved in quarries a distance away and merely mounted on the granite towers. The outstanding church in this group with noble towers is the cruciform fourteenth-century church at Widecombe-in-the-Moor, described by W. G. Hoskins as 'one of the finest in the west of England'. There the octagonal pinnacles have crocketed spirelets rising from them. Inside the church, the remains of a rood-screen with 32 figure paintings on it is preserved. Similar churches built by the tinners are found as far west as Poughill (Poffill), St Cleer, and St Erme in Cornwall. Although tin had been worked by surface streaming on Dartmoor since pre-Roman times, and had been exploited commercially since the twelfth century, underground mining was not introduced until the sixteenth, and it flourished for little more than a hundred years.

To understand the rough life of these mining communities we need to read such records of old-time life long after the mining had virtually ceased as the *Reminiscences and Reflections of an Old West Country Clergyman* by W. H. Thornton, who ministered at North Bovey and other moorland parishes, and of Baring Gould who knew Devon for 90 years and acquired a vast amount of inherited knowledge of life on the Moor from his visits to old settlements of quarrymen and tinners. Baring Gould's own family church at Lew-trenchard was restored twice in the nineteenth century, once by his grandfather and once by himself, and although not done on the 'make do and mend principle', it was patched with all the Devonian's enthusiasm for saving anything that might prove useful. The screen was built from sections of one Baring Gould had himself salvaged as a boy, and throughout his life he continued to pick up what he could where he could and to restore these fragments to dignified use whenever opportunity was presented. He was deeply affected by the Oxford Movement in religion, and keen on restoring Catholic symbols. Not everyone would approve of the way he did this; but the West owes him an unpayable debt.

The churches in the southern foothills of Dartmoor derived benefit from other forms of mining. Bovey Tracey, where the china clay industry has flourished so long, has a wealth of woodwork, including a rood-screen in 11 bays and a coloured stone pulpit. Bridford, a hilltop granite village, prospered so lucratively from quarrying and barytes- and lead-mining that it has an even finer display of medieval woodwork, including richly carved pulpit, stalls and bench-ends, and a delicately coloured early sixteenth-century screen. Higher Ashton has another gem of a church which, like Bridford's has a screen with panels retaining much of their original colouring and a font with a bar to protect the water from witches – yet another feature typical of the superstitious spirit of old Devon. The pulpit is said to be Elizabethan. Since preaching was not common in Elizabeth I's reign these claims should always be treated with reserve. Most pulpits claimed to be Elizabethan turn out on investigation to be Jacobean; but the West of England does have several sixteenth- and even fifteenth-century pulpits.

Along the southern fringe of the Moor limestone comes into use – most impressively at Ashburton, one of the West Country towers with its own distinctive style of window stonework. But Ashburton's importance is not confined to decorative stonework. Its tower is as representative of local style south of Dartmoor as those at Hartland and Combe Martin are of style in the north of the county. It was from Ashburton's that Totnes's magnificent tower, the finest in south Devon, was planned.

East of Exeter we find two contrasting stones: white Beer stone and Old Red Sandstone, which at Kentisbeare are used

36 St Buryan's, Cornwall: elaborately traceried and vaulted Cornish screen with richly carved beam

stone when we reach Cornwall. But as most of the churches along this coast have been over-restored they are less relevant to local style than inland churches.

Fortunately, the preservation of ancient woodwork and church treasures of every kind no longer depends on patching and anti-quarian enthusiasm in Devon and Cornwall. Craftsmen like Herbert Read, who did such sensitive work at Kenton and has a memorial in the south aisle of Exeter Cathedral, have pointed the way to a better understanding of

together to produce a chequer effect in the tower. Both are familiar to summer visitors in the characteristic but insecure cliffs, the red soil, and the cob-and-thatch villages around the most favoured resorts. As we travel westward along the coast we find bands of slate, sandstone, and limestone, with volcanic

what can be done to achieve genuine restoration and continuing care in churches. Having listed a few of the places where the best of the old may be seen, at least one place where modern work worthy to be named with the best in the county's tradition must be mentioned before crossing the Tamar into Cornwall. The choice is simple. It must be St Petroc's, Lydford, a fifteenth-century church; but with a beautiful rood-screen designed in 1904 by Bligh Bond and carved by Violet Pinwill of Ermington, together with between 60 and 70 bench-ends portraying prophets, saints, eminent ecclesiastics and servants of the church from Samuel to Archbishop Temple, designed in the 1920s by Herbert Read and cut by two fine craftsmen, one doing the figures, the other the borders.

After crossing the Tamar into Cornwall the first impressions are of greater austerity in the landscape. Cornwall is a grey county, and the tourist has to attune himself to the delicate gradations that do exist in local stone. Granite continues to dominate church fabrics across Bodmin Moor, while from Newquay to St Ives in the north, and Looe to Falmouth in the south, the cliffs are of dark slate with yellow Pentewan stone providing colour in several places – most impressively in the tower of Holy Trinity, St Austell, which is lined with granite and faced with Pentewan.

If I follow the habit I have found useful so far, of sorting out from a complexity of churches visited those that have left the strongest visual impression in my memory, the one that immediately comes to mind in Cornwall is St Anietus at St Neot, a village in a valley on the southern fringe of Bodmin Moor built entirely, as I remember it, of slate and granite. The massive fourteenth-century tower is as individualistic in its own way as Ashburton's is in Devon, and both south wall and porch are built of large blocks of Cornish granite with pinnacles on the buttresses. Perhaps it remains prominent in my memory because like St Petroc Bodmin, St Mary Truro, and St Mary Magdalene Launceston, it is remarkable for exterior as well as interior

decoration, without going to the eccentric lengths found at Launceston. Pevsner points out the significance of Cornwall recovering in the second half of the fifteenth century the feeling for elaborate decoration, illustrated at St Neot, which had its roots in the county's Celtic past. The same spirit is expressed in the carving of the bench-ends at Launcells and Gorran.

Despite the cathedral being at Truro – and rightly for administration – Bodmin, 'the abode of monks', has the strongest claim to be regarded still as the religious centre of Cornwall. Before St Petroc founded a priory there in the sixth century St Guron, a hermit, had a cell close to the present church, which is the largest parish church in Cornwall. When it was rebuilt in the fifteenth century Thomas Luccomb, the mayor, acted as treasurer of the 'Fabric Fund', as we should now call it, and all the parishioners contributed according to their means, the vicar giving one year's salary, and the local guilds – in particular the Millers, Cordwainers, Smiths, and Skinners – in proportion to their wealth. Bodmin's is in every respect a typically large Cornish church and one in which the Celtic spirit finds full expression.

In some respects, however, it is less impressive than the great medieval church at St Germans, basically Norman, which was formerly that of an Augustinian priory, and has the distinction of having two west towers with a gabled doorway between them. But St Germans could not be described as typical. Nevertheless it must have had considerable local influence since it was the head of the original See of Cornwall, the opposite number, as it were, of Crediton in Devon, with which it was merged. Most of the fifteenth- and sixteenth-century churches in Cornwall conform to the style already established in Devon; in some of the older churches, like those at Fowey and Lostwithiel, Breton influence can be traced.

Many of the wells found in so many Cornish churchyards have cells built over them, and are of the greatest significance in accounting

37 St Neot, Cornwall: austerely built of large blocks of granite, with a massive fourteenth-century tower and fine windows of medieval glass

for the strong superstitious element in Cornish religion. Although they now bear the names of Christian saints these wells are pre-Christian. In view of man's dependence on water to sustain life it is obvious that they should be. 'Where a spring rises or a river flows', declared Seneca, 'there ought we to build altars and offer sacrifices'. The local well came to be regarded as the home of the god, and the water supply might be cut off if he were not regularly propitiated with sacrifices. For more practical reasons the well became the daily meeting place of the villagers, as it continued to be throughout rural England before water was supplied by pipe to every cottage in most villages. What more natural, then, than that the first Christian missionaries should preach at them and baptise converts in the water. But in no other part of England did the old superstitions continue to anything like the same extent to colour local religious attitudes, with Derbyshire coming closest.

R. S. Hawker's churchyard at Morwenstow has both a preaching cross and St Morwena's

75

38 Bodmin, Cornwall: the largest parish church west of the Tamar, rebuilt by townsmen in the fifteenth century

Well. Unquestionably Hawker's hold on his huge congregations was due to the intermingling of Celtic superstition with Christianity in the sermons he preached. And if it is interjected that Hawker of Morwenstow was the county's most eccentric vicar, there is the factual record that the Methodists made concessions to local superstitions in *The Ancient and Holy Wells of Cornwall* by M. and L. Quiller-Couch, where we read: 'At the present time people go to the well in crowds on the first Sunday in May, when the Wesleyans hold the service there, and a sermon is preached; after which the people throw in two pins or pebbles to consult the Spirit or try for sweethearts. If the two articles sink together they will soon be married'.

It cannot be merely fanciful to see a connection between this Celtic attitude to places of baptism and their tutelary spirits and the peculiar style of personalised carving found on two groups of Norman fonts in Cornwall. In the group seen at their best at Bodmin, Roche, and St Austell, elaborately carved cup bowls are set on strong central pillars, with four or five shafts on the outside of the bowl carved at the corners with curious faces. A second group, with carved heads, can be seen at St Thomas-by-Launceston, Laneast, and St Nonna, Altarnun, a church worth visiting both because the respectful use of granite can be seen so impressively in the nave, where the piers, their bases and capitals are axed out of single blocks of granite, and in the tower, which is one of the tallest in Cornwall. Altarnun has also a remarkable series of 79 sixteenth-century bench-ends carved by a Cornish craftsman named Robert Daye.

The dominance of the moors in Cornwall is shown in the way tall granite towers were built to succeed ancient crosses as landmarks for travellers. Many of the tracks leading up to them are as ancient as the crosses, and it is significant that many towers are not only detached from their churches but stand at a distance from them. At Launceston, Callington, Looe, and Wadebridge the whole church was originally a mile or more away from the settlement, a detached 'sanctuary' as it were.

'There is', as J. D. Sedding wrote in 1884, 'in the older Cornish churches an undefinable something which makes them seem more identified with the local surroundings than is the case with church architecture in other parts of England. These simple structures seem to be part of the simple nature of the moor and down which surround them . . . they are essentially human, and eloquent of the character of the men who reared them'. They are not, in fact, as unique in these characteristics as Sedding made out. Their nearest counterparts are in Cumbria. In both regions the churches are wild and rustic. The difference between them is that there is a brooding Wordsworthian solemnity about the churches in Cumbria, which has its roots in Norse culture, whereas in Cornwall there is the wild moorishness that Sedding found undefinable but palpable and which leaves the tourist with so many memories of magnificent granite towers like those at Ludgvan, St Column Minor and Probus, the finest of them all; and simple moorland buildings all finding unity in being built from rock broken from tors or quarried from the Moor, bearing marks of centuries of harsh weathering, and reached along churchyard paths between the gravestones of men bearing names, many of which are, in fact, unique to Cornwall, and most of them as distinctively Cornish as the churches they built.

5 The West Midlands: South

GLOUCESTERSHIRE – OXFORDSHIRE – HEREFORDSHIRE – WORCESTERSHIRE – WARWICKSHIRE

Cloth was woven in the Cotswolds before the Norman Conquest. Before the end of the twelfth century Flemish weavers were settled in strength there, giving unique importance to churches in such regions as the hills north of Cirencester, where a college of Saxon canons was established in the ninth century, and where one of the longest Saxon naves in England was excavated in 1965. We see these survivals especially at Bibury, Quenington, Bagendon, Daglingworth, Stratton, Elkstone, and the Cerneys – all in a region which enjoyed prosperity under lay patronage before the abbots gained power.

The wealthiest of the lay landowners in the south-west of the region were the Berkeleys, who owned among other estates Nympsfield, Beverstone, Dursley, Wotton-under-Edge, Westonbirt, Syde, and Uley. All these parishes benefited from their patronage, accounting for the preservation of such features as the Saxon carving of the figure of Christ now built into the south wall of the tower of Beverstone church, which dates from the first half of the eleventh century and resembles one in Bristol Cathedral. The Berkeleys were later to make an interesting if limited contribution to local styles in the 'Berkeley arch', introduced by the reigning Lord Berkeley into the Great Hall of Berkeley Castle between 1340 and 1350 and afterwards used in the construction of chantry chapels endowed by the family, as well as in Bristol Cathedral and in the many cusped arches of

the ambulatory screen in Gloucester Cathedral. It may be described briefly as a double arch, polygonal in form, with four or more straight supports enclosing a cusped inner arch, usually with slightly ogee-shaped foils. It is one of the earliest and most interesting of the many eccentric features in church furnishings derived from lay patronage. The most handsome of these Berkeley arches are in the chapel built south of the chancel in Berkeley church for the tomb of James, the 11th earl.

In discussing Norman churches in *The Vale and the Forest of Dean* volume of Pevsner, David Verey draws attention to the group of churches without east windows in the country north of Cirencester, and poses the question which no-one is better qualified than he to answer: 'Do they represent the rare unaltered survival of an early plan which is of Celtic origin?' One would suspect that they do, although its source may remain in doubt. They are all in a confined area, and comprise the group made up of Notgrove, Aston Blank, Baunton, Winstone, and Brimpsfield. Local conservatism is shown in that when east windows were introduced into this region at Elkstone, Edgeworth, Tarlton, Hampnett, and Clapton, they were small.

39 Cirencester, Gloucestershire: the three-storeyed fifteenth-century south porch formerly used as the Town Hall

The survival of such features as these, and of others such as the stone-vaulted chancels at Hampnett, Avening, Elkstone, and Coln St Dennis is a tribute to both the early prosperity of the region and the superb quality of local oolitic limestone, which made possible the decoration of so many of the fonts and local-style tympana for which the Cotswold churches around Cirencester are renowned. The two examples in the group just mentioned that should not be missed are at Elkstone and Quenington, the one for the carving depicting Christ in Majesty, the emblems of the four Evangelists, the *Agnus Dei*, and the hand of God the Father, the other for two elaborately carved tympana, both *c.* 1150. The carving above the south doorway, depicting the Coronation of the Virgin witnessed by two seraphs and the symbolic beasts of the four Evangelists, is of more than local importance. Its source is a mystery, chiefly because the treatment is so much cruder than that of other carvings in the Cotswolds, and the subject is only known to have been used here and in the carvings of a capital from Reading Abbey, now in the Victoria and Albert Museum, also of superior workmanship. Eight other churches in the Gloucestershire Cotswolds are decorated with elaborately carved tympana of so rare a quality that they can only be explained by the early introduction into the region of a remarkably advanced school of stone carvers. For a scholarly examination of their work the reader is referred to *Cotswold Churches* by David Verey (Batsford, 1976), in which the various styles are traced back to their places of origin.

The other great landowning family from the point of view of ecclesiastical patronage in the region is that of St Clare, which tooks its name from Clare in Suffolk, but is associated with the West Midlands in the earldom of Gloucester. Walter de Clare founded Tintern Abbey as a Cistercian monastery in 1131, and Tewkesbury Abbey was on one of his manors. It was from the building of Tewkesbury Abbey and Gloucester Cathedral in the

twelfth century that the West Midlands gained pre-eminence in Norman architecture. The two buildings have much in common. Both dominate with their tall cylindrical piers and low arches, a style that for a long time remained restricted to the counties of Gloucester and Worcester. The tallness was probably derived directly from the late Saxon style seen locally in the narrow nave at Deerhurst.

Bristol and Gloucester quickly eclipsed Chichester and Winchester as sources of local style in the South-West of England by establishing schools of masons that became the most renowned in the country and in Gloucester's case gave rise to the saying 'As sure as God's in Gloucester', which Thomas Fuller explains as being due to the number of churches in the county. He might have said 'Norman churches', since there is hardly one ancient church in the region that entirely lacks Norman features. Sixty of the best are in Gloucestershire, and to those should be added the churches in the Oxfordshire Cotswolds.

At Cirencester, 'the Cathedral of the Cotswolds', we see how developing liturgy made its contribution to architecture. The original church was built *c.* 1180 with aisles flanking both nave and chancel. When it was rebuilt in the thirteenth century the south aisle was widened to provide a chapel dedicated to St John the Baptist, the north aisle to provide one dedicated to Our Lady. This Lady Chapel was again widened in 1450, and the nave was reconstructed in 1515–30. With each stage the expansion of the Catholic liturgy was recorded in stone until the dissolution of the monasteries, completed in 1540, brought this line of development to an end as Protestantism took over.

That Gloucester and Tewkesbury should have abbeys erected simultaneously is marvel enough; but the wonder increases when at Malvern and Pershore in Worcestershire we find two other inexplicably noble churches within a few miles of each other with similarly distinctively local features in common. Apart from the exceptionally tall piers, it is only in

40 Fairford, Gloucestershire: famed for its exterior tracery and for having the best fifteenth- and sixteenth-century glass in England

this region that we find uncommonly small round capitals on tall Norman piers as a local characteristic, and just how local these characteristics are is brought home to us when we visit Hereford Cathedral and find that although the piers there are of the same diameter as those at Gloucester and Tewkesbury they are only half as tall.

In Norman times the structural comparisons that best repay study in the West Midlands are between Gloucester and Bristol, where the masons attached to the Augustinian abbey, of which little remains, left their mark on churches over an area that enjoyed early prosperity. Worcester's influence on architec-

tural style was small because the county was late in developing. Hereford's, as we shall see presently, was great and extended into the north Midlands; but it was not revolutionary except in decorative stone carving. In comparing churches built by masons from Bristol with those built by masons from Gloucester we find that the main preoccupation of the Bristol masons was with the earth-bound horizontal effects we noted as being characteristic of the churches of Devon and Cornwall as well as of those in north Somerset and Dorset, whereas all the feeling that emanated from Gloucester was for vertical lines that gave height to buildings and a sense of towering nobility to the larger churches, so that eventually Gloucester was the birthplace of Perpendicular architecture.

Seen in purely practical terms, the Bristol style was in keeping with the West of England's preoccupation with broad-based styles of construction suitable for regions in which stone was intractable and weather severe, especially along the coast, while the Gloucester masons could revel in the availability of stone that fulfilled every ambition they could cherish in working it. Given also patrons to finance their ambitious projects it is not surprising that the development of ecclesiastical architecture in the fourteenth and fifteenth centuries should have been concentrated in the West Midlands and have found such inspiring expression, first in the building of Bristol Cathedral, followed by the remodelling of Gloucester, where the eastern parts of the Cathedral were to point the way forward by evolving the style that was to become England's major contribution to architectural styles internationally. In addition to being the birth-place of the Perpendicular style, the introduction of fan vaulting into the eastern range of the cloisters at Gloucester between 1351 and 1377 is claimed to be the earliest date for fan vaulting in Europe so far authenticated, although work in the Chapter House at Hereford cannot have been much later, and the fourteenth-century vaulting at Tewkesbury might be thought to anticipate the fans that opened out fully at Gloucester.

The wealth of the Church along the western fringe of the Cotswolds is shown in that within a circuit of less than 30 miles there were eight flourishing monasteries: Gloucester, Tewkesbury, Malvern, Worcester, Pershore, Evesham, Winchcombe, and Hailes, all deriving features from Gloucester. The first of these to attract the attention of the visitor as he opens the churchyard gate at Gloucester is the tower. The blind surface panelling that is so striking a feature, and one seen also at Malvern and Evesham in Worcestershire and Cirencester and Chipping Campden in Gloucestershire, was the Gloucester School's main contribution to local style in tower construction. The ultimate was achieved at Evesham, where panels cover the whole of the east and west faces of the bell tower, including the outer face of the buttresses. It must,

however, be added that not everything in Evesham's bell tower was derived from Gloucester. Professor Allen believed that the parapet and pinnacles were copied from York Minster. However that may be, we must regret that this remarkable tower, started by the last abbot of Evesham in 1528 was never completed with the groined ceiling he intended it to have.

It must not be thought that the West Midlands are exclusively, or even primarily, remarkable for the grandeur of their churches. From the point of view of local style the great charm of the Cotswold churches is that they harmonise so perfectly with the buildings around them. 'Cotswold Gothic' applies as much to Cotswold manor houses and cottages as it does to churches. We see this in all the villages, and nowhere more attractively than at Bibury, where the three classes of building just named are clustered together, not autocratically separated as they are in so many villages rebuilt in the eighteenth century. The unifying element is, of course, the stone – particularly in the roofs, which conform to the one pattern for cottage, mansion, and church: stone slabs of varying thickness laid with the thinner ones along the ridge and the heavier ones in descending order. The object of this arrangement is that the heavy slabs along the eaves shall be strong enough to hold the whole roof in position.

The man who loved this unity between ecclesiastical and domestic architecture in the Cotswolds above all others was William Morris, who used to drive all his visitors at Kelmscott to see Great Coxwell barn. Professor Lethaby tells us that Morris loved this barn 'not only deeply but excitedly'. On one occasion he went so far as to declare it the finest piece of architecture in England, its merit being that it grew strongly and simply to meet the daily needs of the people who built it, which is how so many Cotswold village churches grew.

This unity came about in the Cotswolds because the barns were built to store grain from the demesne lands and tithes in kind

Despite the wealth of the wool staplers, which was so great that some of them were able to pull down existing churches like the foolish man in the Bible who pulled down his barns to build greater, scores remain as faithful records of the generations in which they were built. At Burford, extensions made over a period of 400 years have given the church an irregular form which makes it look as though its construction, magnificent as it is, had been haphazard. At Witney, the plan as we see it now straggles through all the periods from Norman to Perpendicular to meet the ambitions of local guilds wanting to set up altars in its aisles. In fact, it is estimated that before the chancel of the south transept was taken down the church had been expanded to four times the size of the original Norman church with simple rectangular nave, short square chancel and axial tower out of which it grew. This may suggest that in this case the process of historical accretion had gone too far, so completely had the original church been overlaid by a complex of aisles, transepts, and chapels. But better that than the arrogant zeal of the academic purist too ignorant to know that one generation's fashion may be the next generation's folly.

The two churches most closely associated with the wealthy wool staplers of the Cotswolds are those at Northleach and Chipping Campden. John Fortey, d. 1458, paid for the nave of Northleach to be rebuilt; William Grevel rebuilt Chipping Campden. The brass to William Grevel at Chipping Campden describes him as 'the flower of the wool merchants of the whole realm of England'; but as Dr Johnson remarked, 'in lapidary inscriptions a man is not upon oath' and no doubt something equally laudatory could have been claimed for John Fortey. What is so interesting is that their churches have so many features in common, suggesting that both these wealthy men were guided by the masons they employed and did not adopt the principle of 'the man who pays the piper calls the tune', which proved so disastrous in the nineteenth-century rebuildings of many

41   Burford, Oxfordshire: the tower, spire, and parvised porch of a majestic church in several styles

from the monastic granges by the same hands as built the churches. So just as when we look for an interpretation of the *genius loci* in Sussex we turn to Kipling, for Dorset to Hardy, and for Cumbria to Wordsworth, in the Cotswolds we turn to William Morris. It was while travelling through Burford in September 1876 that he saw the restorers doing what he regarded as their devil's work. In the following March he found them threatening Tewkesbury Abbey with 'scraping and scouring', and in the heat of his indignation the Society for the Protection of Ancient Buildings was forged, with himself as first secretary.

42 Chipping Campden, Gloucestershire: the stately 'wool church' of an unspoiled Cotswold town

churches in the North Midlands. So at Northleach and Chipping Campden we see features that have come to be particularly associated with Perpendicular style in the Cotswolds: concave pier mouldings, depressed arches, windows inserted above the chancel arch to allow the nave to be flooded with morning light. Another feature rare elsewhere is a niche in the east wall of the porch, which formerly contained a figure set there to give solemnity to contracts made in the porch, including marriages. Readers of Chaucer will remember that the Wife of Bath had husbands five 'at the church door', evidence that the legally binding contract of marriage was made before witnesses in the porch before nuptial mass was celebrated inside the church.

With local stone producing such beautiful fan vaulting in roofs, its use became popular for every kind of church furniture. I don't remember seeing a single one of the ubiquitous Purbeck marble fonts in a Gloucestershire church, and Purbeck marble monuments are rare in them. The local oolite fulfilled every need for dignified use and commemoration. So despite the popularity of alabaster, freestone continued to be used for effigies in Cotswold churches until the middle of the seventeenth century, and when in the eighteenth Italian marble took over for monuments inside churches the local masons continued to do fine work in the churchyards

43 Witney, Oxfordshire: the thirteenth-century tower crossing and chancel

with upright headstones and chest tombs, the best of which are at Painswick and Burford.

Painswick is recognised as having the most beautiful churchyard in England. Its 99 yews figure in every account of it. But they are not the only, or even the principal justification for its fame. This, surely, is the fine series of Georgian gravestones commemorating the leading citizens in the town's most affluent period carved by such accomplished masons as the Bryant family, who were attracted to the neighbourhood by the excellence of the local stone. Some headstones, however, have weathered badly and brass plaques have had to be fixed to them to preserve their identity.

Much of the decoration, like that on the Swithland slate headstones in Leicestershire, is derived from patterns found in the books of writing masters. At Burford the interest is in the way the lids of the chest tombs are carved to represent corded bales of wool. Other churchyards have their own distinctive features of this kind. At Dumbleton in the Vale of Evesham the headstones are sculptured with Resurrection scenes, at Newnham there are 13 angels carved on a single stone, which looks excessive for the guardianship of one poor soul!

It is not surprising that Gloucestershire should have little to show for itself in rood-screens, which were a feature of the county in the Middle Ages. Their removal was at the behest of the reforming Bishop Hooper, who suffered martyrdom under Mary I at Gloucester in 1555. Fortunately a few remain: notably at Fairford, Rendcomb, and Cirencester, as well as the well-known stone screen at Berkeley. Stone pulpits are a different story. With 30, Gloucestershire ties with Somerset for them. The local style is goblet-shaped, with the traceried panels and crocketed gables seen at Chedworth, Cirencester, North Cerney, and Naunton.

Travelling masons – freemasons – worked their way across the South Midlands in the thirteenth and fourteenth centuries, leaving their marks on pier capitals carved with grotesque heads appearing out of foliage as far east as Woodstock, Bloxham, Adderley, and Hampton Poyle in Oxfordshire, where portrait heads are a county feature. Eventually new styles that are now more closely associated with the Home Counties than with the West Midlands came into use. As in all regions, styles spill over from one county to another, and in styling the West Midlands certainly cannot exclude the Oxfordshire Cotswolds. Clerestory lighting, for example, reaches its highest development at Chipping Norton, where each bay is filled with square windows of five lights, each light divided at the head into two long panels to produce the effect of woodwork – treatment that would

44 Great Tew, Oxfordshire: showing typical tall rectangular clerestory windows with heavy hood moulds

have incurred the wrath of Ruskin, who held that each material should be used in accordance with its own natural character, which meant that stone should not be used as timber, a purist point of view that many would say can be carried too far.

As in Somerset, many Gloucestershire churches have towers that were originally designed to carry spires; but these were either never built, or if built were not rebuilt when they crumbled, as so much of the soft stone in the west of the region is liable to do. Fortunately, the limestone of the Oxfordshire Cotswolds is usually hard, so we have splendid spires at other places besides Burford and

Witney. The most typical are thirteenth-century, and take their design from the spire on Oxford Cathedral, which has a strong claim to be the earliest true spire in England. Spires of this type are seen at Kemble, Bampton, Broadwell, and Shipton-under-Wychwood. As a group they are certainly early. The fine spires at Adderbury, Bloxham, and St Mary the Virgin, Oxford, are fourteenth-century.

The opinion that spires are most effective on low towers finds much support in Herefordshire, a county of massive towers that are broad rather than lofty. Most of them are built of the Old Red Sandstone that is typical of the county. The tall slender spire at Yatton rises from such a tower. Although Herefordshire may not be thought of as a county particularly remarkable for its spires it has, in fact, more than might be expected, and they

45 Pembridge, Herefordshire: late fourteenth-century detached belfry in three stages

have the common feature of being recessed, not broached. The spires at Weobley and Ross-on-Wye are good examples. Herefordshire is also the only county so far as I know that has flying buttresses to link the spire with the pinnacles of the tower.

As we are now near the border with Wales, original features may be expected in Herefordshire, and they are to be found in many places, but might be considered more appropriately in relation to local styles in Wales than in England. One of the most curious is the fourteenth-century bell tower at Pembridge, sometimes referred to as the 'bell-house'. It is a suitable one to include because it har-

monises so well with the black-and-white cottages round it. The steeple rises from a squat stone stage with chamfered corners to a roof sloping up to a wooden second stage, which in turn slopes upwards through a shingled stage capped by a pillar carrying a weather vane. This odd-looking structure is supported on the inside by four pillars rising from the ground to the top of the second stage. But although unique, Pembridge's bell-tower 'belongs', since it is similar in character to others on the Welsh border and expresses the Celtic independence of mind which must be the explanation of so many original features in Herefordshire, and which spills over into Worcestershire in the half-timbered tower in three stages at Warndon, which looks more like a dwelling house than a church. More typical of Herefordshire are the detached late fourteenth-century wooden belfries at Hol-

46 Leominster, Herefordshire: fourteenth-century south aisle and east window with ball-flower encrustation

mer and Yarpole, which look like those on market halls. Detached towers are a Herefordshire feature. There are eight of them, of which the finest are at Bromyard, Ross-on-Wye, and Ledbury, to which may be added as another Herefordshire curiosity the gaunt, gabled tower at Kinnersley, which is attached to the church by the corner only. The long windows seen at Ross-on-Wye and Ledbury were apparently inspired by Hereford Cathedral.

Another structural curiosity in Herefordshire is the carrying up into a gable of either the south or north wall of the easternmost bay of the aisle in order to introduce additional light by the insertion of a window that may be even larger than the east window of the aisle.

The effect of this is similar to that gained by a transept window. It is seen at Almeley and Lyonshall. Windows on both sides of the chancel are another local characteristic designed to maximise light.

Where Herefordshire really excels, however, is in the astonishing range and quality of its decorative stone-carving. This virtuosity of the Hereford sculptors is seen particularly in the exuberance of the ball-flower decoration – sometimes likened to a sheep-bell – seen most profusely at Ledbury and Leominster, where there was a school of stone-carving associated with the Benedictine abbey. It seems probable that it was there that so much of this decorative work originated, including the elaborate stone-carving at Kilpeck, which is world-famed, and the remarkable group of Herefordshire goblet-shaped fonts covered with symbolic designs in which Irish, Scandinavian, French, and Italian influences have been identified by experts. The most exuberant are at Castle Frome and Eardisley. The best of this work is Norman, with Abbey Dore, a thirteenth-century fragment of an influential Cistercian abbey, the outstanding exception, although Herefordshire long continued to be a county producing supplementary work of the highest merit. Katharine Esdaile, in *English Church Monuments* (Batsford, 1947), describes the work of such skilled sculptors as Epiphanius Evesham, born in Herefordshire, whose work is found extensively in the West Midlands and at Felsted and Stanstead Mountfitchet in Essex, and John Gildon, who introduced Italian motifs into memorials. We see the work of these two in Herefordshire at Much Marcle, Ross-on-Wye, and many other places.

Although not on the same scale as at Gloucester, there are distinctive styles of church building that so far as England as a whole is concerned do appear to have originated at Hereford. From the city there appear to have been freemasons travelling about the county from late Norman times, and many of them wandered into Worcestershire from the west as masons from Gloucester did from the south. We can often recognise their influence on approaching a short sturdy tower, usually unbuttressed, that has weathered to a greyish pink, which in the hills between Hereford and Ledbury may be varied by the use of the Silurian limestone quarried near Woolhope.

The sharp wiry folds of the draperies at Fownhope are typical of the work of the Herefordshire school, although different hands can be identified in work of the same period at Rowlstone, Brinsop, Stretton Sugwas, Leominster, Eardisley and Castle Frome. In all the work of the pioneer Herefordshire masons there is bold variety of treatment in the recurring use of Viking dragons, birds, and human figures on medallions strung together on interlaced beaded bands. It is this figure sculpture that most attracts attention in Herefordshire craftsmanship, starting with the Cathedral.

Experts find the mid-twelfth-century ruins of the dismantled church at Shobdon a fascinating study, although they amount to no more than two doorways and a chancel arch resited near the present church, with an interior transformed in 1753 by Lord Bateman in 'Strawberry Hill Gothic' style. The motifs are now so defaced that they can only be deciphered with the help of lithographs done in 1852 by G. R. Lewis, but racial origins can be identified in them that were later to be developed in all the work of the Herefordshire freemasons. In no other part of the country is the combination of Celtic, Scandinavian, French, and Italian motifs achieved with such confident dexterity.

The explanation arises from the consideration of two distinct double strains of influence. The Celtic and Scandinavian must have been derived from St Aidan's Northumbrian missionaries, who made their way down the west of England, integrating successfully with native craftsmen along the Welsh border, where Irish influence was already strong. The French and Italian strains, which combined another Scandinavian element, are explained by the power of the French marcher lords who were established on the border after the Norman Conquest by William to defend the region against the Welsh. Their ruined castles continue to give a romantic, if feudal, air to the landscape of the Wye Valley, and are to be seen in association with the churches architecturally.

The precocious element in the work is attributed to the influence of a master mason who was given to showing off his skill by introducing figures in highly improbable attitudes, such as angels flying upside down, and carving his birds and beasts with ferociously long claws. His work can be recognised at Kilpeck in the carving of the south doorway, considered to be his best work. The same mastery has been identified at Fownhope in the tympanum of the carefully preserved doorway, where the Virgin is seated with one hand raised and feet apart.

A little later came that other characteristically Herefordshire feature, the trumpet or

48 St Margaret's, Herefordshire: the wide
galleried rood loft above a bressummer
with delicate lace-like carving

stiff-leaf capital seen in more than 20
churches, including those at Bromyard,
Colwall, Ledbury, Ross-on-Wye, and Abbey
Dore, to recount a few that most tourists of the
county would want to see anyway. Of these
Abbey Dore is far too important a church for
any attempt to be made to summarise its
features in a book looking only for local
styling. Suffice it to say that the ceilings
(1633) are by John Abel, the king's carpenter.

The two features that go a long way
towards accounting for the lack of distinctive
styles in Worcestershire churches are the
dense afforestation of the county in the

Middle Ages, and its geological structure as a
shallow basin rimmed by hills. The effect of
the latter is that the centre of the county,
eventually to become the main region of
growth, had no good building stone, while the
villages along the hill ranges were built in
styles closely akin to those of their neighbouring counties. Malvern's kinship with Gloucester has been mentioned. Broadway,
Worcestershire's showpiece, where the old
church is a mile out of the village, is Cotswold
Gothic in the Gloucestershire idiom. The red
sandstone in the west links Worcestershire
with Herefordshire, with which it is now
united administratively. On the northern
border timber towers and bell-cotes are in
Shropshire style. Between these marginal
features are soft sandstones and muddy
limestones which are so characteristic of
village churches in the Midlands. Few are
built in the distinctive styles found under the
Malvern hills, Bredon, and the Cotswolds.

47 Kilpeck, Herefordshire: richly
decorated twelfth-century south doorway

Although there is Norman work in about 90 churches in Worcestershire it is seldom dominant, and in any case such instances of sculpture as the chancel arch at Rock, or the ornate font at Chaddesley Corbett are attributed to Herefordshire stone masons. St Andrew's, Droitwich has fine thirteenth-century work; but there is little else from the period that can be considered noteworthy, and when we turn to the cathedral, which is the county's glory, we find that it has had to be refaced repeatedly.

So how do we start looking for what is characteristic if not uniquely local in Worcestershire? The answer, as in all densely wooded counties, is to follow the courses of navigable rivers. It was from these that heavily forested counties were settled. This was doubly so in the West Midlands, which in the Severn and its tributaries had waterways that carried more transport than any other in England except the Thames. Examples that come to mind of churches in places of early settlement are Cropthorne and Fladbury between Evesham and Pershore, where unbuttressed Norman towers with small windows match each other, and where decorative motifs are found that may also be seen at Shrawley, overlooking the Severn.

The Teme, which gave its name to the lovable little market town of Tenbury Wells, is another stream running into Worcestershire at its most characteristic. Above it, on hill sites looking towards the Clee hills of Shropshire, there are several churches with strong family resemblances. Bayton, near a tributary of the Teme, must have been a forest church comparable with Besford before its restoration, and Eastham, near Tenbury is important because it is built of stone described by Mervyn Blatch in *Parish Churches of England in Colour* (Blandford Press, 1974), as 'tufaceous limestone . . . formed of spring water bubbling up through another limestone and precipitat-

ing calcium carbonate upon it; in time this hardens and assumes a sponge-like appearance with many holes in its surface. . . . It is used in two or three churches in Worcestershire, the best known of which is Shelsley Walsh'. Eastham has another local characteristic in the way the Norman south door projects from the wall. It has also a curious, much weathered representation of Sagittarius and Leo on the south wall.

In touring the county in search of specifically local features, instead of merely doing a 'Cook's Tour' to inspect national monuments, we may be astonished to find how rich Worcestershire is in minor features that surprise and delight by their unexpectedness. The zig-zag design at Elmbridge, for example, is claimed to occur in no other county. Timber towers figure more prominently than in any of the other counties so far discussed, and five are of special interest: those at Pirton, Dormston, Kington, Cotheridge, and Warndon. Bell-cotes over the west end of the nave, which have already been noted along the south coast are common in Worcestershire, so become a local feature to be recognised. We see them at Knighton-on-Teme, Mamble, White Ladies Aston, and Himbleton.

A seldom-visited church that I always see – rightly or wrongly – as the sole survivor of what for centuries must have been the local style is at Besford, three miles south-west of Pershore. Its timber nave is both framed and roofed in oak, and inside the church is an interesting sixteenth-century rood loft. Among churches that have lost their original character on the outside, but have retained much of it inside must be mentioned Peopleton, north of Pershore and near White Ladies Aston.

When we move into Warwickshire we find that the Avon forms a natural dividing line between the large, over-restored churches with smoky red sandstone towers to the north of it, and the churches built of oolitic or lias limestone to the south, which merge into those of the Cotswolds. As Warwickshire is the midmost of England's shires it is cut through

49 Pirton, Worcestershire: typically West Country timbered tower

50   Pershore, Worcestershire: the interior
of the tower from the ringing platform

by Roman roads producing elongated street
villages, and the county as a whole lacks the
composure and settled character that gave
rise to so many distinctive local styles in the
southern and western counties. Those to
whom local styles tend to be personalised –
and I am one – may feel that Warwickshire's
most distinctive churches are in the mood of
George Eliot's novels. They may see it
reflected in such churches as Astley's St Mary,
where the nave is the chancel of a collegiate
church that was remodelled as a parish

church by Thomas Astley in 1343, to which
Richard Chamberlain added a red sandstone tower and chancel in 1608. In 1700 local
industry made its own contribution of a
wrought-iron communion rail. Another collegiate church in Warwickshire is St Edith,
Monks Kirby.

The completeness of the change in atmosphere found near Birmingham is the result of
prosperity reaching the district late and
lasting longer. Fourteenth-century work,
which is rare in other West Midlands counties
becomes prominent, and is often mixed, as at
Coleshill and Solihull, with fifteenth-century
work. Even the chancels, which in most parts
of England were enlarged by the clergy

51 St Mary's, Warwick: the fine pseudo-Gothic nave which needs to be seen in relationship with the castle

South of the Avon, St George, Brailes, 'the cathedral of the Feldon', with a nave 150 feet long, a west tower 110 feet high, and clerestories with 12 windows on each side would be a good introduction to the many churches built in the grand style for the prosperous Midlands, which reach their peak in Holy Trinity, Coventry, and their most splendid exhibition of pride in the rich carving of the Beauchamp Chapel at St Mary's, Warwick, which in localising style has to be seen in relation to Warwick Castle. For churches simply reflecting the use of local iron-bearing limestone, All Saints, Burton Dassett, with a south arcade of octagonal piers and a north aisle with thirteenth-century carving might be selected. It has a churchyard with fascinating if somewhat heavily carved headstones. For a different style of church in Warwickshire, Wootton Wawen, with four Saxon arches in the tower, should not be missed. It was described by George Gilbert Scott as 'an epitome in stone of the history of the Church of England'.

In conclusion it must be acknowledged that the churches of the West Midlands are so complicated in character and design that students could argue interminably as to which features are most representative of local style. I can only say that for me the outstanding feature is the beauty of the stone fan vaulting throughout the entire region. Timber fan vaulting reached its peak in the rood-screens of Somerset and Devon; stone fan vaulting still remains most closely associated with the West Midlands despite Kings Chapel, Cambridge, and perhaps half a dozen churches in East Anglia. The only medieval fan vaulting in the North of England is at Manchester and Rotherham. Nationally, the concentration is west of a band running southwards from Warwick to Christchurch. Every cathedral in the area has it, as well as such parish churches as those at Evesham, Tewkesbury, Cirencester, Burford, Minster Lovell, Maids Moreton, and Fairford.

during the thirteenth century, were most often enlarged in Warwickshire during the fourteenth. Solihull and Aston Cantlow are notable examples. Warwickshire had no school of masons to compare with those at Gloucester and Hereford. What it did have was an important school of builders who developed a local style of steeple seen most impressively at Coleshill on the Chester Road. This is probably the Warwickshire church best worth studying for local style.

6 The East Midlands: South

NORTHAMPTONSHIRE – HUNTINGDONSHIRE – BEDFORDSHIRE – BUCKINGHAMSHIRE – HERTFORDSHIRE

It is claimed for Northamptonshire that it has the most unbroken record of church styles of any English county. The early Saxon church at Brixworth is described by Sir Alfred Clapham as 'perhaps the most imposing architectural memorial of the seventh century surviving north of the Alps'; Earl's Barton's massive unbuttressed late Saxon tower must be the most photographed monument of its period in Britain. The twelfth-century tower of St Kynburga, Castor, has all the strength of the Norman combined with richness of ornamentation that foreshadows what was to be achieved there in the thirteenth century, and shows in its open work parapet and short fourteenth-century spire how harmoniously Barnack stone could be adapted for use in every period and style, in contrast to the ironstone of the region, which needed limestone support for tall steeples.

This architectural pioneering, which is so conspicuous a feature in Northamptonshire and the Soke of Peterborough, originated in the founding of Peterborough's Benedictine monastery by Peada, son of King Penda of Mercia in 650, and continued through a succession of rebuildings made necessary by sackings in 870 and 1070, and destruction by fire in 1160, which meant that over a period of more than 400 years there were masons of the highest skill at Peterborough, whose influence inevitably spread across northern Northamptonshire, particularly in the thirteenth century, when the Church was at the height of its monastic power.

Early evidence of the coming into use of the chisel in stone carving is seen in the nave and aisles of the cathedral, which date from the second half of the twelfth century and have all the characteristics of late Norman styles in both form and enrichment. Consequently, Norman style in Northamptonshire is advanced to the degree of flamboyance seen at Castor, where the pier capitals are decorated with interlacing between animal and leaf mouldings cut with a lighter touch than at Peterborough. Altogether, Castor is an admirable example of how period styles were introduced into provincial churches in orderly succession under the influence of a great abbey. In the south wall of the chancel round-arched Norman sedilia figure alongside dog-toothed double piscina. For later thirteenth-century work we turn to the south transept, for fourteenth-century to the north arcade, and finally to the east window for fifteenth-century work. Similar work may be seen at Haddon and Maxey; but unfortunately Northamptonshire suffered more than most counties at the hands of Victorian vandals.

As so much of what was achieved in the East Midland counties depended on the availability of such splendid stone for the masons to work in, we instinctively visit the

52 Earls Barton, Northamptonshire: bold Saxon tower with exceptionally elaborate strip decoration

53 Brixworth, Northamptonshire: interior of an internationally important pre-Conquest church dating from the seventh century

church at Barnack itself, where the most famous of all the Midland stones was quarried from Norman times until the eighteenth century. The stone came out of the quarries in huge masses that were broken into manageable size and carried to lean-to sheds called lodges, where they were roughly shaped with a two-headed axe ready to be carved by the masons on the building site.

After Peterborough and Castor there is no better place than Barnack for studying the evolution of period styles in the region. From its Saxon tower, decorated with scrolls branching off a stem carved with figures which include a cock, it summarises admirably the entire history of ecclesiastical architecture throughout the East Midlands. The early fourteenth-century chancel and east window are of rare excellence. But the greatest treasure at Barnack is the late Saxon figure of Christ in Majesty seated. Pevsner, commenting on its 'exquisite quality' says 'the draperies are managed as competently as never again anywhere for a century or more, and the expression is as human, dignified, and gentle as also never again for a century'.

St Giles's church in the county town is obviously of the same family as Barnack's and Castor's; but from the historian's point of view the most interesting churches in Northampton are those of St Peter and Holy Sepulchre, both twelfth-century. The special interest in St Peter is in its association with the castle of this shire capital, while Holy Trinity is one of several round churches dispersed across England that were built for the Knights Templars and Knights Hospitallers on the plan of the Holy Sepulchre in Jerusalem. Like

54 St Peter's, Northampton: ornately carved twelfth-century arcades and chancel arch

the one at Cambridge, it has always been a parish church.

The completion of the west front of Peterborough Cathedral by 1238 inspired advances in church style in Northamptonshire at Etton, Hargrave, and Polebrook, and even more impressively at Warmington, three miles north-east of Oundle. But thirteenth-century influences are most readily studied through tracery. In Northamptonshire the most marked feature in tracery is the early introduction of the pointed trefoil, which first appeared in England at Westminster Abbey, *c.* 1250–60, shortly after the completion of Peterborough's west front. It appeared at Longthorpe, near Peterborough, as early as 1263–4 when William de Thorpe rebuilt the

parish church there, giving rise to the speculation that the work was done by masons from Westminster, as it may well have been, since work of similar character and excellence was done about the same time at Higham Ferrers, which was granted by Henry III to his son, Edmund Crouchback, Earl of Lancaster.

To these influences from Peterborough and Westminster must be added Ely's influence seen so impressively in the lantern towers at Lowick and Fotheringhay, where the octagon rises from a plain tower, with a large four-centred window bisected in what came to be adopted as the Northamptonshire manner. In his survey of Northamptonshire towers Professor F. J. Allen declared that the church at Titchmarsh had 'the finest parish church tower in England outside Somerset'.

The usual thing to say about Northamptonshire is that it is a county of squires and spires. Despite its triteness the tag is inescapably true.

99

Many of the villages built of local stone – some of them as perfect in their way as any in the Cotswolds – have the manor house in the main street, imposing its own dignity on the scene and inspiring similar standards of care and maintenance for the cottages. Privacy for the family at the manor is gained by having parkland extending from the rear. As the stone for the churches as well as for the cottages came from the squire's own quarries it was always at hand, and when spires came into fashion and local stone proved so perfectly suited for them, it was inevitable that the county should become as famous for its spires as it already was for its squires, although in fact, neither word had assumed its present meaning. Spires were incorporated in steeples in the Middle Ages, and local landowners were lords of manors.

Most of these famous Northamptonshire spires are in the Nene Valley and will be more conveniently dealt with in connection with the North Midlands. Oddly enough, if we were to classify by quantity and not by quality we should discover that not more than one-third of Northamptonshire's churches do have spires! But what must be said at once is that the emergence of the recessed spire from the broach is an outstandingly local feature. It can be studied particularly at Deene, near Corby, at Woodford, Denford, and Newton-in-the-Willows, where the recessed spires incorporate broaches in true Northampton-shire style.

The most typical Northamptonshire spires are seen at their best at Higham Ferrers, Oundle, and Kettering. The first of these is thirteenth-century, the second fourteenth, the third fifteenth. All are crocketed, but so are many broach spires. The most prominent feature, and one that runs through various stages of development is the arrangement of lucarnes. Those at Ringstead and Hargrave have the unusual characteristic of starting at the foot of the spire. At St Raunds, tower and spire are unified by tall lancets running through two stages of the tower to the spire, with broaches pointing upwards again to high

lucarnes, which must be accounted a typical feature of Northamptonshire spires. They occur also at Higham Ferrers and Oundle. As some lucarnes are set in cardinal and others in alternating directions they were probably designed with a view to reducing wind resistance.

On the east, Northamptonshire has common boundaries with Huntingdonshire, Bedfordshire, and Buckinghamshire. Huntingdonshire, the most northerly of these has few characteristics that distinguish it from Northamptonshire on one side, or from Cambridgeshire on the other. The Great Ouse meanders through its clays, sustaining its three most important towns: St Neots, Huntingdon, and St Ives. Its other two important towns are Kimbolton on the Northamptonshire border and Ramsey in the Fens to the east. All these five towns derived their medieval importance from monastic patronage: Ramsey grew up round a powerful Benedictine abbey on an island in the Fens, St Ives and St Neots round priories of the same Order, Huntingdon and Kimbolton round Augustinian priories. The present parish church at Ramsey was originally the *hospitum*, or guest house, of the abbey.

The religious foundation at St Ives was originally a cell of Ramsey, but the bridge enabled a town to develop round it which eventually became so prosperous that it eclipsed Ramsey as a market town, and by exploiting its situation on one of the great historic trade routes of England established an Easter Fair which became one of the three largest in England. So when the church was rebuilt in the third quarter of the fifteenth century it was to a size and dignity befitting the town's industrial status. The tower has a spire rising from within the pinnacled battlements, but with low broaches attached to it before soaring upwards in a form that makes it comparable with the best in Northamptonshire. The furnishings inside the church are the most luxurious in the county. They include a richly painted rood-screen, statues, organ, and stained glass by Sir Ninian

55 Oundle, Northamptonshire: the south transept, porch, tower, and base of the spire of one of the county's noblest fourteenth-century churches

Comper. The town's medieval bridge, c. 1415, has one of the best bridge chapels in England.

Besides having the finest tower in the county, St Neots has a church which in Sir John Betjeman's words is 'almost everything that a good town church should be', while of the two churches that sprang from Augustinian foundations, Kimbolton's is as famous for its broach spire as St Neots' is for its tower; but as Huntingdonshire is more famous for spires than for towers, and particularly for

ashlar-faced broach spires, Kimbolton has more rivals for pre-eminence. The chief contender for the honour of being the best would probably be the fourteenth-century broach spire at Spaldwick. Both are of the same period and equally well-proportioned. Two other fine steeples are those at Buckworth and Warboys, both thirteenth-century and with three tiers of lucarnes.

As Huntingdonshire has no local stone of the first order, the stone for the best churches had to be brought in by barge, and as the towns in which they stand have remained small, the inaccessibility of stone for their restoration has meant that they have suffered less than most at the hands of the Victorians. So all are now both dignified and pleasantly encrusted with the patina of centuries. Away from the rivers, most of the village churches of Huntingdonshire are built of rubble and the brown cobbles called carstone.

It was the remoteness of Huntingdonshire that made it so conducive to Nicholas Ferrar's cultivation of the contemplative life – that and having his friend, George Herbert, as parson of Leighton Bromswold, where he rebuilt the nave of the church to accommodate the large congregations attracted by his preaching. The church at Little Gidding was also built to George Herbert's specifications, and although it suffered at the hands of the Puritans it still retains the symbolic feature of having pulpit and lectern of the same height, reminding readers of Izaak Walton's *Life* of Herbert that 'he would often say, they should neither have a precedency or priority of each other'.

Conservative features are a characteristic of Huntingdonshire churches. Double piscinas, for example, like the one we found at Castor, are seen at Hemingford Grey, where the arches are on Purbeck shafts, and in the south aisle at St Ives, where each has a pointed arch within an enclosing dog-toothed round arch. There is another at Houghton. These double piscinas are now comparatively rare. They ceased to be built towards the end of the thirteenth century when a papal edict ordered that the rinsings of the chalice after Holy

Communion must be drunk by the officiating clergy and not poured down the drain. Even in the county town, where All Saints in the Market Place is over-restored, St Mary's in the High Street retains all the features of its historical development. Its fine tower has corner-clasping buttresses in the Northamptonshire style, richly carved, with niches for statues like those in the tower at St Neots. Remains of Norman buttresses prove that a large aisled church originally occupied the site. The chancel is thirteenth-century, and the position of the priest's doorway shows that the earlier chancel was longer, indicating collegiate use. The arcades are thirteenth-century, but were altered after part of the tower collapsed in 1607. The fine mouldings of the arches, the waterleaf capitals and features like the decoration of the west tower doorway with niches for such images on brackets as a Pelican and a Green Man make the church one to provoke endless speculation.

As we see so often, because rivers form the boundaries of so many counties the question of whether neighbouring churches fall into one or other county is frequently irrelevant to their style. We have an instance of this in the Ouse Valley at Olney, which is in Buckinghamshire but might be regarded as an outstanding example of a Northamptonshire church in its steeple. When we reach the southern part of Bedfordshire the question of whether the churches are in Bedfordshire, Buckinghamshire, or Hertfordshire becomes practically meaningless if we confine our attention to style. Once we have left the main stone belt of the famous quarries, the distinguishing features, apart from districts where local wealth could overcome such limitations, were conditioned by the building materials available. This is particularly true of Bedfordshire, where the geology is exceptionally mixed. Bands of stone cross the county, with heavy clays between them from which carstone could be extracted. In the north there are the ironstone churches of the Ouse Valley, with stone spires indistinguish-

able from those of Northamptonshire, in the south there is an abundance of flint rubble.

Local sources of wealth are indicated frequently in the dating of church benefactions. The fourteenth-century spire at Wymington proclaims the wealth of the wool merchant, John Curteys, one time mayor of the Calais staple, who rebuilt the church there. As an exporter of wool he is interesting in that his money was made when spires were at their peak of popularity, not in the fifteenth century, when so many church benefactors derived their wealth from woven cloth and celebrated their success in church towers. Other fourteenth-century spires in this carstone district are at Swineshead, Yelden, and Dean, which local pride saved in the nick of time from becoming derelict. It is now lovingly cared for as a perfect example of a Bedfordshire country church of the thirteenth century onwards.

South of this group we have the fascinating churches at Harrold and Felmersham, where thirteenth-century work can be seen at the county's best. Harrold got a thirteenth-century north arcade uncommonly early, as we see from the stiff-leaf capitals carved on pillars contrived out of the wall. Its west tower is fourteenth-century, with a fifteenth-century recessed spire. It is thus another church in a county not pre-eminent for its architecture, in which records of progress are preserved simply by the necessity to adapt to new period styles because there was neither the wealth nor the material available for complete rebuilding.

Felmersham tells a different story. Wymington depended on lay patronage, Felmersham came under monastic care in the second half of the twelfth century, and was entirely rebuilt between 1220 and 1240, at the time when the Church in England was rising to its greatest period of power. Pevsner examines the result in the detail in relation to that in other churches in the county, after posing the question that thrills every local historian when it is asked: the simple question of 'Why is the work here so different?' Nothing exas-

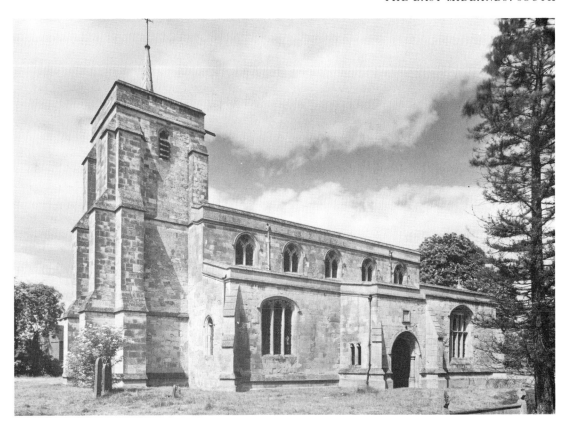

56 Eaton Bray, Bedfordshire: exterior of an outstanding fifteenth-century church to be studied for its use of Totternhoe stone

perates a local historian more than a long antiquarian description of an object, of the

I've measured it from side to side
'Tis three feet long, and two feet wide

kind, without a hint of what is either historically or artistically significant about it. So, as Felmersham is unique, the reader must be referred to the 'Bedfordshire and the County of Huntingdon and Peterborough' volume of *The Buildings of England* series for a full examination of the question: 'What can the reason have been for Felmersham receiving the noblest parish church in the county during the noblest age of medieval churches, and moreover a church in spiritual scale, even

if not in size, vying with any abbey or priory church?'

Moving southward again we find a green-sand ridge running across the middle of the county, giving character to the villages around Woburn and to the east of them. Husborne Crawley has a fifteenth-century tower built of a remarkably green stone, interestingly mixed with ironstone. Of churches hereabouts that are mainly of ironstone there is Eversholt, but in many, as conspicuously at Tingrith, freestone is introduced and use made of outliers of chalk.

South of this ridge are the only really important quarries in Bedfordshire: those at Totternhoe, from which clunch was taken throughout the Middle Ages for building churches. Unfortunately it weathers badly. But for interior use it was so easily worked that it attracted good stone carvers into the district, whose work can be seen especially at Eaton Bray, Dunstable Priory, and Totternhoe St Giles. Totternhoe stone is a darker grey than most chalks. It is gritty, and has a distinctive 'curly grain', best seen at Eaton Bray, which has two arcades of the 1220–40 period. The south one has octagonal piers with stiff-leaf capitals opening into large full leaves at the top of the bells, in the north arcade the development is complete. Pevsner puts it: 'The capitals are of the most dramatic stiff-leaf variety'. It is all unexpectedly splendid. Even the font has stiff-leaf carving.

In a county of so many different styles, none of which can be said to be exclusively local, it is useful to find in the county town the whole record of succeeding styles exemplified in the churches, starting with St Peter de Merton, which appears to be Norman, but has evidence of an earlier Saxon tower becoming the chancel of the later church. St Mary's starts with a Norman crossing tower and transepts, and runs through to Victorian intrusions. St Paul's, the civic church, carries with appropriate dignity a crossing tower with a recessed spire, and has saved from restoration thirteenth-century features in one doorway. The spire is late. There are no medieval spires in south Bedfordshire – due, no doubt, to the unsuitability of Totternhoe stone.

Before crossing into Buckinghamshire from Bedfordshire the one church that should not be missed is All Saints, Leighton Buzzard (now Leighton Linslade) on the river Ouse four miles west of the A5 road. Something of its early importance is indicated by its dedication in 1288 by Bishop Oliver of Lincoln in days when the Lincoln diocese extended from the Humber to the Thames. Money was available that year for its completion, which brings the later stages of the original building into the Golden Age of church architecture. Externally the rest is fifteenth-century and fully worthy of the earlier work, completing a great cruciform church with a magnificent spire, strengthened by big broaches ventilated by three tiers of lucarnes, making it what is generally considered to be the finest church in Bedfordshire.

The interior is on the same scale of collegiate dignity, with flying ironwork scrolls on the west door, similar to those at Eaton Bray and Turvey. They are the work of a native, Thomas Leighton, who forged the finest piece of ironwork in England: the grille protecting the tomb of Queen Eleanor of Castille in Westminster Abbey.

Entering Buckinghamshire from Leighton Buzzard we find ourselves crossing the vast expanse of the Vale of Aylesbury criss-crossed confusingly – or so they always are to me – by roads running south-west to the Cotswolds and south-east to the Chilterns. But before crossing the Vale we should spend time along the Bedfordshire–Buckinghamshire border examining the work done by local freemasons in decorating with foliage the pier capitals at Ivinghoe, Marsh Gibbons, Pitstone, and Wingrave on the Buckinghamshire side, and Eaton Bray, Chalgrave, Elstow, and Studham on the Bedfordshire side of the river.*

There is no distinctively Buckinghamshire style of church. The county's geological structure is as varied as that of Bedfordshire. In the north, like Bedfordshire and Huntingdonshire, it has a common boundary with Northamptonshire and churches built of the limestone common to all three counties; on the west the long boundary with Oxfordshire gives it churches of such exceptional interest as those at Hillesden (nearly entirely fifteenth-century), Twyford, and Chetwode.

The best known local feature in Buckinghamshire is the set of Aylesbury fonts: a late twelfth-century group found at Aylesbury, Bledlow, Great Kimble, and Weston Turville, and without the original base at Chearsley, Chenies, Haddenham, Linslade, Monks Risborough, and Pitstone. Pevsner describes the Aylesbury font as looking like a reversed scalloped capital, and I know of no better description. The bowl is circular and fluted to the shape of a chalice, with a broad band of foliage scrolls at the rim and a short banded

* Mervyn Blatch: *Parish Churches of England*, Blandford Press, 1974.

and flint, which in Buckinghamshire came mainly from the Princes Risborough and Wendover Gaps. On the broad Chiltern plateau, as in the Vale of the White Horse south of the Thames, sandstone conglomerates called sarsens are found in use as church foundations. We find them trimmed to serve in this way at Chesham, and as corner stones at Hartwell. North and west of Aylesbury, Jurassic limestone could be extracted. Generally speaking, however, the best work in the north of this curiously elongated county is in stone brought in from quarries in the North Midlands.

The one important early church in Buckinghamshire is the Saxon church at Wing, where aisles, which have disappeared from the church at Brixworth, Northamptonshire, have survived as they have at Great Paxton in Huntingdonshire, while at Fingest we have another interesting example of a tower that was originally the nave of a Saxon church.

There were only two large medieval churches built in Buckinghamshire: those at High Wycombe and Beaconsfield. High Wycombe was always the largest and is the more interesting because it stands on the site of a Saxon or early Norman church of which nothing is left except a rough piece of walling in the west wall of the north aisle. Despite the restoration of 1893, thirteenth-century work remains in the arch and jambs of the original west window (now one of the tower arches), the south doorway, porch, and the pillars and arch dividing the north side of the nave from the chancel arch. Obviously the original tower was central.

Beaconsfield provides no such opportunity for detective work. It was practically rebuilt in sumptuous style in 1869, when most of the flint was covered with stone dressings. From the historian's point of view Stoke Poges is more interesting. Like all the churches in this part of the county, including the town churches, the setting is in perfect harmony with the building, of which the piers of the nave are Norman, the tower thirteenth-century and completely unspoilt except by the

57 Olney, Buckinghamshire: tower and fourteenth-century broach spire with local-style lucarnes

stem with zig-zag carving to connect it with a base of carved half-circles with deep indentations between them.

It is only when we reach the Chilterns and the fertile valleys of the Thames Plain that we realize that whereas the early settlement of the valleys to the north-east was from the Great Ouse and its tributaries, in Buckinghamshire and Hertfordshire it was from the Thames, the Lea, and ancient trade-routes across the Downs, particularly the Upper Icknield Way, which carried settlers from the Thames crossing at Streatley into East Anglia. So in south Buckinghamshire as in Hertfordshire, the ancient churches are built of chalk rubble

58 Fingest, Buckinghamshire: Norman tower with double saddle-back roof. The lower stages may have been the original nave

removal of the original spire. Some of the glass, however, seems to have come from another church.

For the most typical local composition of church, inn, manor house, and rectory at the heart of a village we cannot do better than visit Little Missenden. The present church replaces a Saxon one, but is small and friendly, with whitewashed interior and a pleasantly designed dormer window. But the chief delight is the series of wall paintings discovered in the 1930s and brought to the notice of Professor Tristram, who was then the leading authority on them. The St Christopher, St Catherine, and the Crucifixion are fourteenth-century; but these are part of a long tradition shown in fragments dating from the twelfth to the eighteenth century.

The reason why Buckinghamshire has not more monastic churches is that it had no abbey sufficiently wealthy to produce a local school of craftsmanship in either wood or stone. The only one of note was at Chetwode, where we see the best thirteenth-century stone work in the county in the nave that was the chancel of a small Augustinian priory church of *c.* 1250. The clustered columns seen at Bierton and Wavenden might be thought local in style, and to some extent they are. But we find them along the Thames, where they seem to have been introduced from Oxford. But what Buckinghamshire lacks in magnificence it gains in the simple charm which remains as attractive as ever while magnificence in our modern world is so often becoming fossilised. Flint is the most ageless of building materials, and when restoration is carried out in it the original effect is seldom lost. Another charming feature in the landscaping of churches in this part of England is that where they do not stand in the heart of a village, they tend to be on the edge of escarpments affording wide prospects across well-wooded farmland and peaceful villages quite unspoilt despite their proximity to London. We may think of Shillington in Bedfordshire, Little Gaddesden in Hertfordshire, or Penn in Buckinghamshire.

Some of the unspoilt charm of Buckinghamshire is due to the Thames on the south

59 Penn, Buckinghamshire: large village-style church in perfect relationship with its setting

having few river crossings, ensuring that development has been channelled away from the beech woods. Penn itself, as the name might lead one to expect, stands on such a hill top, and here again all the additions to the original church have been sympathetically introduced under a particularly fine oak roof reminding the visitor that this is forest country.

The same charm extends into Hertfordshire, described by E. M. Forster in *Howards End* as 'England at its quietest, with little emphasis on river or hill; it is England meditative'. Since those words were written Hertfordshire has had to take more than its share of new towns and motorways; but they are still a true description of the whole of the county north of a line drawn from Tring to Sawbridgeworth. Hertford is still an unspoilt market town bypassed by traffic, unselfconsciously keeping its old houses in good repair as befits the centre of Charles Lamb's 'hearty, homely, loving Hertfordshire'. Unhappily the

ecclesiastical authorities went sadly astray in allowing its medieval churches to fall into decay, and the proud church of All Saints to be built by a Lancaster firm at the beginning of the present century of red Runcorn stone in a style that would enhance the dignity of any northern town, but can never look right in Hertfordshire. No other town in the county, however strong the forces of 'progress' may have been, has made the same mistake. Even Watford, the county's most populous town and one from which most memorials of the past have been obliterated, keeps its old parish church of St Mary screened from the busy High Street with all its local character intact, and the planners of Hemel Hempstead's new town have gone to great lengths to cultivate pride among new residents in the county's most historic parish church outside St Albans. In these, as in all the old parish churches of Hertfordshire, the walls are of flint. Only on the fringe of the county is any other material used. Ashwell at the northern tip has the only tower in Hertfordshire built entirely of stone, and there the church is of clunch and flint.

To most of those for whom Hertfordshire has inexplicably strong appeal – and I am one the defiantly countryfied character of the churches must be one of its main attractions. There are two main reasons for this county characteristic. The first is that as there was no good building stone to hand every odd scrap of Roman brick and rubble was packed into the mortar of the church walls of even the largest churches. St Albans Cathedral, with a nave nearly 300 feet long, seems to have surprised Sir Nikolaus Pevsner with its odd proportions and incongruity of materials. His description is far from being complimentary. 'In approaching the building and getting a close view of its Norman parts', he writes, 'the most striking peculiarity is the russet and blackish-grey colouring of the Roman brick and flint. . . . As it is, the building has a sombre tone, decidedly joyless'. To those of us who never cease to be impressed by the southern aspect of this mammoth pile, recumbent on its hill above the river Ver, the exclamation on reading those words must be: 'What did he expect to find?' The use of Roman brick from the buried city of *Ver-ulamium* in the crossing tower is surely one of the marvels of English architecture. The fabric of the walls, raised from material dredged from the valley below, matches the fragments of masonry on the hill slope opposite, and harmonises with the Abbey gateway alongside it. The whole mass of this great abbey church stands as a mighty monument to the evolution of the city from the Saxon royal manor of Kingsbury, situated by the ford and bridge across the river, used by pilgrims before climbing the winding track that is now Fishpool Street in order to kneel at the shrine of Britain's protomartyr. So long as we avert our eyes from the absurdity of the Grimthorpe accretions, that is what makes St Albans Cathedral uniquely impressive.

All this would have been understood better if St Albans Abbey had lived up to the glory of its foundation. That it failed to do so explains why we do not find local styles of tracery and decoration in Hertfordshire similar to those established in the West Midlands, or at Peterborough and Ely in the East, where wealthy abbots and bishops had schools of masons under their patronage. Despite the early wealth and importance of St Albans, the abbots managed their estates so badly that their influence declined to nothing. Their building record is lamentable. So in Hertfordshire we tend to find such elements of local style as the county does possess in the post-Dissolution period under the influence of families like the Cecils and others who benefited from the Tudor distribution of lands. In these circumstances we look for such features as the Jacobean strapwork at Albury, and most outstandingly in the screen between the nave and the south chapel at Hunsdon, with the manorial pews behind it. In the use of materials, perhaps the most significant feature is the acceptance of brick for use with flint and stone. It appears in the south porch at Meesden, *c.* 1530, the north aisle and north chancel chapel at Wyddial, the chapels at Hunsdon and Stanstead Abbots – both Elizabethan – and other churches near the border with Essex, the county in which brick became most important in church fabrics. It is even used unashamedly in the upper stages added in 1812 to the church tower at Bishops Stortford at the time when many towers were being built of brick, but cased in ashlar – as St John's was at Epping.

The best-known Hertfordshire feature is the slender, leaded *flèche*, perched on the top of scores of broad-beamed flint towers in every part of the county. They are now commonly referred to as 'spikes' or even 'candle snuffers'. The embattled tower at Hitchin has one. So has the great tower at Much Hadham. St Mary, Hitchin, would be my own choice of the most assertively characteristic church in Hertfordshire – a great hulk apparently grounded rather than built on the mud bank of the River Hiz. This is all the more impressive since Hitchin is the one town in Hertfordshire, apart from the county town, which displays evidence of medieval wealth in the buildings along its main streets. As Hitchin was always a great place for lawyers, it is not surprising that its parish church should have two double-storeyed porches, the

60 St Paul's Walden, Hertfordshire: ornate Renaissance screen (1727)

south one being traditionally the place where Hitchin folk settled their debts, signed contracts, and plighted troths. As Hitchin was also a great place for Quakers, the settling of debts and signing of contracts were important elements in the local way of life!

Porches are important in Hertfordshire. It was the carpenters who provided most of the skill in differentiating churches from other buildings in the county. Their work is seen not so much in ornamentation as in the strong jointing of roofs and in the simple strength of the pews, pulpits, and plainly constructed screens – with such ventures into finer work as the screens at Hitchin and the village church at Gilston. The old church at Stanstead Abbots, no longer the parish church, has box pews and double-decker pulpit that must give a fair impression of what the average Hertfordshire village church looked like 300 years ago.

From Stanstead Abbots, which can be opened by arrangement, we can visit within the short space of a summer afternoon as fair a sample of Hertfordshire churches as could be found anywhere in the county. Nearby is what is left of the Great House at Hunsdon, described as being 'of stones called bricks' when it was in the possession of Henry VIII. The church alongside it has brick chapels and a porch with the heavy timbers typical of the county. Although it might not be regarded as an architectural showpiece, the whole of the fabric and furnishing of the church is full of Tudor and Jacobean character, with tombs commemorating the First Lord Hunsdon, Sir Francis Pointz, and Sir Thomas Forster in his robes as Justice of the Queen's Bench. Most of the churches in this part of Hertfordshire, as in those in other Home Counties, have sixteenth-, seventeenth- and eighteenth-century monuments to courtiers as well as to retired City merchants, whose names are only preserved in the churches they supported and the records of the City Livery Companies. But Hunsdon has something more. It has a brass dated 1591 on the north wall depicting a man shooting a deer with a cross-bow.

The next church of call on this brief tour is St John Baptist, Widford, built by the Cluniac monks of Bermondsey, owners of the manor since 1118; but only fragments remain of the original church. The present building is mainly fourteenth-century, and is interesting in being so spacious and representative of the Cluniac attitude to the religious life. The east window is a memorial to John Eliot, the 'Apostle to the Red Indians'. In the west wall of the churchyard there is a four-centred arched doorway, known locally as 'the manor gate', which formerly led to the monastic buildings.

Much Hadham, the next to be visited, is the pride of the group. It is the kind of village that although it frequently finds itself voted the county's 'Best Kept Village', continues to conduct itself with the well-bred ease of one that somehow manages to give the impression that it wasn't really trying! Nevertheless, it has to be reminded occasionally that when William Morris used to visit his mother there in a seventeenth-century cottage with overhanging eaves he was given to commenting on the way some of the houses had been 'faked up' and denounced one particular effort at church restoration as a 'wanton piece of stupidity'. Setting these things aside, we may feel that no church in Hertfordshire has a more beautiful setting or is in itself more completely Hertfordshire at its best. Overlooking the churchyard on the north is the long low mansion, now divided into three gracious homes, that for nearly a thousand years has been built, rebuilt, and altered to serve as one of the country palaces of the bishops of London.

At Little Hadham the church stands close to yet another Elizabethan mansion, associated with the Capel family. A stone in the church to Arthur, Lord Capel, records that he was 'murdered for his loyalty to King Charles the First'. All these monuments are part and parcel of church styling in this part of England. At Bishops Stortford the association is with Cecil Rhodes, whose father was vicar of St Michael's. At Sawbridgeworth some of the Jocelyns are buried, of whom it was written in 1728 that 'this family have been longer in Hertfordshire than any other that are now possessed of an estate here'. Other families are remembered at Sawbridgeworth, and given greater honour than the Jocelyns, of whom strange tales are told of their quarrels with the vicar, most of them arising out of nothing more sinister than mild eccentricity and built-in Hertfordshire Nonconformity.

7 Essex and East Anglia

ESSEX – SUFFOLK – NORFOLK – CAMBRIDGESHIRE and the ISLE OF ELY

Like its neighbouring Home Counties north of the Thames, Essex has no local style that is exclusively its own. There is certainly none to be identified in its major churches. Waltham Abbey, with piers comparable with those in Durham Cathedral, is architecturally unique in the south of England. The great churches in the north of the county, from Dedham and Lawford in the east to Thaxted, Saffron Walden and Clavering in the west are East Anglian in style, and Essex is not and never was part of East Anglia. Kentish styles cross the Thames in the south of the county, and fine towers of Kentish ragstone dominate the eastern marshes and chalk escarpments above the estuaries. We see them at Canewdon, traditionally believed to have been built to celebrate Agincourt, at Burnham-on-Crouch, on the hill top at Rettendon, at Runwell and Fobbing. The Cluniacs, who owned Prittlewell in the Middle Ages, sent their masons from Lewes to build in Essex a tower comparable in style with those at Lydd, Ashford, and Tenterden in Kent. Other fine towers, such as those at Chelmsford and Bocking, are closely related to towers in Hertfordshire and Cambridgeshire.

Where Essex, in common with Hertfordshire scores is in the use of every available scrap of material during the period in which it remained poorer than its neighbours to the south and north. As evidence of this we find that Essex masons used more Roman bricks and bonding tiles in their churches than can be found in those of any other county. So the medieval churches of Essex – and there are nearly 500 of them – are fascinating medleys.

The reason for this failure to develop a local style in Essex is the same as Hertfordshire's. Both counties lacked the quality of stone that attracted masons from Westminster and Canterbury to display their skill in the parish churches of Kent, those from Ely in Cambridgeshire, from Bury St Edmunds in West Suffolk. The only local stone for which Essex is famous are that renowned, but often despised, trio: pudding-stone, septaria, and clunch. Pudding-stone and septaria are conglomerate stones composed of nodules of ancient rock, or calcareous clay, held together by a kind of natural concrete. In pudding-stone these are mere fragments of rock and small pebbles or gravel held together by a siliceous cement, which has become so immensely strong that blocks of pudding-stone held together by hard mortar show no sign of crumbling after eight or nine centuries of exposure to weather. Clunch is hard chalk. Of these three, pudding-stone is only found in churches in the east and north-east of Essex and up the Suffolk coast as far as Orford.

A county's character, like a child's, is formed early, and research is increasingly showing that long before historical records were started indigenous skills in the use of this jumble of rubble, timber, and flint in building was acquired by natives of the East Saxon kingdom – which formerly included east

61 Saffron Walden, Essex: tall arcades with lozenge-shaped piers, to be studied in relation with East Anglian churches and St Mary's, Cambridge

Hertfordshire – who survived successive invasions by retreating into dense forest in mid-Essex or demon-haunted marshes along the coastal fringe.

This skill in the use of indifferent material was to give Essex churches uncommon attraction both for artists in search of interesting texture and archaeological sleuths. In recent years the county has been exceptionally fortunate in gaining the attention of both, with the result that it is no longer the poor relation of neighbouring counties, but one that has become pre-eminent among them for its use of two building materials in the late-medieval period: timber and clay. From the first we get the remarkable series of timber belfries in the old forest belt, from the

second brickwork of quality and quantity that no other county can match. The outstanding work of C. A. Hewett on timber buildings has made it necessary for the dating of many Essex belfries to be revised and their importance in the history of carpentry to be reassessed. The timber tower at Navestock, for example, which was formerly attributed to the fifteenth century, has been carbon-dated *c.* 1190. The belfry at Bradwell-juxta-Coggeshall has also been confirmed as Norman.

The most characteristic Essex timber towers are in the heart of the county. Those in the Lavers and the Roothings are fourteenth century. So are the free-standing belfries at Little Burstead and Black Notley. Then in the fifteenth century came the group that raised Essex to the highest rank in the construction of timber belfries: those at Blackmore, Stock, Margaretting, and Bulphan, a group of churches that came as near to giving Essex a local style as can be found. Their designs, however, are varied. Blackmore is in three,

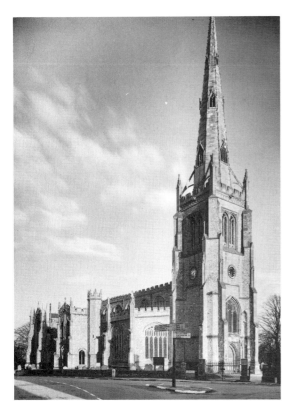

62 Thaxted, Essex: the county's finest church, mainly fourteenth-century, remarkable for the effect of a tall narrow nave and wide aisles inside, and for having the only medieval spire in Essex

Navestock, Margaretting, and Stock in two diminishing stages. Others are in a single stage, while the belfry at West Hanningfield is on the plan of a Greek cross. The style that Cecil Hewett calls 'the ultimate type' was achieved at Shenfield towards the end of the fifteenth century, and no greater tribute could be paid to it as a genuine Essex type than Sir Thomas Fowell Buxton's choice of Shenfield in 1902 as the basic style of the church he built that year at Upshire in Epping Forest. I recall Harry Batsford's delight on visiting it more than 30 years ago. It really belongs!

The tower frame most favoured in Essex is the 'four-poster', with four stout balks of timber resting on the nave floor, locked together with cross pieces. At Laindon the framing has a two-storeyed priest's house attached to the west side. Thanks to Cecil Hewett's investigations we now know that the timber frames supporting the belfries at Blackmore, Stock, Navestock, and Margaretting were originally the timber frames of tall Saxon naves, confirming the feeling that many of us have long had, that carpentry skills developed by the Saxons in the county were continued under the Normans, and not – as in counties where stone was abundant – abandoned in favour of masonry. The only surviving Saxon timber nave in England is at Greensted-juxta-Ongar; but as it is so different in its proportions from those at Blackmore, Stock, Navestock, and Margaretting, it cannot be taken as representative of local style in Saxon church building in the county generally. On the other hand it could be representative of the first Saxon churches, of which those just named were the successors. We may be sure that many of the first Saxon churches would be destroyed by the Danes in their various forays.

For later examples of skills that Essex carpenters had acquired we have the ten oak effigies in Essex churches, which is a larger number than any other county can claim. There is the priest at Little Leighs, *c.* 1300, three knights at Danbury, late thirteenth-century, two knights and a lady from Little Horkesley, now in Colchester Museum, a civilian and lady at Little Baddow, *c.* 1300, and a knight at Elmstead. The finest timber porch in the county is the fifteenth-century one at South Benfleet. Margaretting has two, the one on the south being a contender for top honours. Others of outstanding merit are found at Doddinghurst, Danbury, Broomfield, Stondon Massey, Blackmore, White Notley, Munden, and Shenfield.

The pre-eminence of Essex in the use of brick in its medieval churches may be attributed to the county lying on the direct route between London and the Low Countries, where brick was in early use. So Essex has examples of thirteenth-century use in the

63 Greensted-juxta-Ongar, Essex: the sole survivor in England of the original Saxon log churches. Carbon dated *c.* 845 but mutilated in an unfortunate restoration of 1848

moulded arches at St Nicholas's chapel, Coggeshall, and in the three-light lancet window at Chipping Ongar. But the question still remains unanswered as to why, with so much Roman brick in its church fabrics, building in brick was abandoned in Essex for the best part of a thousand years after the withdrawal – which was gradual – of the Roman legions, although its use continued on the Continent. However, what we do know is that its reintroduction was due to the influence of the Hanseatic League, which explains its early occurrence in the neighbourhood of the East Coast ports, including Hull and King's Lynn as well as those in Essex. In all of them the styles adopted are those associated with Flemish immigrants, many of whom were refugees.

The great period of brick building in Essex churches was the last quarter of the fifteenth century. There are 21 brick towers of the Tudor period in the county: the best at Ingatestone, Fryerning, Rochford, Castle Hedingham, and Sandon. Features of both Ingatestone and Sandon are combined in the parapet at Fryerning; but unquestionably the finest brick tower in Essex is at In-

gatestone. It has been calculated that more than half a million bricks were used in building it. To the towers must be added the fine brick porches at Feering and Sandon, while Great Baddow, the most interesting church in the county for the use of brick, has not only the best brick porch, but a clerestory wall with the Flemish stepped parapets found on the towers of Ingatestone and Fryerning, and more modestly at Woodham Walter.

Essex has more churches built entirely of brick than any other county – all of them Tudor, many with Jacobean features added. The list would be too long to give here. The two most remarkable are át Chignal Smealey, which goes so far as to have both font and piscina of brick, and Woodham Walter, which has the rare distinction of being built entirely during the reign of Elizabeth I.

Turning from the local use of these two specific materials, timber and brick, to the county's historical development through ecclesiastical patronage and influence we find an unbroken thread in the southern half of the county, which was settled from the rivers while the northern half remained dense forest penetrated only by ancient trackways and the

64 Sandon, Essex: tower and south porch of Tudor brick with blue diaperwork

River Stour. The record begins with Cedd's two minsters built on fortified sites at Bradwell-juxta-Mare and Tilbury – probably because they had good communications and material at hand for building. The Normans endowed upwards of 50 religious houses, most of which were cells of Continental abbeys. This led to the bypassing of remotely sited churches. Warwick Rodwell has done valuable archaeological research into these abandoned sites, which may reveal that there are more remains of deserted villages in Essex than had been suspected. At the same time the lack of building material meant that ancient foundations were re-used where possible, and Gordon J. Copley, in *An Archaeology of South East England* gives more than 50 church sites in Essex that are closely related to sites of archaeological importance. Alphamstone's church is on the site of a Roman building. There is a plateau fort round the church at Asheldham, Danish earthworks at Ashingdon, Early Bronze Age beaker burial at Berden, Roman cremations at Birdbrook and Boreham. Danbury church is within an Iron Age fortification. At Chipping Ongar there is Roman building material under the church as

well as in the walls. Warwick Rodwell is at present engaged on a full archaeological survey of Essex churches, and his findings are bound to contribute many sidelights on building styles, if only in the use and re-use of existing material, which appears to have been an important feature in Essex church maintenance.

The strongest religious Order in the county was that of the Augustinian Canons, whose rule permitted them to serve as priests. Their Houses included St Botolph's Priory, Colchester, the first of the Order in England, and Waltham Abbey, the most important. The dominant character of Essex churchmanship to this day, and consequently the liturgical styling of its church furnishings, is attributable to so many of them being served during their formative years by Augustinian Canons. Unlike the Benedictines they were not ambitious, so simplicity remains an engaging feature of Essex village churches. The Cistercians, who were even more austere, had three houses in Essex. So it is only where de Vere influence was strong, as at Castle Hedingham, Earls Colne, and Hatfield Broadoak – which enjoyed other munificent lay patronage – that we get churches built in the ambitious styles associated with the Benedictines. And nowhere in Essex was there the autocratic rule exercised in Suffolk by the proud abbots of St Edmundsbury. Nor during the Middle Ages was there anywhere except at Coggeshall and Dedham, the dominance of such wealthy clothiers as the Springs of Lavenham. In Essex the traditional link was between the church and the manor house.

In travelling northward, however, we begin to recognise East Anglian influence long before we reach the Stour Valley. The most important new feature is the round tower. It is true that there is one at South Ockendon; but it may be regarded as an outlier. The first to be encountered in a northward journey from Chelmsford is at Broomfield. The others are at Lamarsh, Great Leighs, Bardfield Saling, and Pentlow, making a total of six in Essex, against

65 Lavenham, Suffolk: the most visited of East Anglia's great wool churches, celebrating the wealth of the clothiers and the pride of the De Vere lords of the manor

41 in Suffolk and 129 – not all of which survive – in Norfolk. As there are only seven in the rest of England, neither these nor the foundations of others reported from time to time are sufficiently numerous to affect the claim that in England round towers are distinctively East Anglian. Nor do they resemble either those in Ireland or the Romanesque types on the Continent sufficiently to establish relationship. They are all built of sea or river pebbles bonded together with rubble and mortar into walls four to five feet thick; with entrances originally reached by ladders that could be drawn up when the women and children were safely inside. They were to East Anglia what pele towers were to the North. In the Middle Ages, several of them were given an octagonal top stage. We see examples of these at Mutford, Theberton, and Ricking-hall Inferior, while at Little Saxham the top storey has Norman arcading.

The churches associated with these round towers were originally thatched with Norfolk reeds – as many still are – and the contrast between these simple thatched churches built of flint and rubble and the great 'wool churches' of East Anglia is even greater than that between the shepherds' churches on the Sussex Downs and the ironmasters' churches of the Weald. In fact, the development from the seventh-century churches of St Felix to such great Perpendicular churches as those at Lavenham, Southwold, and Long Melford in Suffolk, and those in Norfolk to be mentioned presently, has no parallel anywhere. East Anglian flushwork is unique as a local style. The flints for the best work were not pebbles raked from the fields or dredged from the streams. They were obtained from shafts 40 to 50 feet deep dug into the clay until a layer of suitable stones was reached. Galleries like those in coal mines were then driven along the layers and the flints extracted. When these were split to obtain a flat surface many were found to be jet black, others pearly grey, and all with a tendency to fade on exposure. They were then further shaped by flaking until they were reduced to the required shape and size by the knappers.

The ideal method was to cut them into the rectangular form of small blocks of ashlar. Normally they were squared on the outside and left slightly conical behind so that they could be pressed into the mortar. They were then fitted into frames of freestone, both flints and frames depending for survival on the quality of the mortar behind them. The best effects were obtained by first constructing a facing of freestone, with panels into which mosaics of black flints could be inserted. A cheaper method was to insert panels into existing walls of flint. This was done along the parapet at Long Melford.

Apart from the simple chess-board patterns seen in other counties – notably at Steyning in Sussex – flush tracery is the peculiar glory of East Anglia, with a few examples, such as those at Colchester and St Osyth, in north Essex. The best work was done in the second half of the fifteenth century, probably starting with St Peter Mancroft, Norwich, 1455, and Southwold, Suffolk, 1460. Full-scale work on the naves of Lavenham and Long Melford churches was not started until the closing years of the century, although some of the work at Lavenham is dated 1473. But there may have been experimental work done in domestic buildings earlier. Traceried panels on a house in St Andrew's, Norwich, are in fourteenth-century style. In these the flints are fully squared, not flaked on one side only. To see the full expression of local pride in this uniquely regional style the churches should be visited at Redenhall, Eye, and Laxfield, where the panelling covers the whole of the west front of the tower. Elsewhere some of the best work is in the parapets.

From simple emblems, like the crowned 'M' for Mary, heraldic devices were developed, and finally long pious inscriptions to run round porches and clerestories. Eventually the masons became so skilled in the flaking of flints to fit the panels that the blade of a penknife cannot be inserted between them. The use of decorative flushwork is an indication of which church features gave masons the greatest pride. They were, as we might expect, towers, porches, and clerestories. The source of this pride was the wealth of the merchants of Norwich and the great monastic foundations of the region, both of which were influenced to a degree greater than elsewhere by immigrants from the Low Countries. Undoubtedly the similarity of the East Anglian terrain to that from which the settlers came contributed to this unique expression of religious aspiration in architecture. In short, it was the same feeling of

66 Castle Rising, Norfolk: late Norman, with central tower and narrow crossing

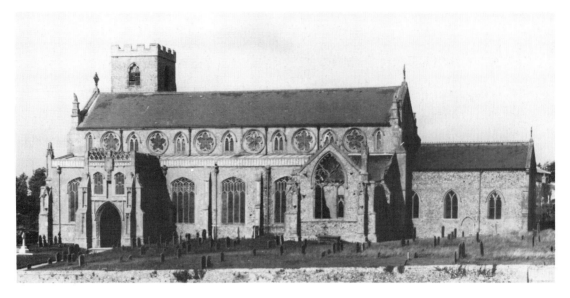

belonging as that which led to the Dutch landscape painters influencing so profoundly the work of Constable and the Norwich School of painters.

Light was all-important to the builders of these great East Anglian churches, as it was to Constable among painters. Every device was used to flood the churches with it. That is why in East Anglia we see the full development of the rectangular interior, which contrasts so sharply with the triple-nave plan of the west of England. The chancel arc disappeared to allow a continuous middle avenue extending with the same roof pitch to terminate in a towering gable above the High Altar. This lofty roof was usually flanked by aisles with windows so large that slender buttresses had to be built between them externally for support. Above them were built clerestories which reached their daring maximum for the admission of light at St Mary's, Bury St Edmunds, where there are 20 clerestory windows on each side of the nave – which is only two a side more than at Long Melford, Blythburgh, and Southwold, each with 18. It is amazing to find how many of the largest churches in East Anglia were being built almost simultaneously: Long Melford, Southwold, and Saxmundham among them.

Towers dominate the East Anglian land-scape. There are more than a thousand of them in the two counties of Norfolk and Suffolk together, and they are so unlike the great towers built elsewhere that when G. F. Bodley built a new one at Long Melford in his most accomplished style it was seen at once that it didn't belong. The typical East Anglian tower is a plain massive structure in either four or five stages, often with the peculiarity of having openings with tracery locally called 'Norfolk air-holes' in the stage below the bell chamber. Stair turrets are less common in East Anglia than in most regions – perhaps because there is usually nothing at the top of the tower to need regular attention. It is a curious feature of East Anglian towers that so many of even the finest – such as those at Southwold, Lavenham, and Beccles in Suffolk, and Wymondham, Dereham, and Cawston in Norfolk – have straight parapets, without even the adornment of battlements, and that pinnacles are rare. Where they do occur they are sometimes in the form of

68 Grundisburgh, Suffolk: magnificent double hammer-beam roof

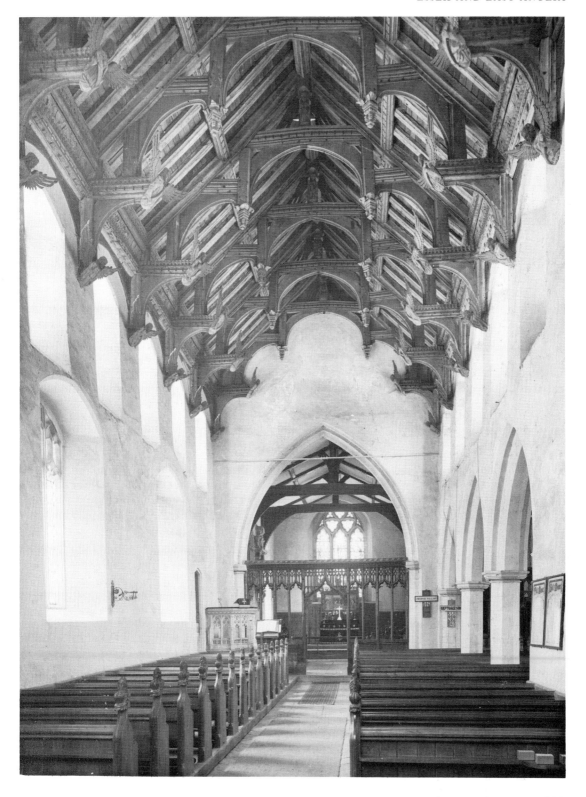

figures, as at Woodbridge in Suffolk and East Harling in Norfolk. Lack of money can seldom have been the explanation. Could it be that some of them were originally intended to have spires? Size seems to have been their dominant characteristic, which may well have been a feature imported from the Low Countries.

Whatever started the style, here as everywhere else copying explains the spread of it. The nave and clerestory at Cavendish, for example, are derived from Long Melford, the adjoining parish. Walberswick's flint tower was built by Adam Powle of Blythburgh and Richard Russell of Dunwich in 1426, taking Tunstall's as their model for the tower, and Halesworth's for the lights. When in 1487 Thomas Aldrych of North Lopham undertook to build a tower at Helmingham it was to be on the model of a tower that was named in the contract. But in that case ambition outran capacity, and the tower was not completed until 56 years later. The most strongly individualistic tower in Norfolk is at Blakeney on the coast. It is in the form of a 'lantern' to guide mariners into the harbour, and rises from the north-east angle of the chancel, with a window in each face through which the beacon light could shine.

East Anglian churches are fascinating to the local historian for the light they throw on the brief period during which the three dominant orders of society, the ecclesiastical, the aristocratic, and the industrial, were thrown together before separating to take their different ways. Nowhere is this better illustrated than at Lavenham while the landed aristocracy were represented by John de Vere, 13th Earl of Oxford and lord of the manor, the industrial by the rich clothier, Thomas Spring. On the massed plinth of the great tower, 141 feet high, there are symbols of the Church, the Nobility, and Commerce respectively in the crossed keys of St Peter and the crossed swords of St Paul, the badges of the earls, and the merchant mark of Thomas Spring. But when we look up at the proud display of the quartered arms of the earls

above the entrance arch of the porch we cannot help feeling that they are displayed to proclaim that John de Vere, 13th Earl of Oxford, was the most important person in Lavenham and not this upstart clothier, Thomas Spring.

As in the West Midlands, the aisles in these great churches were cluttered up with guild altars. The guilds, in fact, appropriated ecclesiastical ritual to their use and based their constitutions on that of the Church. This, however, would be inevitable since the first guilds were entirely religious. In course of time these religious guilds were superseded by craft guilds who built halls for themselves like the one preserved by the National Trust at Lavenham, in which their business could be conducted more conveniently than in church.

With the removal of guild altars the vertical lines of the nave piers directed all eyes upwards to the lofty hammer-beam roofs that are so typical of East Anglia. There the impression of height is further emphasised by the hammer-beams, which project from the walls to carry the narrowed arch of the roof, reducing the outward thrust. From simple hammer-beams evolved double hammer-beams adorned with flights of angels, of which there are more than a hundred in some of the larger churches. Among dozens of these angel roofs in East Anglia there are outstandingly beautiful examples at Cawston, Gissing, Knapton, and Swaffham in Norfolk, and Woolpit, Badingham, Earl Stonham, Grundisburgh, Hopton, and Worlingworth in Suffolk, with outliers at Great Bromley in Essex and March in Cambridgeshire. With the unexpectedness which makes the study of churches everywhere so fascinating, the finest of these roofs is at Needham Market in Suffolk, where nothing about the exterior of the church could lead anyone to expect such a display of craftsmanship. Although magnificently carved roofs are to be found in medieval palaces and great halls in and around London, they reached a perfection in the churches of East Anglia only to be found in isolation elsewhere. The best are in Suffolk.

69 Needham Market, Suffolk: a *tour de force* by East Anglian carpenters in bridging a wide span with a minimum of outward thrust

'For open timber roofs', declares Pevsner, 'Suffolk stands supreme'.

The polarisation of styles found in the extreme west and the extreme east of England has always seemed to me odd in view of the way the most highly skilled craftsmen moved about the country under royal and episcopal patronage. There were exceptions, like the triple-naves of Kent and Cornwall; but such features as the elaboration of pinnacles, which is so prominent in the West, being practically absent in the East must have a deeper explanation than mere fashion. The difference is seen most prominently in the rood-screens. This was mentioned in describing those of Devon and Cornwall and need not be repeated in detail; but to appreciate the effect of the spare ribs of fan vaulting above slender pillars in East Anglian screens we do need to see them in contrast to those of Devon. The point is that the geometrical tracery of East Anglia emphasises the loftiness of the churches, whereas the naturalistic of the West Country emphasises width. There is rightness about this to anyone sensitive to the fundamental difference between East and West in that in the one the sun rises into a vast sky, in the other it sets into an earth-bound landscape. A particularly pleasing feature of East Anglian screens is that the cusping is attached to both sides of the arched openings. The colouring, apart from one or two exceptions, is more delicate in the East than in the West, and there is nothing in the West of England to

compare with the gesso work at Southwold, the finest screen in Suffolk.

Splendid gesso work is seen in several Norfolk screens, and the similarity in the figures of the Apostles suggests that they were all done by the same hands. The thing that continues to trouble admirers of the Southwold screen is that the panels do not fit. This is usually explained, and no doubt correctly, by the belief that they were salvaged from the lost church at Dunwich, now under the sea, or from roofless Covehithe or Walberswick, where only the tower and one aisle of the former great church survive. The *Victoria County History* of Norfolk gives a long list of painters who were permanent residents in Norwich between 1373 and 1579. Much of the work must have been done by them, and for the best work they would have associates on the Continent with whom they had links. It is pointed out by art experts that the panel depicting the Temptation of St Anthony on the Ranworth screen has Flemish furnishings and closely resembles a painting of the same subject by Rufus van Dycken, who was working at Antwerp in 1509.

An invariable characteristic of East Anglian screens is that the lower panels are solid. Usually, they are painted either red or green, sometimes with these colours alternately. As Francis Bond commented: 'To this day the districts where the finest painted screens are found – Ranworth, Barton Turf, Ludham, Marsham – where the soil is dry, are incarnadine with poppies; where it is marshy, with lush green grass. The colour system of the screens is just that of Poppyland and marshland blended'. If we add to this that the gold of East Anglian grain and the blue of its skies are reflected in the gesso work we see how regional the inspiration for these Norfolk and Suffolk screens was.

70 Wymondham, Norfolk: the magnificent Norman arcades and triforium windows of the part of a Benedictine Abbey that was always a parish church

71 St Clement, Terrington, Norfolk: the interior of a great marshland church with a detached tower

Stalls, misericords, and bench-ends in East Anglia are only in degree less impressive because they are less awe-inspiring; but nowhere is vernacular art more spontaneous in its expression or craftsmanship superior. At Framsden a saint bears the gift of a church, at Norton a woman is shown carding wool, at Stowlangtoft a hawk is depicted killing a hare, at Denston a crane holds a stone in its uplifted claw, and so we might go on. Poppyhead bench-ends in contrast to the square-headed

72   South Creake, Norfolk: Perpendicular
nave with hammer-beam angel roof and
seven-sacrament font

commonest is, of course, the *fleur-de-lys*.

Fonts are the other distinctively local
feature. There are two types of them, one
dating from the fourteenth century, the other
from the early sixteenth. All have richly
carved octagonal bowls on octagonal plinths,
which culminated in the sixteenth-century
series of Seven Sacrament fonts with the
eighth panel depicting the Crucifixion. Of
these Norfolk has 23, Suffolk 13. Blythburgh,
however, asserted East Anglian independence

noted in the West of England, are found in
about 140 Suffolk churches and I don't know
how many in Norfolk. Everywhere, where
subjects are taken from popular bestiaries the
treatment reflects local occupations and
humour. Among conventional subjects the

by depicting Seven Deadly Sins instead of the Sacraments! Most of the faces were so disfigured by Cromwell's men that on only a few – of which Badingham is one – can the subjects be recognised. In the designing of font-covers the carpenters, not to be outshone by the masons who produced the fonts, achieved the finest tabernacle work to be seen anywhere in England, with the best at Ufford in Suffolk.

It is inevitable that in looking for clues to the most distinctive styles in Cambridgeshire churches we should turn to Ely Cathedral, which Pevsner describes as representing 'in terms of the highest architectural quality, a complete synopsis of the development of the Norman and Transitional styles'. The alternative piers at Bourn, Chippenham, Downham, Sawston, and Soham, are obviously derived from that source; but only the chancel of St Radegund, now the chapel of Jesus College, Cambridge, approaches the quality of the best work at Ely. It was the magnificent fourteenth-century octagon that had the greatest influence, inspiring the addition of smaller copies to crown so many twelfth- and thirteenth-century towers in the county until at the end of the medieval building period Cambridgeshire had more octagons on its towers than any other English county, Northamptonshire following with five, Norfolk and Huntingdonshire with three each.

Seen in relation to East Anglia, Cambridgeshire has the distinction of being the only county in the region that developed a local style of tower in the thirteenth century. The best of these are at Bottisham, Leverington, and Orwell. All three have blank arcading and the further distinction of not having been inspired by Ely. In fact, it is claimed for the thirteenth-century tower at Elm that it influenced the designing of Ely's late fourteenth-century west tower. This thirteenth-century activity in Cambridgeshire continued into the fourteenth century, making the county especially interesting to those who wish to study transitions from Early English to Decorated styles. One particularly notable characteristic is the insertion of large transomed windows on the south side near the west end of the chancels. Spires seem to have been notably popular in Cambridgeshire in the fourteenth century; but Whittlesey's is the only one retained east of the River Cam. In the Fens thirteenth- and fourteenth-century towers dominate great churches built of oolite, with tall naves flooded with the light that pours through the clerestory windows to show off the magnificent carpentry of the roofs.

In the south-west corner of the county, between Cambridge and the Icknield Way, which crosses the county at this point, there are about a score of churches that have long had a peculiar fascination for me, both for their variety and their atmosphere of belonging to an immemorial past that lingers on into the present. They are all encompassed within an area that in the West and North of England might be included in a single parish, bearing witness to the prosperity of this part of the country when the wool trade was at its zenith. The first two on leaving Cambridge are Trumpington and Grantchester, which seem to exhibit pride in being so near an ancient university city. Pevsner calls Trumpington 'sumptuous' and says of Grantchester that 'what raises it high above the run of Cambridgeshire village churches is its splendid chancel'. Both have been extended and renewed.

Great Shelford comes next, with an unbuttressed plastered tower crowned with an octagon. On entering it we are arrested by the sight of a low-pitched roof with tie-beams and hammer-beams alternating, the latter with angels. Little Shelford church is a mere stone's throw away, and again bears evidence of Norman origin, but with the difference from Great Shelford that its tower carries a Hertfordshire-style spike. Histon and Cherry Hinton nearby are claimed to be the finest thirteenth-century parish churches in Cambridgeshire, Cherry Hinton with blank cinquefoiled arches derived from Ely. At Hauxton, less than two miles from Little Shelford, we find a Norman nave and chancel which promptly extend our time-scale on this short tour. Newton may be visited to see the remains of a thirteenth-century wall painting, and Thriplow, a thirteenth-century cruciform church with a Norman font and fragments of a screen referred to in a stipulation made when Great St Mary was built at Cambridge that it

73 Swaffham, Norfolk: double hammer-beam roof with angels bearing shields

should be like that 'within ye parisshe chirche of Tripplow'. Turning north-east from Thriplow we should on no account pass by Whittlesford, a typical pebble-rubble building with a Norman nave and crossing-tower, before turning south to Duxford, with another pebble-rubble church with a local-style unbuttressed west tower in which we can test our detective skill through thirteenth-, fourteenth- and fifteenth-century features before going on to Hinxton, where we may trace the development of the church from the outside, starting with the blocked Norman doorway before turning to the tower which begins as Transitional and rises to a Perpendicular top stage, now capped with a lead spire, while inside we have a Norman font as our starting point, and from that can make our way through time to the Jacobean pulpit. At Ickleton, again a mere two miles away, we have the church of which Pevsner says: 'As a parish church of the Early Norman decades Ickleton has few equals in the country. It is far too little known'. Alas, the chancel of this noble church was burnt out in a disastrous fire in August 1979. Its restoration is being carefully and painstakingly carried out while this book is being written.

From Ickleton we reach the Essex border at Great Chesterford, to turn north and back to Cambridge through the villages between the A139 and A604 roads, visiting Pampisford, with an extraordinary tympana of small arches formed radially along a rim and filled with figures, Great and Little Abington, and Sawston, all with Norman features that are so strong in the district; but not missing Babraham in its park, with Georgian family pews to bring our time span to its final stage in local styling.

There are other regions in which as many features in the development of local styles can be traced; but few in which character remains so strongly conserved in its various forms in so compact an area.

8 The East Midlands: North

LINCOLNSHIRE – RUTLAND – LEICESTERSHIRE – NOTTINGHAMSHIRE

Despite its size, Lincolnshire is geographically the most isolated and least known of all English counties, yet when its historic churches were being built it was the heart of a major ecclesiastical division covering the whole of the East Midlands. So to be understood its churches have to be related to those of its inland neighbours on the west, and as a great maritime county to those of Norfolk and south-east Yorkshire.

As in Cornwall and Cumbria, this geographical separateness is reflected in church dedications that are either unique, as St Medard at Little Bytham appears to be, or as rare as those of St Genewys at Scotton, St Sebastian at Great Gonerby, St Firmin at Thurlby, St Cornelius at Linwood, or St Hybald at Hibaldstow, Manton, and Scawby. As always, place-names provide the best clues to early settlement. That one third of them end in -by or -thorpe explains the vigour of Scandinavian sculpture found in Lindsey, while the influence of the Dutch is seen in Holland. Only in the western division of Kesteven is the link with the inland counties dominant. Nevertheless it is there that most of the architecturally outstanding churches are found, as distinct from the great marshland churches of Lindsey, which are the most characteristically local in style.

Lindsey, by far the largest of the three divisions, includes the Wolds, which are unlike those in other counties in the way deep ravines are cut into them by rivers, and also in the quality of the light which plays on them continuously as great clouds pass like chariots across the sky. No doubt this characteristic arises from the tilt of the land towards the east, which has the effect of enhancing colour and accentuating detail. The scenery around Tennyson's birthplace at Somersby is summed up in his lines:

Calm and deep peace on this high wold,
And on these dews that drench the furze,
And all the silvery gossamers
That twinkle into green and gold:
Calm and still light on yon great plain
That sweeps with all its autumn bowers,
And crowded farms and lessening towers,
To mingle with the bounding main.

The 'crowded farms' testify to the fertility of the soil, the 'lessening towers' to the need for these to be less conspicuous as landmarks for invaders. That is why they are markedly low and broad, while at the same time strong enough to serve as places of refuge.

Minor features in Lincolnshire are reminiscent of Suffolk. I remember vividly my impression of the contrast between the Fens and the heathery pine-clad country round Woodhall Spa when I visited Boston many years ago to see for the first time the Stump. Along the Welland the churches resemble those of Norfolk and Cambridgeshire. So how, in the face of this complexity, do we start dividing up this great county into regions with groups of churches in which local

style is crystallised? The answer does not appear to be in river valleys as it is in most counties; but in the two ridges that run southwards from the Humber: one of chalk, expanding in the Wolds before merging with fenland near Spilsby and Horncastle as described so well by Tennyson, the other a narrow ridge running for 40 miles or so down the county towards Grantham and Stamford. Along this ridge ran the Ermine Street of the Romans, locally called the Ramper, and from its quarries at Ancaster came the grey limestone used for the county's most visited churches after Lincoln's: those at Grantham, Heckington, and Sleaford, as well as upwards of 20 ashlar-faced spires around Sleaford.

Lincolnshire's spires, like Northamptonshire's, are so famous that they obscure the fact that the county has far more towers without than with them, to say nothing of the hundreds of bell-cotes along the eastern marshes from the Humber to the Wash, where spires are rare. The only spires on scores of towers along the eastern border of the county are at South Brocklesby, North Ulceby, Haugham, Faldingworth, and Louth, which makes Louth, the most perfect spire in England, all the more remarkable as being completely unrelated to its neighbours. It is also out of line with Lincolnshire's other fine spires in being late-Perpendicular in style in a county in which the best work is usually thirteenth- or fourteenth-century. The influence at Louth was from the North of England, a feature we shall find in Nottinghamshire and Derbyshire, as a result of the overlapping of the diocese of York. The first master mason at Louth was succeeded in 1505 by Christopher Scune, who was too fully engaged at Ripon and Durham to spend much time in Lincolnshire.

The concentration of Lincolnshire spires is in Kesteven. Their distinction is that they have small lights for ventilation, introduced in tiers placed alternately on the cardinal and intermediate sides of the octagon, whereas in Northamptonshire and Huntingdonshire they are larger, and usually, although not invariably, in the cardinal faces.

It was the suitability of Ancaster stone for carving that made possible the superb

75 Grantham, Lincolnshire: stately Early-English church with spire 272 feet high

tracery in the church windows at Grantham, Heckington, and Sleaford, which is ack-knowledged to be unsurpassed in any county. The styling is derived from the Angel Choir at Lincoln, started in 1256 and completed in 1280. The same influence produced the tracery at Spalding, begun in 1284, the trefoils at Norton Disney, and the pointed quatrefoils at Fishtoft. But the church we return to most frequently is Heckington's, which is all the more remarkable in being the parish church of a village. The explanation of its magnificence appears to be the devotion of a wealthy rector, Richard de Potesgrave, installed in 1307. The south porch is the finest of its period to be seen anywhere, and Pevsner describes the six-light east window as 'one of England's greatest displays of flowing tracery'. The Easter Sepulchre and tomb recess of the presumed benefactor in the chancel attract the same superlatives. This and other Easter Sepulchres in Lincolnshire were inspired by the appearance of one in the cathedral to-wards the end of the thirteenth century. From Lincoln they spread to eight churches in the county and four in Nottinghamshire.

It would be tempting to attribute the many splendid churches in Lincolnshire to the large number of monasteries in the county; but it is doubtful whether a good case could be made out for this even with stronger documentation than we possess. That so little is left of the 50 or more monastic foundations strewn across the county is un-questionably due to their ruins in the low-lands being used as quarries for repairing farm buildings. M. W. Barley in *Lincolnshire and the Fens* (Batsford, 1952) says: 'There is only one non-monastic church for which the monks can truthfully be given the credit. At Kirkstead, the Cistercian monks built a chapel for lay folks outside the entrance to the precincts, and it remains today, after a

precarious and varied history, a most exqui-site example of Early English design'.

The relationship between the abbeys and the parish churches was similar in Lincoln-shire to that in many other counties. Where livings were appropriated to a monastery in the fourteenth century it was usually with a view to getting hold of the tithes, seldom to confer so great a benefit on the parish as the rebuilding of its church, except where monastic and episcopal powers were merged, as they were at Ely and Peterborough. At Ely monastic and episcopal functions were combined from the beginning of the twelfth century. At Peterborough the last abbot be-came the first bishop of the new See, which implies an existing good relationship. As Lincolnshire had so many abbeys and priories relationships must have been more complex; but we may be sure that many parishes took advantage of the Dissolution in the sixteenth century to purchase the old monastic church, or part of it, for their own use. We certainly know that they did this at Bourne, South Kyme, Fretstone, Deeping St James, Thornley, and Crowland. Churches that survived in this way might be expected to provide clues to established local styles in Lincolnshire as in other counties; but they seldom do. Pevsner owns to finding dating difficult in Lincolnshire.

The evolution of towers in Lincolnshire starts with the Saxon one at Barton-upon-Humber, originally the nave of the church, which has the tall bell-openings with mid-wall shafts characteristic of many Saxon churches. Above these bell-openings in early churches in Lincolnshire is a through-stone set at right-angles to the wall, which projects as a lintel. There are several of them in the city of Lincoln, at least ten in Lindsey and five in Kesteven and Holland. A curious local custom is to combine two traceried lancet tower openings under a single arch in the top stage. We see it at Stamford, Easton, and Folkingham.

Most of the churches in the east of the county are built of rubble, and were ori-

76 Louth, Lincolnshire: the ultimate in spire construction in England

ginally plastered. As in so many other places the plaster has been scraped off; but in Lincolnshire the operation has had the advantage of revealing the extent to which herringbone masonry was used before as well as after the Conquest, and also how much brick was used for repairs in days when every parish in the lowlands had at least one pit from which clay was taken for firing into bricks. At Stow, between Lincoln and Gainsborough, the county's principal monument from the Norman period, and in churches to the south of it, skerry from across the Trent was widely used for building, while north of Lincoln, where blue lias disappears and honey-coloured oolitic limestone similar to that of the Oxfordshire Cotswolds comes into use. To many eyes this is more attractive than the dull grey of the Ancaster stone. The stone quarried along the ridge north of Lincoln was seldom good enough for ashlar dressing, but Clipsham was at hand on the Rutland-Lincolnshire border.

From a great deal of pioneering work done in the thirteenth century Lincolnshire went on to become the county that surpassed all others in the fourteenth, with Grantham, Sleaford, Heckington, Holbeach, Gedney, and of course Boston as its showpieces. The development starts with the building of the crossing tower of the Cathedral in 1307 to 1311, in which ogee arches and ball-flower decoration come into vogue, followed by reticulated tracery. Some of the best work of the period is to be found in the pleasant countryside of the upper Witham. Brant Broughton is especially worth visiting, not only for its elegant spire, nearly 200 feet high, but for the evidence of the care lavished on it by a succession of three squarsons of the Sutton family who lived at the dignified rectory in the village street. Most of the stained glass was designed by one of them. The ironwork was done by a local firm still carrying on a fine tradition. At Beckingham every period from the Norman of the doorways to the Perpendicular of the tower can

be admired in the church, while in the late-Georgian-faced rectory, with pedimented north front, and beautiful cast-iron entrance gates, we get the feeling of what the Church of England represented in local communities during its period of greatest affluence.

These impressions, however, can be matched in other counties. The Lincolnshire churches that linger longest in the memories of those who value them as records of local history are the big lonely churches of Lindsey and especially of the marshes, standing out like sentinels on their mounds, so many of which, alas, on approaching are now found to be decayed and crumbling. Churches on mounds are found in all counties; but there are so many of them in Lincolnshire that one cannot help suspecting that they may be connected with a Scandinavian predisposition for burial places to be on heights.

There are two main reasons for the sustained magnificence throughout the Middle Ages of the south Lincolnshire churches. One is that unlike East Anglia, Lincolnshire had stone. The other is that the eastern marshland was less affected than most parts of England by the decline in mixed farming that led to the depopulation of so many regions. The 1397 poll tax returns show that Holland at that date was the wealthiest part of England, sustained as it was by the port of Boston, from which the wool from the sheep that grazed the marshes produced the great parish church 282 feet long, with a steeple, the Boston Stump, that is one of the wonders of England.

The best of the new churches built early in the fourteenth century were cruciform and without aisles, which meant that the four arches supporting the central tower abutted solid walls, not nave arcades. The optimism generated by this medieval prosperity is preserved in scores of tales illustrating the

77 Boston, Lincolnshire: St Botolph's tower and 'Stump'

local enthusiasm with which these rebuildings were undertaken. One relates that at Leverton the owner of the local quarry allowed the church-wardens to help themselves to all the stone they needed to build the tower. Another that when the stately tower at Great Ponton was built, Anthony Ellis, a merchant of the Staple of Calais, sent his wife a cask labelled 'Calais Sand', which was placed in the cellar pending his return. She then learned that it contained a store of wealth for the building of the tower as a thank-offering to God for having prospered his concerns so abundantly. When the tower was built his arms were carved on it with the inscription: 'Thinke and Thanke God for all'.

When we cross the Great North Road out of Lincolnshire into Rutland we leave the exciting complexity of Lincolnshire behind us and enter the most unspoiled of the east Midland counties, and one in which the buildings are all in perfect harmony with the landscape in which they sit in such well-bred ease. Where in other counties we seek explanations for splendid churches in small villages, in Rutland we should want explanations of their absence. Several of the grandest churches in England are in this smallest of all our geographical counties. How could it be otherwise in a county blessed with such quarries as those at Ketton and Clipsham, yielding the limestone that W. G. Hoskins so happily describes as 'sheep-grey'? With this stone Rutland was able to add its own soaring spires to those of south-west Lincolnshire, and as they continued along the Nene Valley into Northamptonshire and Huntingdonshire they became the principal architectural glory of the East Midlands.

Rutland's importance in the history of distinctive styles is in the way it illustrates the emergence of the Early English from the late Norman or Transitional. Pevsner points out that 'of the fifty-odd churches in the county two dozen contribute to the illustration of this problem in one way or another'. To

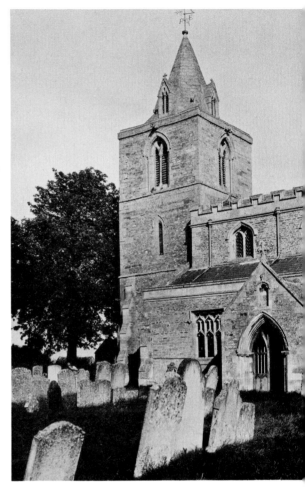

78 Upper Hambleton, Rutland: squat broach spire in local style

trace this development through we start with either the south arcades at Clipsham near the Lincolnshire border in the north or Wing in the south, both dating from the second half of the twelfth century. With their short round piers and scalloped capitals both are severely Norman. A little later in date come the waterleaf capitals at Preston and Little Casterton, and later again, but all within the same half century, the capitals with leaf volutes at Brooke and Burley-on-the-Hill. From these we go on to the waterleaf capitals at South Luffenham and Seaton, and the leaf and animal capitals at

Morcott. All these churches have arches with roll mouldings.

Apart from the specialised architectural interest of these churches, they are all distinctively local. Clipsham, two miles east of the Great North Road, has a remarkable late thirteenth- to early fourteenth-century steeple of a design I have seen nowhere else. There are two short frontal buttresses on the west face, the one on the right finished off with a short frieze decorated with human heads. Capability Brown is reputed to have said that 'Nature abhors a straight line'. So did the builders of Clipsham spire! But architectural individuality appears to have flourished in Rutland. At Preston, instead of the usual triple-sedilia in the chancel there is a single sedile, introduced as part of an unconventional but successful composition in which the south windows of the chancel and the priest's doorway form a single harmonious whole. Everything about this church is well-designed, and the attractive ironstone village it serves lives up to it in neatness and good style.

At Little Casterton, two miles east of the Great North Road near Stamford, there is one of Rutland's local-style double-bellcotes, and inside the church a re-set Norman tympanum with a Tree of Life in the middle. As at Preston, the chancel is distinctive. Here the feature is the piscina, reminding one of the sedile at Preston in its shafts, with naturalistic foliage supporting an arch and an outer crocketed gable. Both are reminiscent of the Chapter House at Southwell. However, like the tympanum, it is not *in situ*. This fine piscina came from the dismantled church at Pickworth.

Another of Rutland's thirteenth-century double-bellcotes is nearby at Essendine, which has one of the finest Norman south doorways in the county, and certainly the most remarkable. Pevsner ascribes it to the second third of the twelfth century. The tympanum has a demi-figure of Christ with angels left and right in a form unusual in England, and still rare – although the

chancel arch at Stoke Dry in Rutland may be thought related – are the elaborately carved jambs of the Essendine doorway. Among the figures that can be recognised are two under a tree, which we may take to be Adam and Eve, while inside the doorway are two men with crooks. This fine carving is probably explained by the church having been the chapel of a castle that formerly stood on an adjacent site.

Rutland had only one monastic foundation. In most of the churches the association is with the nearby castle or manor house, and this, no doubt, explains both the dignity of the churches and their frequent unconventionality. Norman round arches, for example, may appear on thirteenth-century-style capitals, and pointed arches on round Norman piers with plain capitals. This architectural unconventionality of the churches in the villages is just as evident in those of the towns. The squires who built them, like the Northamptonshire squires, would own the quarries from which the stone came and employ their estate masons to carry out most of the work to their own individual taste. After all, variety of style is not surprising where there was such a variety of stone in the county: marlstone, ironstone, and all the varieties of limestone from quarries at Clipsham, Casterton, Edith Weston, and Ketton, with Barnack and Ancaster to draw on from across the county boundary. Splendid as the church at Ketton is, early and late style mouldings are found together in the west front in apparently unrelated assembly. But this does not detract from the magnificence of the church – with its great crossing-tower supported on four arches with triple-shafts rising to a beautiful late thirteenth- or early fourteenth-century spire. The bell stage of the tower is one of the finest to be seen in any county. Three exceptionally tall two-light openings with tracery and rich shafting carry the eye upwards through a frieze of cusped arches to the tall broach spire. The whole took about 50 years to complete.

135

Oakham's fourteenth-century tower dominates the town, but may be thought to fall short of what has come to be expected in Rutland. The tall bell-openings on the west and south faces are out of centre to allow space for the stairs. The parapet is out of harmony, and has heavy Berkshire-style turrets, leaving the spire to contribute little to the overall design. Whissendine's fourteenth-century tower is far more satisfactory, although both turrets and parapet are related to those of Oakham, and the harmony of the whole is destroyed as at Oakham by wilfully placing the bell-openings on the west and south faces out of line in order to accommodate a staircase. Interesting and impressive as these towers and spires are in their individual way, it is not until we reach Uppingham that we find perfection of grouping. There the church porch opens on to the market place of the town, while on the south the whole church is seen in profile from the fields. And although the church was restored and enlarged in 1861, the tall recessed spire, with three tiers of lucarnes facing in cardinal directions, remains perfect. But it must not be thought that all the recessed spires of Rutland are tall. Low spires are equally typical of the county as we see them at Empingham and in broach form at Upper Hambleton.

In Leicestershire the division of the county is between east and west, with the east predominating as it runs towards Rutland. In the west are the coalfields around Ashby-de-la-Zouche and Coalville; but they are not extensive. Although Charnwood Forest has rocks that are probably pre-Cambrian, the entire area measures only seven miles by four. The 'mountain limestone' of the Peak and the Craven dales of Yorkshire breaks through at Breedon-on-the-Hill, where a building of exceptional archaeological interest dramatically caps the landscape. Tempting as it would be to describe it, as it was a monastic not a parish church, it is outside our survey. In the short space available the parish churches of the green, rolling countryside east of the Soar, with its ironstone villages and churches in which ironstone and limestone are so attractively combined to produce a distinctively local style, must be the field of enquiry for Leicestershire.

But before turning to them, the value of the slate from the Swithland quarries for headstones must be mentioned. There are upwards of 1100 of them at Loughborough alone. This remarkable slate comes from a vein found in the volcanic rocks of the southern half of Charnwood Forest. Its widespread use for this one purpose arises from its hardness, which made it unsuitable for use as a building freestone, but admirable for inscribing with elaborate decorative designs and lettering. In the second half of the eighteenth century tablets of Swithland slate even superseded black marble ledger slabs for memorials inside churches. A feature especially valuable for family historians is the Loughborough custom of recording the trade or profession of the deceased.

The lettering, enmeshed in the kind of elaborate scroll work and interlaced capitals seen on old legal documents, is as legible today as when it was carved. From Charnwood the use of this stone for memorials and gravestones spread across the whole of the north-east Midlands and produced a superb craftsman in James Sparrow of Radcliffe-on-Trent in Nottinghamshire, whose work can be recognised not only in meticulously inscribed memorials but also on lists of parochial charities and Biblical texts in town and village churches throughout the 'Shires'.

The characteristic stones in Leicestershire churches east of the Soar are taken from the marls, or ironstones, of the Triassic and

79 Melton Mowbray, Leicestershire: the finest parish church in the county and one of the half-dozen or so finest in England. The tower and long clerestory of 48 windows sumptuous in both design and execution

Jurassic systems that are the bedrock of this part of the county, including the sandy layers of sandstone called skerries. A ridge of ironstone runs from Market Harborough to the plain of Melton Mowbray, and is worked near Waltham-on-the-Wolds. But attractive as this ironstone is, much of it needs limestone for strengthening. Leicestershire is not itself well stocked with good building stone. The only marlstone that can be used with confidence for exterior work is confined to a narrow strip between Market Harborough and Melton Mowbray, and a short strip east of it. Consequently, the two churches of Market Harborough and Melton Mowbray are the best parish churches in Leicestershire.

Pevsner considers the steeple at Market Harborough, where the dedication is to St Dionysius, 'the final answer to the question of how broaches can be handled without imparting any heaviness to the outline and proportion of the spire'. The broaches here are tall, sparingly crocketed, and the total effect is one of restrained elegance. Although the main body of the church is of ironstone, the steeple is ashlar-faced in grey limestone.

Melton Mowbray belongs to the select class of parish churches that includes St Mary Redcliffe, Bristol, and Patrington in Yorkshire. As we approach it, and see the long clerestory with 48 Perpendicular style windows extending above both nave and transepts, with a sumptuously designed tower rising in stages from a thirteenth-century base through a bell stage with Norman style windows to a superbly designed parapet with a quatrefoil frieze and eight pinnacles, we must feel that this is the ultimate in English church design. The one reservation may be that within this elegant parapet is set a spirelet of the Hertfordshire type, which here looks out of place.

The main body of Melton Mowbray church is of the *c.* 1280 to *c.* 1330 half-century into which most of the best work in Leicestershire falls. That it goes so much beyond what is normal in the county is no doubt due

to the living being owned by the proud Cluniacs of Lewes Priory in Sussex. Nevertheless, Melton Mowbray is rightly regarded as the supreme achievement in the county's distinctive style, with all the typical features of intersected tracery in the north aisle, geometrical in the south, and tracery of a slightly later date in the south transept. In summarising the evolution of these tracery styles Pevsner says: 'Melton Mowbray is a whole pattern-book of them'.

Leicestershire has little good fifteenth-century work. Its great period was the early fourteenth century, when spires were at their best and towers of a type completely different from those of Somerset were coming into vogue; but in St Margaret's, Leicester, 1448, the county pioneered fifteenth-century tower development in the Midland counties, which culminated in the tower of All Saints, Derby.

Another church worthy of study for both tracery and the effect of patronage is St Luke's, Gaddesby, where the west tower is of ironstone with an ashlar-faced spire. The whole church is of quite outstanding interest, which in this case is no doubt due to the munificence of the Templars of Rothley, who were lords of the manor. Pevsner finds its famous window, with intersected tracery broken by an insertion of a circle at the apex, 'filled with three cusped spherical quadrangles and their display of niches, crocketed canopies, and ornate battlements and pinnacles' so superb as to be 'amazing'.

An architectural characteristic of Leicestershire churches that must strike visitors to the county is that so often naves seem unusually high in relation to their length. We notice this at Church Langton, another ironstone church with limestone dressings, at Claybrook, and Staunton Harold where an inscription over the entrance reads: 'When all things sacred were throughout ye nation either demolished or profaned Sir Richard Shirley Barronet founded this Church whose singular praise it is to have done ye best things in ye worst

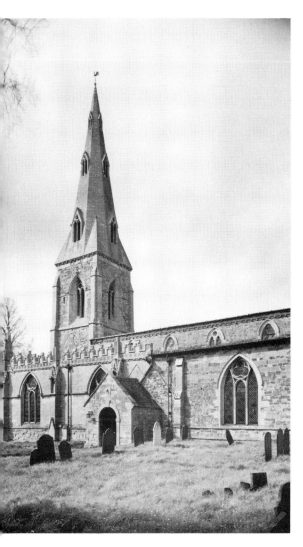

80 Gaddesby, Leicestershire: local ironstone tower with ashlar-faced spire. The whole church is of exceptional interest

leaves. One capital has a row of small heads below a row of leaves. Another has figures of a knight, of ladies wearing wimples, and of an impudent youth sticking out his tongue. Pierced quatrefoils in square panels decorate the parapet of the south aisle, a motif repeated in the parapet of the west tower, from which soars a tall recessed spire. Wyndham St Peter is another example of Leicestershire's free-lancing in its church architecture. It has transepts, but the tower is not at the crossing but at the west end.

Nottinghamshire from the point of view of local style is disappointing. This may seem surprising, since Nottingham St Mary and Newark St Mary Magdalen are among the 20 or so grandest parish churches in England, and Southwell Minster, which was raised to cathedral status in 1884, is in a class of its own for the beauty of the carved foliage on its pier capitals. The truth is that none of these could be said to be in locally generated styles. The explanation is that in the Middle Ages the whole of Nottinghamshire was merely the southern archdeaconry of the diocese of York, although Southwell, like Ripon and Beverley in Yorkshire, had a chapter that was largely independent of episcopal control. Nevertheless, the relationship with York was so strong that Nottingham St Mary and many smaller churches in the north of the county show kinship with the churches of south Yorkshire. In the smaller churches this is shown in their having plain towers, with single windows of two lights in each belfry stage and battlemented parapets with slender pinnacles at the angles. Apart from being the finest fifteenth-century parish church in the county, St Mary's, Nottingham, is unusual for its period in that it is cruciform, with tall central tower and long transepts.

The churches in the wapentake of Newark all derive their style from Lincolnshire, and the grandeur of Newark's own church is directly attributable to its having been built on one of the Bishop of Lincoln's manors, and to successive bishops refusing to allow

times and hoped them in the most calamitous'. Sir Richard died in the Tower in 1656.

For a church that is outstanding both in total design and ornament we cannot do better than visit Stoke Golding near the Warwickshire border in the south-west of the county, where the bays of the south aisle and chapel have superbly moulded arches, with pier capitals carved with naturalistic

the developing town to be divided into separate parishes. The Lincoln Chapter owned large estates in the wapentake, which explains why so many of the towers built there after about 1480 are so different in style from those of north Nottinghamshire. This Lincolnshire style is characterised by having double window openings at the belfry stage, with depressed arches, prominent hoods, and more than one string course projecting boldly from the wall. The type is best seen at Hawton, an unspoilt fifteenth-century church with a fine tower on the outside and good woodwork in simple pews inside. Its Easter Sepulchre – again a Lincolnshire derivative – is claimed to be the finest in England.

In a scholarly essay contributed to *Memorials of Old Nottinghamshire*, Professor Hamilton Thompson attributed the lack of local style in north and east Nottinghamshire to the best masons being attracted out of the county by the exciting work being done in the fourteenth and fifteenth centuries in Lincolnshire and Yorkshire, both with schools of craftsmen of high distinction. His arguments are convincing as regards style. Craftsmen trained in the schools at York and Lincoln must have come into Nottinghamshire to work, just as those trained at Gloucester and Hereford carried their skill across the Cotswolds. Only by this means can we explain the excellence of much thirteenth- and fourteenth-century work, particularly in the Bassetlaw wapentake in the north of the county, where the carving of pier capitals is often of rare beauty. Much of this is especially appropriate and locally inspired. The foliated capitals at North Collingham, East Markham, and South Leverton, are particularly appropriate in forest country. The style of the carving at South Leverton indicates that it was done by the Lincoln trained masons who carved the foliated capitals at Newark.

Nottinghamshire undoubtedly suffered architecturally from so many of its churches belonging to monasteries outside the county. So, as in many similar cases, the money for building the churches came normally from individual benefactors, usually wool merchants. One example is Holme St Giles, rebuilt by John Barton of Newark, who is said to have had inscribed on one of the windows of his house:

I thank God and ever shall
Its the sheepe hath payed for all.

Above the porch entrance at Holme are seven shields displaying the arms of Barton and the Staple of Calais, with bales of wool and John Barton's initials.

The length of the county from north to south also contributed to the variety of styles in its ecclesiastical buildings. Perhaps the one monastic foundation within the county that did have strong influence on its buildings was Worksop Priory, which owned churches in the north-east, where the Fens, called 'Carrs', produced churches with family resemblances that are clearly traceable to Worksop. And, of course, it must be borne in mind that when we reach the Trent we are on the historic boundary for both legal and ecclesiastical purposes separating the north from the south of England. The two strategic crossings from the one to the other were the bridges at Nottingham and Newark, both with castles to guard them. So it is not surprising that such northern features as the square-headed windows found also in Derbyshire are found in about 40 fourteenth-century parish churches in Nottinghamshire.

9 The West Midlands: North

SHROPSHIRE – CHESHIRE – STAFFORDSHIRE – DERBYSHIRE

Shropshire is conveniently divided into two distinctive regions by the Severn. On the north and east are the lowlands of the Midland plain, on the south the uplands of Long Mountain, Stiperstones, the Long Mynd, and Wenlock Edge. Each division has its own building material as well as its own landscape. New red sandstone, which is distinguished from the old of Herefordshire by having an orange tint derived from iron, is quarried in the north, where it can be supplemented from a few outcrops of limestone. In the south, pre-Cambrian rocks break through the thin soil of the Long Mynd, which is broken by a series of ravines called 'batches' or 'gullies' as it runs down to Church Stretton. To the south-east are the hog-backed ridges of the Clun Forest, with rivers serving small communities in the stone villages under Wenlock Edge, where limestone full of fossil corals is quarried, while the Clee Hills yield old red sandstone capped with hard igneous rock called dolerite. From these we reach the villages north-east of Ludlow: Aston Botterel, Clee St Margaret, Stoke Milborough and the rest of them, all with strong local character.

This is the district that introduces us to the sandstone churches of Shropshire, and enables us to see how they differ from the village churches of Herefordshire and Worcestershire to the south and Cheshire to the north. Their particular local style originated along the Welsh border and in the Clun Forest region when the Marcher lords were dominant. Like

their castles, their churches were built of a hard pinkish-grey sandstone, with squat, thick-walled towers of undressed stone, and were obviously designed for defence. Several of them were later given wooden bell-turrets built in diminishing stages, with short roofs rising in a broken pyramid to a wooden cap pierced by small lights, or louvre-boards, to allow the sound of the bells to come through. They are similar to the towers at Brookland on the Romney marshes and Pembridge in Herefordshire; but away from Wales and the Marches belfries of this type are rare. In Shropshire the best are at Clun, Hopesay, and More. Of these the Clun and Hopesay pyramids are on Norman towers. The one at More is entirely medieval and attached to a church that harmonises well with the black-and-white buildings surrounding it – Church Farm to the east, which would formerly be farmed by the parson, and Manor Farm with its weather-boarded buildings completing the composition. The consensus of informed opinion seems to be that the weatherboarding of West Country turrets was originally vertical, and that the horizontal now common, which is so much more pleasing to the eye, was introduced in nineteenth-century restorations.

As we would expect, we find many fine roofs in this forest region. They include early ones at Hopesay and Clun, which have collar-beams on arched braces cusped into quatrefoils; but most of them are late – some as late

81   Heath Chapel, Shropshire: a plain Norman building without tower or bellcote

as the seventeenth century. The typical Shropshire roof is low-pitched, with moulded beams and carved bosses. Some, like the one at St Mary's, Shrewsbury, are enriched by panels with quatrefoil decoration. One of the finest is at Ellesmere in the north-west of the county.

In the country around Cleobury Mortimer shingled spires, or shingled roofs between the stages of pyramidal towers, are common. But while fine timber-work, usually simple in form, is universal, Shropshire has only two completely timber-framed churches: one on the river bank at Melverley, with ancient yews in the churchyard, the other at Halston. Melverley is particularly well sited for our purpose of identifying local styles because it is so perfectly related to its farming environment. Halston was built as a private chapel for Halston Hall, once the home of 'Mad Jack Mitton', the fox-hunting squire and Member of Parliament who died in 1835 in the King's

Bench Prison after squandering a fortune. Like so many other small churches connected with local manor houses it is an unrestored gem, with box-pews facing each other and a double-decker pulpit.

Away from the Welsh border and the medieval Royal Forests surprisingly few distinctively designed churches from any period are found in Shropshire. There are, however, common features that suggest influences from outside the region. According to Dean Cranage, the greatest authority on Shropshire churches, fewer than half the ancient ones have chancel arches. Even churches as large as those at Hodnet and Stottesden are without them. This indicates that the clergy were not pointedly segregated from the congregation as they usually were where monastic influence was strong. The simplicity of this Shropshire plan was probably due to Celtic influence from Ireland outweighing Norman influence coming from the south. The same characteristic will be found in churches in the North of England, where Norse influence that also reached England from Ireland was strong.

Like Worcestershire, which the southern part of the county closely resembles, rural Shropshire has little outstanding Saxon work for inspection except the late Saxon nave at Diddlebury and the chancel at Barrow, two miles from Much Wenlock, where excavations have exposed Saxon foundations. But despite this lack of outstanding Saxon work above ground, about 40% of the county's ancient churches are in round churchyards, which almost invariably indicates pre-Norman siting, and in several there is supportive evidence of early origin in that the church is not only situated at the highest point in the village but on a mound – again suggesting Scandinavian settlement. Cardeston and Church Pulverbatch are examples. Unfortunately from the point of view of historical research Cardeston was rebuilt in 1749 and over-restored in 1844; Church Pulverhatch, apart from the tower, was rebuilt in 1793. The cruciform church at Stanton Lacy fortunately escaped rebuilding, so the whole of the original part can be reliably attributed to the eleventh century, although it was enlarged in the fourteenth century, when the ball-flower decoration typical of the West Midlands was introduced. In conservation, poverty has its uses!

The barrier of the Welsh mountains and Offa's Dyke have protected west Shropshire from the destructive effect of through traffic and industrialisation. So the eastern region has remained one of small settlements, with an exceptionally large number of unspoilt Norman churches serving vast parishes, some of which are so large that they were originally co-extensive with Hundreds, and where smaller parishes have been carved out of them the reduction in size has been marginal. When churches had to be built in these new parishes local style was so strong that it took care of them – and in any case the hardness of the stone kept them simple.

There are, of course, exceptions to this prevailing simplicity. The one that must spring to everyone's mind is Much Wenlock, although it is exceptional in that it was not built as a parish church. It was the church of a wealthy Cluniac Priory that could afford to bring in good workable freestone from the centre of the county to be carved with motifs, both geometric and figurative, by masons whose work reflects Herefordshire influence and is quite alien to Shropshire vernacular. There is another exceptional piece of work in the tympanum over the west door at Aston Eyre, between Much Wenlock and Bridgnorth, which is in fact the best stone carving in Shropshire.

The genuine parish churches that soar above the general run in Shropshire are west of Much Wenlock at Church Stretton, at Shrewsbury, where St Mary's church has one of the tallest towers in England, and at Ludlow, which in the great church of St Laurence has the largest parish church in Shropshire, with a pinnacled tower only 30 inches shorter than Shrewsbury's. The significance of this great tower at Ludlow is that the cost of building it was borne entirely by local guilds of carpenters, smiths, butchers, bakers, tailors, dyers, and cordwainers. When these guilds were in their glory there were three guild chapels in the north aisle of the church, four in the south aisle, five under the arches of the nave, and two in each transept, all enclosed by screens. The knell sounded nationally for such chapels in 1529, when an Act was passed forbidding the founding of any new chantries, and on the accession of Edward VI all their endowments were confiscated. With the loss of this provision for their maintenance the parcloses fell into decay and were dismantled when they became dilapidated.

Both town and church at Ludlow are now national monuments. The layout of the streets on a grid plan, with some of the finest medieval and Georgian houses in England, testifies to Ludlow's civic pride in having been for centuries the seat of the President of the Marches. The defensive pre-eminence of the castle, where Milton's *Comus* was first performed, testifies to the strength that made it the last Royalist stronghold to fall to the

Roundheads. But splendid as it is, Ludlow's church cannot be claimed to represent the climax of local style in Shropshire. The stone came from Hollington, near Uttoxeter in Staffordshire, the source of the stone used by Sir Basil Spence for the new Coventry Cathedral; the hexagonal porch gives away the source of much of the style of the building, since this and the porch at St Mary Redcliffe, Bristol, are the only two in England in this form.

Ludlow's great value for the local historian is in such features as these. St Laurence, Ludlow, like the great churches at Shrewsbury, Wroxeter, Witney, Burford, and one or two others in the West Midlands that have been mentioned, preserves the record of its growth from the simple Norman rectangle from which it developed into the spacious fifteenth-century church with clerestories and tower that we admire today. Such churches are so much more fun to explore as well as rewarding to study than those that were rebuilt from their foundations by purse-proud benefactors. And fun, which is so essential a part of vernacular art, is seen everywhere at Ludlow – most impressively in the stalls and misericords made in 1447, of which the most exciting depicts an ale-wife being carried off by a demon.

In St Andrew's, Wroxeter, at the north-west end of Watling street, the progression starts with the Roman masonry incorporated in a Norman building. The font is believed to have been made from part of a Roman column, and there are Roman remains outside the church. The pulpit and box pews are Stuart, and figure with Victorian features. The brick flooring of the nave is homely and local, giving the whole church an air of continuity which nowhere violates the *religio loci*, whatever architectural purists may regard as being violated.

When we reach Shrewsbury in search of evidence of continuity and belonging, we have A. E. Housman's lines to set the scene:

High the vanes of Shrewsbury gleam
Islanded by Severn stream.

The island mound on which Shrewsbury stands has kept the county's capital gratifyingly small by Midland standards. Its two bridges, the English and the Welsh, symbolise its strategic importance. The pink sandstone of the castle is typical of public buildings in Shropshire, including the churches, and in St Chad's, Shrewsbury, we are reminded that Shropshire is the English county in which the Industrial Revolution, which seems so remote from the countryside of the Marches, made its most distinctive contribution to local style in church buildings.

After searching Sussex for mementoes of the iron furnaces, and finding few except grave slabs, it is exciting to find in Shropshire not only cast-iron table-tombs, or chest-tombs, elaborated with plinths and urns, as at Madeley, but reminders from every age of the traditional skill of Shropshire blacksmiths. They start with such minor details as the wrought-iron hinges, believed to be Norman, on the door at Edstaston, and reach their peak in the art forms used so impressively in the complete system of tracery produced in 1800 for the rebuilding of the church at Adderley. At Tilstock iron was used in 1835 for most of the framework normally constructed of wood or stone. St Alkmund's, Shrewsbury, 1793–5, has windows with Perpendicular tracery in cast-iron. But the masterpiece is St Chad's, Shrewsbury, built to an original design by George Steuart in 1790–92, with a flat ceiling and a gallery supported by graceful cast-iron columns. In appreciating this unique church we have moved a long way from Murray's *Guide* for 1897, which described it, a hundred years after it was built, as being in 'execrable taste'.

With such exciting work being done in Shropshire at the end of the eighteenth century while Thomas Telford was county surveyor, it was inevitable that the master should try his hand at church building. He accomplished the three at Madeley, Bridgnorth, and Malinslee, which was based on the Madeley design. Pevsner writes of them admiringly, and refers to Telford's apparent 'full awareness of recent developments in France'. St Michael's, Madeley, is of ashlar, and is octagonal in form, with a square west tower above an arched entrance with an arched window above it. The upper stages are free-standing, the body of the church, which is not octagonal, has two tiers of windows.

These are very different churches from the small unrestored sandstone and half-timbered churches built by the hunting squires who owned most of the land in Shropshire until the county was invaded by Victorian ironmasters.

From Shropshire we go north across the Cheshire plain where not only the walls of the churches are black-and-white half-timbering, but in some places the nave arcades also. The timber arcades at Lower Peover, which is grouped with an inn and a school at the end of a cobbled lane, must be typical of many churches that have now been dismantled and replaced. Some of the box pews have the fixed panels below the doors that were fitted to hold in the rushes strewn across the floor for warmth. In those days the traditional association of Christmas with the Babe in the manger and the cattle in the stall meant more to village worshippers than it does now. In such churches we can still sense fully the simple beauty of Thomas Hardy's poem, *The Oxen*.

To Fred Crossley, the authority on Cheshire's churches, Lower Peover was the county's best in timber, a judgment that may surprise the casual observer, familiar only with its external appearance. The tower is late sixteenth-century, and the triple roof bears no resemblance to the original, which must have spanned both nave and aisles. Indoors, however, the contrasting white walls and dark woodwork, with octagonal piers, adzed into shape, supporting the cambered tie-beams on massive braces of the roof timbers, are all breath-taking. The adzed columns cannot be later than fourteenth-century, and are probably earlier. The rood-screen, parclose screens, and lectern harmonise successfully with the Jacobean carpentry of the north and south chancel chapels, while pulpit and pews are so perfectly of their period that anyone dropping in between services might well imagine himself back in the seventeenth-century, drowsing in one of the pews while the parson in wig and gown droned solemnly through his first, secondly, and thirdly by candlelight, while the sand trickled through the hour-glass.

Those who want to study the development of wood carving in Cheshire might start with the old church at Warburton, where the piers are merely square posts roughly adzed – looking proud to be timber and aspiring to be nothing more ambitious. The tower at Warburton is at the east, not the west end of the church, and the whole is described by Pevsner as 'a lovable muddle'. Of other timber churches in Cheshire, Siddington's original nave has gone; but Whitegate keeps its fifteenth-century-style piers in what may now appear to be no more than a charming Victorian village church, but in fact is one which has traditional local features in the timber-framed gables, the porch and lych-gate, and most importantly in the strongly constructed timber-framed roof that sweeps down into the churchyard.

The best Cheshire roofs are at Astbury, Barthomley, Malpas, Gresford, Witton, and Northwich. All are low-pitched, with camber beams, and are enriched with bosses and open work pendants. Pevsner describes the roofs of St Helen's, Northwich, as 'good enough for Somerset'. The one at Barthomley is noteworthy because it has angels carved with outspread wings in the East Anglian manner.

Timber continued to be used for building churches in Cheshire until well into the eighteenth century. So it is not a clue to Saxon origin as it might be in south-east England. In fact, there is not one Saxon church surviving in Cheshire, and outside Chester and the Wirrall very little Norman work – and even less of the thirteenth century. The ball-flower ornamentation that is so common in West Midland counties to the south does not occur anywhere in Cheshire, where the main influence is not from a cathedral or an abbey but from the gentry, and is therefore largely post-Reformation, replacing the small chapels-of-ease of the vast medieval parishes. Timber dating has only recently reached something approaching precision, and Cheshire is not a well documented county. The most reliable dating therefore is found in wills. From the evidence available the rebuilding by the gentry started with High Legh, c. 1581.

There is evidence of the closeness of the link between the church and the manor house in Cheshire in the exceptionally large number of churches that began as private chapels. Warburton is one. Woodhey is another, and an interesting one because although the old manor house has gone, traces of its location remain in a great barn, and also in the manorial pew in the church, with two fireplaces, panelled walls and white marble floor.

When stone came into general use for church building in Cheshire the vernacular element that is so attractive in the county's timber work tended to be lost. In many churches piers became standardised in octagonal form with double-chamfered arches and plain moulded capitals exhibiting little distinctive style. The traditional black-and-white churches had brought the House of God into close and easy relationship with the houses of the people. Fortunately the traditional tie-beam roofs in oak continued to be in local form. We see them in the larger churches already mentioned, and in many others that come to mind, like Nantwich, Congleton, Gawsworth, and Mobberley. Nor must it be thought that the old link between the church and the manor house was broken when industrialisation began to affect Cheshire. It expressed itself, as in other parts of the West Midlands, in the introduction of classical design into church building. This is seen particularly in places associated with the Mainwaring family, members of which have played such a distinguished part in the history of Cheshire. We have it at Over Peover, and in the local tendency to commemorate manorial connections in brilliantly painted heraldic tablets on church walls.

The explanation of Cheshire's dependence on the gentry for church building, with such

83 Lower Peover, Cheshire: locally styled in every feature: black and white building with sandstone tower at the end of a cobbled lane, with dark oak arcades, box pews, and roof timbers all contrasting vividly with the whitewashed walls

happy results from the vernacular point of view, was the minor character of most of its monastic foundations. Few of them were able to undertake great building enterprises that could be compared with those of the wealthy Benedictines elsewhere. This makes the exceptions so much more important in looking for sources of local style. The most significant of these stemmed from the founding by Edward I in 1278 in the Vale Royal of what was to become one of the largest Cistercian abbeys in England. It was colonised from the Abbey Dore, and masons came out of Herefordshire to build it when the reputation of the Herefordshire masons was at its peak. It was, in fact, in 1278 that Edward appointed a Herefordshire stone-carver to be one of the king's Master Masons, and it was he who brought into Cheshire the 'shouldered', or ogee, arch, 14 examples of which occur in the octagonal tower at Nantwich. When Master Walter, the king's Master Mason, died in 1315, he had started a style that was continued by his successors into the third quarter of the fourteenth century. The churches built under this influence are the most distinguished examples of church building in Cheshire and are very fine. They are characterised by spaciousness, and as the Cistercians always wanted simple churches they are in harmony with traditional styles.

This distinctive style in stone is recognised on approaching such a church by noting that the tower is in three stages, rising to a height of approximately 60 feet, with a plain battlemented parapet. Mason's marks from schools or lodges in the Vale Royal are found at Shotwick, Backford, Handley, and Tattenhall. Fred Crossley sums up the style in his 'County Book' on Cheshire in a sentence: 'We have noticed that in the end Cheshire had a strong individual sense of style shown in the façades, mouldings, four-light high transomed and uncusped traceried windows, deep projecting buttresses and handsome parapets'.

After the first outburst of building in this finer style than Cheshire had hitherto been accustomed to, the county reverted to more practical designs in which novelty was at a minimum even for the larger churches. Perhaps it was this instinct to adopt what was most serviceable that led to the local adaptation of the normal Decorated style to the Perpendicular by providing for more light to be admitted without interfering more than was necessary with existing features. Pevsner seems to have been struck by this. He says Nantwich impressed him as 'taking in the change from Dec. to Perp. in a particularly abrupt manner'. Malpas, although a predominantly Perpendicular church is classed as 'Perp. c14,' although we usually think of Perpendicular as fifteenth- or sixteenth-century styling.

Time has not been kind to many of the stone churches in Cheshire. In most parts of the county the only stone to hand was one or other of a range of sandstones that have weathered badly and lost their freshness of colour. Only on the fringes of the county do we get stones that wear well. For example, the millstone grit from Mow Cap in the south-eastern corner was used for the fifteenth-century church at Astbury, which is still one of Cheshire's finest buildings.

Inevitably, along the eastern fringe of Cheshire we are aware of being in a different environment. Here industrialisation is made more intrusive than it might otherwise have been by the presence of carboniferous stone, which tends to blacken and give the churches a sombre appearance. The window tracery becomes less graceful, and the general character of the buildings seems to prepare us for the greater austerity of the North.

As we move eastward into Staffordshire and Derbyshire we become increasingly conscious of the impact of industry, although both counties have large pastoral areas and traditions of building that are by no means obliterated. Staffordshire is not all Black Country. In the south it merges with Warwickshire, just as Derbyshire merges with Leicestershire, while in the Peak District Derbyshire and Staffordshire join forces so completely that it is often claimed that 'the best parts of Derbyshire are in Staffordshire'. As for traditional style, although along the Nottinghamshire border there is the coal-mining country of Ilkeston, Clay Cross, Normanton, and Bolsover, we see in the region some of the best stone broach spires that are such a feature of Derbyshire. One of the finest is at Horsley, overlooking the road from Derby to Ripley. Others are at Breaston, Calow, and Clay Cross; but many of them, it must be added, were only adopted as a local style in the nineteenth century.

The sandstone of the West Midlands is under the coal of much of Staffordshire, and breaks through dramatically in many places to make the churches conspicuous landmarks, with the distinction in the stone that the new red sandstone, which fades to orange through the presence of iron in Shropshire becomes yellow in Staffordshire. At Clifton Campville, where it is now grimy, the stone was originally grey, and there are parts of Staffordshire where sandstone is quarried of quality and colour that gives some of the small towns and villages a Cotswold appearance. With similar stone we get similar treatment resolving itself into related styles even if they are far apart in date. Thus the octagonal towers at Hodnet in Shropshire and Nantwich in Cheshire have their counterparts in churches to the east, many of which, like Bakewell's and the ornate eighteenth-century upper stage at St John's, Wolverhampton, rise to pencil-pointed spires.

To be studied in detail Staffordshire has to be divided into the two parts already indicated: the west of the county along the Shropshire and Cheshire borders, and the moors of the north-east along the Derbyshire border, to which must be added as a third division the industrialised east of the county, and as a fourth the district south of Lichfield and Cannock, which has its own strongly defined Midland character, with an outcrop of red sandstone round Kinver Edge used for church building.

There is something defiant about the way so many churches in the south of the county – notably those at Brierley Hill, Dudley, and Wednesbury stand out in a craggy landscape. History still bites deep here. Lichfield means 'the field of corpses' because it marks the site where the invading Angles conquered the native British. The king of the Mercian kingdom had his capital at Tamworth, the bishop of the Mercians his seat at Lichfield. When King Alfred's daughter, Ethelfleda, rescued east Staffordshire from the Danes she had a line of forts built between Tamworth and Stafford. That traditions died hard in the region is shown in the inscription in a window in the parish church of Wednesbury, 'Woden's bury':

'In grateful commemoration of the overthrow of a heathen religion, especially the worship of a false god, Woden, and the establishment of the worship of the True God by the inhabitants of Wednesbury'.

These are proud words; but the lectern, which is either fourteenth- or fifteenth-century, is in the form of a fighting cock, which might be thought a heathenish pastime! In fact, there are cockpits in two or three Staffordshire churchyards, and from 1795 to 1834 Willenhall, three miles south of Walsall, had a parson who was so addicted to cock-fighting that the Old Church House had its own cockpit. It is alleged that the church door was always left open during sermons so that the vicar could see his cronies pass by on their way to a cock fight, and when he did so he brought the service to a hasty conclusion. This reference to Walsall is a reminder that, as I remember it, the spire of St Matthew's church there soars challengingly upward at the head of a steep cobbled street.

Dudley's fine church is dedicated to St Thomas, the doubting St Didymus, which is uncommon. It must rank among the best of the county's nineteenth-century churches, and although so late it is true to local style in that the slender recessed spire, the battlements and pinnacles, are all traditional in character; but the east window has remarkably fine tracery moulded in cast-iron, and the whole church is well worth studying for its combination of styles boldly and at the same time sensitively treated. Nevertheless, when the old church was pulled down to build the present one, gravestones had to be cleared from the churchyard to make way for a larger

building on a severely restricted site. These along with stone from the old church were used to build houses and some found their way into bakers' ovens, so that bread came out of them imprinted with fragments of epitaphs!

This is a district for studying bold experiments in church building. Tamworth's St Editha is an enormous collegiate church in a modern shopping development, which has been restored and rebuilt to an extent that defies description, yet evidence can still be found in it of late Saxon origin in the way the outer angles of the crossing tower project into the aisles. The south wall of the chancel is largely of Norman masonry. Most of the rest of the building is fourteenth-century, with a fifteenth-century west tower. An intriguing feature to the most casual visitor must be the double-spiral staircase, with two stairs starting on opposite sides and never meeting. The design, which is said to have come from one of Leonardo da Vinci's drawings, was used also at Much Wenlock and Pontefract. The Tamworth screen is of wrought-iron. The stained glass is by Ford Madox Brown, Burne-Jones and William Morris; but brought into the contemporary world with a memorial window depicting a land girl and a miner. The stone for Tamworth came from a quarry between Hints and Hopwas, which also has a church designed with more than common ingenuity.

Staffordshire has buildings of distinction from every architectural period. It has more thirteenth-century work than either Shropshire or Cheshire. The Norman west front of the parish church at Tutbury, which stands on a site overlooking the town and near the castle, has a doorway of seven Orders so sumptuously carved that there are few in England to equal it. The outermost Order displays the earliest use of alabaster so far identified in the region. At Uttoxeter the

tower continues to commemorate the building designed between 1325 and 1350 by Henry Yevele. Ingestre church is attributed to Sir Christopher Wren. But despite these distinguished examples, there is nothing in the general run of local designs that can be regarded as distinctive until we reach the eighteenth century, which is uncommonly late for the development of locally distinctive styles. The series starts with St Andrew's, Weston-under-Lizard, in 1701, and continues with churches at Burslem, Burton-upon-Trent, Dudley, Forton, Gayton, Stone, Wolverhampton, Longnor, Hanbury, and many others in a sequence that extended into the first quarter of the nineteenth century to produce churches at Bilston, Walsall, and again at Wolverhampton. Among the most distinguished of the local families of architects who worked during this period were the five generations of Trubshaws, starting with Richard, who died in 1745 and ending with Thomas, who died in 1842.

In the gritstone hills of the Peak District, which provided the thin flagstones that roofed so many Midland churches, we reach the gateway to the mountainous North of England. The Peak is the southernmost part of the Pennine range. But as in so many parts of the North, streams that spring from peaty moorland run down through limestone gorges to water pleasant pastoral country in which a surprising number of Great Houses were built in Tudor times. On the banks of these streams Derbyshire's most typical towns were established: Bakewell on the Wye, Hathersage and Matlock on the Derwent. The scenery around them is so romantic that the Dove and Manifold valleys attracted early devotees of the 'Picturesque' to improve the landscape by such plantings as the ashwoods of Dovedale, now often mistaken for natural in the way the Horner woods in the foothills of Exmoor, planted by the Aclands, are thought to be self sown.

The whiteness of the limestone and the greenness of the vegetation in the Peak gives a brightness to the landscape that is peculiarly

84 Melbourne, Derbyshire: the interior of a Norman church on the grand scale, known externally for its twin towers

its own, especially where the rock breaks through the hill-slopes in huge escarpments called 'Edges' in Derbyshire and 'Scars' in Yorkshire, where similar formations occur. It is in this part of Derbyshire that the county's most characteristic churches and villages are found. The old lead-mining village of Bonsall, built of pinkish-grey stone is one. There the cottages cling to the hillside, as in so many Derbyshire villages, where settlements were established in places where fissures in the rocks made a plentiful supply of pure water available. At Bonsall the road climbs up the embankment to the village cross, set at the top of 13 circular steps, the two lowest cut out of the rock, and the nearby King's Head inn. Higher again stands the church, with a low, battlemented profile, Perpendicular tower and elegant spire with two ornamental bands round it. To match this proud exterior all is polished within, with rood-screen, medieval grave slabs – of which more presently – and a monument with weeping cherubs to Henry Ferne of Snitterton, a late sixteenth- or early seventeenth-century benefactor who lived at the manor house.

The churches of the Peak District provide great scope for research into ecclesiastical industrial archaeology, and not only industrial archaeology. Eyam (Eem) has one of the finest early Christian crosses, several of which are at points where ancient trackways converge on Roman roads. They were probably set up at those points by adventurers prospecting for minerals. The point of this for our present enquiry is that metal work is as important an aspect of church furnishings in such places as timber may be in the South. One of the most important centres of lead-mining from prehistoric times to the late Middle Ages was Wirksworth in the Low Peak, an ancient town situated at the crossing of the two port- or market-ways, and the heart of one of the largest early Saxon parishes in Derbyshire. Like Bonsall it was producing lead when the Romans landed. The circular shape of its large churchyard should alert the visitor to its Saxon origin, which is confirmed

inside the church by a Saxon coffin lid, now set in the wall of the north aisle, so elaborately and skilfully carved in panels depicting the major festivals of the Christian year that it could only have covered the body of a greatly revered cleric, probably a Saxon saint. And as it was discovered below the chancel floor directly in front of the altar it may well have been from the coffin of the founder. Guide books attribute it to the seventh-century. It would be unlikely to be later and might be earlier, since the figure on the Cross is the Lamb of God and not the Crucified Christ, which the Council of Constantinople in 603 decreed should be depicted.

To see evidence of continuity in the use of metal we should visit Ashbourne, which is close to the Roman road from Wirksworth to Rocester, and is another of Derbyshire's early Saxon parishes. There we begin at the modern end of the process started so long ago by prospectors for metal and work backwards. The churchyard gates, hung between quaintly turreted pinnacles on massive pillars, look more like the entrance to the drive of a stately home or a municipal park than to a church-yard. Not that there is any danger of a mistake being made about what lies behind them. The church is fully in view before the gates are reached. Its spire, 212 feet high, dominates the town. The lancet windows in the chancel and north transept are reminiscent of Lichfield and prepare us for more in the same style in the North of England. The interior is magnificent but unorthodox. There is no north aisle, which seems strange in so large a church, and the base of the tower juts into the nave on the north side. Victorian windows in the chancel were unfairly denigrated by Ruskin as 'the worst piece of base Birmingham manufacture' that he had seen.

While Ruskin might not be an entirely unprejudiced judge where manufactured goods were concerned, it has to be acknowledged that in the Midlands we do find brash and immature features in many of the largest churches. And even if it is replied that taste is often a question of fashion there is still the

153

feature of skimped workmanship such as we see in expensively built churches in which all the craftsmanship is concentrated on one side of the screen only. Aymer Vallance in his book on screens says: 'In some Midland churches, as for instance at Kirk Langley, Derbyshire, Blore Ray, Staffordshire, and at Solihull, Warwickshire, such fantastic and unusual variations are to be met with in the tracery or in the carved ornament as would not occur in the south, the east, and the south-west of England'.

This was the country of the self-made man, and one in which the old county families – and there were many of them – had a habit of asserting their superiority, as they regarded it, to these upstarts by getting themselves buried in magnificent tombs. Family tombs, therefore, must be considered a feature of Midland churches, and as they frequently required the building of aisles or side-chapels to accommodate them they became a feature of local style in church fabrics. At Ashbourne they commemorate the Cockaynes and the Bradbournes.

The finest of the craftsmen in iron, and one to whom none of the strictures just referred to apply, was Robert Bakewell, a Derby blacksmith who worked in the middle of the eighteenth century and is believed to have made the church gates at Ashbourne. His work is seen in many Staffordshire and Derbyshire great houses as well as in churches. Some of his best work is in the deservedly renowned chancel screen at All Saints, Derby, now the Cathedral, *c.* 1730, the modest but lovely screens at Borrowash (Borrow-ash) and the altar rails at Foremark.

The money lavished on splendid tombs in Derbyshire has given us two contrasting styles in the county that are as far apart as the shepherds' from the ironmasters' churches of the Sussex Weald. In Derbyshire the ironmasters' are of a later vintage than those of Sussex, and the small churches began, not as shepherds' churches but as private chapels for the gentry – even of the nobility, as at Haddon and Chatsworth. At Ault Hucknall,

overlooking the park at Hardwick, is one of these small unrestored churches that take us back to origins as more carefully maintained churches seldom do. Among those buried at Ault Hucknall are the First Countess of Devonshire, Thomas Hobbes, the philosopher, and Robert Hackett, park-keeper, who died in 1703 and is commemorated in the lines:

Long had he chas'd
The red and fallow deer,

But death's cold dart
At last has fix'd him here.

At Kedleston, the entire village was removed when the park was landscaped during the eighteenth century, leaving the church as virtually a private chapel surpassing all other Derbyshire churches for its sequence of family memorials, starting with that of Richard de Curzon and his wife (d. 1275) and ending with the sumptuous monumental tomb of Marquis Curzon, Viceroy of India, who died in 1929.

Many of these churches are visited now with the sole purpose of seeing examples of the alabaster effigies for which Derbyshire is famed. The most remarkable series of them is at Longford – another church in a private park at a distance from the village it serves – where they date from 1357 to 1610. Morley, where the eighteenth-century rectory is now the Diocesan Retreat House, is visited to see brasses to the Statham family, which are unique in my experience in having inscriptions recording the building of the church as well as the virtues of the deceased. The heiress of the Stathams married a Sacheverell, and the tradition of making the inscriptions informative was continued through to the alabaster tomb of Jacynth, who died a hundred years later, and records that he was a Papist.

Alabaster quarried and carved in Staffordshire, Derbyshire, and Nottinghamshire became as famous for monuments as Purbeck was for fonts. Burton-upon-Trent was already a centre for alabaster carvers in the fourteenth century. Other ancient alabaster quarries in Staffordshire were at Tutbury and Hanbury. In Derbyshire, Chellaston was the best known centre. In the fifteenth century its quarries produced slabs of alabaster incised with effigies in which the lines were filled with pitch. These were popular for a time, but when the pitch became defaced the tablets ceased to serve their intended purpose and were often taken down and used for such purposes as repairing altar steps. One of these slabs can be seen against the wall of the north transept of Darley Dale church, bearing the full-length effigies of John Rollesley, 1513, and Agnes his wife. The best of these incised effigies in Staffordshire, which has about 50 of them, is at Sandon, commemorating Hugh and Cecile Erdeswike, 1473. But despite the number in Staffordshire, Derbyshire must be awarded pre-eminence for them.

The Derbyshire town that to me most clearly bears the true imprint of the county is Bakewell. In the church and churchyard every period of its history is represented, from the remains of a Saxon cross in the church-yard, and Saxon masonry in the fabric of the church, through the details of the Norman west front and the evidence of the collegiate church given by King John to Lichfield Cathedral, to the fourteenth-century octagonal tower and spire, which was carefully rebuilt in 1852. In no other church in this county in which local style is most rewardingly found in towns of medium size, is history more faithfully recorded.

If, however, we are looking for the church with the strongest individual character, we should probably agree that the award must go to Tideswell's St John the Baptist, the 'Cathedral of the Peak'. Its situation on the moors saved it from the worst excesses of the Victorian restorers, so it remains a splendid memorial to the fourteenth century in this region of carboniferous limestone. By the generosity of the guilds it was completed between 1320 and 1380, without serious interruption by the Black Death, the pestilence that cut short so many ambitious building projects in the fourteenth century. The nave is in five bays with fourteenth-century windows, the tower is Perpendicular, and the large chancel anticipates later style in having tall square-headed windows of three lights, a feature that links it with the churches of Lancashire and Yorkshire, and with styles found increasingly as we move northwards into parts where carboniferous limestone becomes universal over vast areas.

10 Lancashire and Yorkshire

With the reorganisation of local government in 1974 Lancashire lost some of its most typically northern-style churches to Cumbria. The loss is lamented; but from the point of view of local styling it is easier to understand the churches of Furness – the region transferred – if we relate them to those of Westmorland than to those of Lancashire. In any case, with the Pennines breaking up so large a region into divisions permanently determined by natural barriers, Lancashire and Yorkshire as we have them today form a unit large enough and varied enough for any purpose. Nor are natural barriers the only factors explaining internal differences. We have seen how the arch-diocese of York extended southwards into Nottinghamshire. In the west the diocese of Lichfield extended northwards across Lancashire as far as the River Ribble, bringing south Lancashire into closer affinity with Derbyshire and Staffordshire than with the country to the north.

The churches of south Lancashire have little attraction for tourists in search of local style. They discover it most significantly at Whalley, in the north of the region lying south of the Ribble, the mother church of a parish which in the Middle Ages covered about 165 square miles. Whalley is still a village and full of rural character, while its daughter, Burnley, is now one of several mill towns of which Whalley was the parent settlement. This is interestingly illustrated in the stipulation made when Burnley's original parish

church was built, that it should have finials surmounting each buttress 'according to the fashion' of those on 'the chapel of Our Lady at Whalley'. In common with most ancient parish churches in Lancashire and Yorkshire there is nothing surviving in the present church at Whalley of the first Anglo-Saxon building, and only a doorway from the Norman church. Most of the oldest existing parts are thirteenth-century; the bulk fifteenth-century. But Whalley has three churchyard crosses elaborately carved with designs that are conclusive evidence of ninth- or tenth-century infiltration into the Ribble Valley from the Lancashire coast.

The commonest style in the churches of south Lancashire, and not least in those in the old Whalley parish, is 'Commissioners' Gothic' – a name derived from the Church Building Commission appointed in 1818 to identify the areas of greatest need of new churches in the 'working-class' districts created by the Industrial Revolution, and to make grants to build them. The first grants were made in 1819 of amounts totalling one million pounds, followed in 1825 by grants totalling half-a-million. From first to last Lancashire got more Commissioners' churches than any other county. Nineteen were built before 1830, 62 between 1830 and 1856. Two of those within a few miles of Whalley are Darwen, 1827–8, and Clitheroe, 1829, both of carboniferous limestone by Thomas Rickman, the architect chiefly associated with

85 Heysham, Lancashire: the thirteenth-century parish church of St Peter, successor to an earlier church dedicated to St Patrick, marking the place where the Norse shepherds landed from Ireland

Commissioners' Gothic churches in Lancashire.

The man who initiated the style adopted by the Commissioners was an ironmaster named John Cragg, who in 1812 employed Thomas Rickman to build churches for him in which the tracery of the windows and every possible feature in the furnishing would be of cast-iron. The style was taken up with characteristic Lancashire enthusiasm, and several churchwardens of the period – notably those of St James's, Oldham – really 'went to town'

with cast-iron tracery. Among the larger parishes that benefited from Commissioners' grants were St Martin's, Liverpool, St George's, Hulme, and St Thomas's, Pendleton. Preston in the north of the county, the 'Coketown' of Charles Dickens, got two churches under the scheme, Burnley one. These churches can be recognised by being Gothic in style, with long lancet windows separated by thin buttresses, which means that their narrow, pinched proportions are in sharp contrast to the low, broad-beamed churches of either north Lancashire or the Yorkshire dales.

The Greater Manchester area got outstanding examples of contemporary Victorian architecture by employing some of the best architects of the day and encouraging them to produce revolutionary designs. One of the

157

most remarkable of these is St Stephen's, Lever Bridge, Bolton, by Edmund Sharpe. The open-work spire is of terracotta made by John Fletcher, a colliery owner, whose name should rank with that of John Cragg as a champion of the pioneering spirit of Industrial Lancashire. Bodley, who was not a Lancastrian, achieved one of his masterpieces in brick at Pendlebury. Paley and Austin followed with majestic churches at the end of the century.

Crossing the River Ribble north of Whalley we enter the well-watered countryside that leads into the hills of north Lancashire at Mitton, which takes its name from the 'meeting of waters' celebrated in the local rhyme:

Hodder, Calder, Ribble and rain,
All meet together in Mitton domain.

Although so near in distance, when their respective churches were built Whalley was in the diocese of Lichfield and the province of Canterbury, Mitton in the arch-diocese of York. As I was born in Mitton, then in Yorkshire, and know the district well, I have always cherished a local tradition which illustrates how strong the impressions made by exceptional natural features are in the minds of countrymen. At Withgill Knowle in Mitton there is an outlier of the famous Derbyshire 'Blue John' stone. Near it is the base of an ancient cross and an old quarry. According to local tradition the first church at Mitton stood there, and when the present parish church was built on an eminence above the Ribble bridge towards the end of the thirteenth-century stone was carried from Withgill to build it.

Mitton, like Whalley, has far more fascinating features than can be summarised here; but it is eminently worthy of mention as an example of true northern style: a long low building with a squat battlemented tower, and with good plain woodwork inside, as befits a church built to serve a parish stretching across the vast Forest of Bowland,

which must have been almost as extensive at one time as Whalley's. It was the westernmost point of the great Deanery of Craven, which extended from Mitton and Slaidburn on the Hodder in the west to Hubberholme in Wharfedale and Bingley in Airedale in the east. The sixteenth-century screen has a representation of the Annunciation carved on the nave side, copied in cast-iron on the chancel side. The cresting also is in cast iron. These, like so many other features in the churches of Craven, serve as reminders that long before John Cragg's time country craftsmen in these parts were constructing their pulpits and church screens as they constructed their farm carts.

At Chipping, north-west of Mitton, is another church built on a mound in the same sturdy style. If Lancastrians were reproached for having failed to preserve many of their Saxon and Norman monuments, they might well argue that such conservation would have been irrelevant since every rebuilding was done in the same country style by local masons who would have resented workmen from other parts of the country being brought in to teach them their job. The pride of inherited possessions, however humble, goes deep in the North. When in 1240 a rector of 'Proud Preston' claimed that Chipping was no more than a chapelry of Preston he was quickly put in his place. A hundred years later an abbot of Whalley found the inhabitants of this rugged countryside 'few, intractable, and wild'. Perhaps they were. Perhaps they still are. But where we look for clues to local style in the south of England in liturgical influences by bishops, craft styles favoured by the monastic patrons of schools of masons or carpenters, or the wishes of wealthy benefactors, in the North it is the native character of the men who farm the land and practice basic skills in village forges and workshops that determines building styles.

We have decided to leave the churches of Furness to be looked at in relation to Cumbria, to which geologically the region belongs. But before looking at the rest of

86 Sefton, Lancashire: apart from the fourteenth-century spire, a mid-sixteenth-century church remarkable for its carved fittings: stalls, canopied pulpit, and screens

Craven, we should cross the grouse moors so much loved by George V to look at the churches between the river Lune and Morecambe Bay if only because it would be churlish to pass through Lancashire without paying our respects to Lancaster, its proud capital – reached from Mitton through an ancient pass, The Trough of Bowland, and

some of the finest scenery in England. Along this north-west coastal fringe magnesium limestone breaks through the moorland in the kind of rocks that gave Silverdale its name. Place-names and personal-names become increasingly Norse, and the dialect spoken by farmworkers is different from that of industrial Lancashire. The clue to these differences is found at Heysham, where the Norse shepherds who settled the Lakeland fells landed in the ninth and tenth centuries from Ireland. The base of a ninth-century cross is preserved there, and the ruins of a church significantly dedicated to St Patrick stand in the same churchyard as the thirteenth-century parish church of St Peter.

This part of Lancashire is still rural and retains features that can be traced to other ancient ports besides Heysham. In the porch at Heversham, now in Cumbria, there is a beautiful example of early work in the sculptured representation of the tale of 'the little foxes that spoil the vines'. The bunches of grapes hang from graceful stems, the foxes have bushy tails and pricked ears, which experts tell us are clearly derived from the work of stone-cutters who landed at the ancient ports of Ravenglass and Workington.

There are few signs of similar schools of craftsmen being established in the ports of south Lancashire, or the inland villages, where the general impression is of poverty and insecurity during the period in which churches were being built elsewhere in distinctively local style. The bleak hills between the village settlements, where the bleating of sheep and the crying of pewits are still the most evocative sounds heard, brought no wealth to Lancashire during the Middle Ages.

On the east of industrial Lancashire the Craven Gap, which extends from Clitheroe in Lancashire to Keighley in Yorkshire, leads out of the region of carboniferous limestone into one of magnesium limestone as effectively as The Trough of Bowland does on the north. Although not the most typical of either Lancashire or Yorkshire building stones, magnesium limestone is the brightest and most interesting, especially when full of the fossil remains of sea creatures that swam about here when water gushed through the Craven Fault. All the parishes in the Craven Deanery except Linton and Burnsall were appropriated to religious houses too far away to take any direct interest in them, with the exception of Kirkby Malham, which although appropriated to Dereham in Norfolk maintained a link with its owners because they always appointed one of their own canons to the living. It cannot, however, have been a happy arrangement, since a glance at the list of incumbents shows that the shortness of their stay was in sharp contrast to that in neighbouring parishes, where down-to-earth parsons bearing honest-to-God fellside names, stayed on for the best part of their lives, farming their glebe and attending local cattle sales along with their parishioners.

However, the general effect of this remote control, such as it was, meant that the maintenance of the buildings was assumed as a local responsibility, resulting in the churches of Craven conforming to a common style: long, low buildings, with battlemented west towers approximately 50 feet high, pierced by a single window at the bell stage and a wide-gabled porch. There is a local tradition that the low pitched roofs of the Craven churches were introduced after a high-pitched one at Gargrave slipped and collapsed at the beginning of the sixteenth century when churches were roofed with stone slabs, locally called flags. There may have been another contributory cause in that few Craven churches have chancel arches, and when the larger churches acquired aisles along the sides of both chancel and nave the outward pressure of the roofs was too great. This was countered in some churches by building great balks of timber into the walls for support. Where roofs were raised and clerestories introduced these were given the same square-headed windows typical of Lancashire and Yorkshire churches, but under hood-moulds strong enough to support the roof directly above them.

Most of the towers in these larger churches, many of which are unbuttressed, have small pinnacles at the corners of the battlements. In a few, open work of a local type runs round the parapets, and there are twin-lights at the belfry stage of the towers. The largest churches in Craven are those at Giggleswick, the mother church of Settle, and Kirkby Malham, formerly serving an area that included seven civil parishes. Other churches in Craven and the country west of the Pennines that are authentically local in character are at Arncliffe, Kettlewell, and Rylstone. But the most visited church in this part of Yorkshire is the ancient chapel of St Oswald, Hubberholme in Wharfedale, first mentioned in church records in 1241, when William de Percy gave it to the Premonstratensian canons of Coverham, with a chamber and garth for a priest. One of the two features that attract so many visitors there is the unfinished rood loft, six feet wide, with a railing on each side and 13 panels pierced with rudely cut Gothic tracery painted in red and black. The other feature is the overpowering cave-like arches of the south arcade: great slabs of undressed stone supported by roughly cut octagonal piers with chamfered abaci and wedge-shaped mouldings at the four corners. When the outer walls at Hubberholme had to be rebuilt in 1863 the greatest care was taken to re-lay the stones in exactly the same order as before. It is sometimes claimed that this is the only rood loft left in Yorkshire; but this is not quite true. There is one at Flamborough, believed to be the work of Ripon woodcarvers. But rood screens are certainly rare in the North.

In trying to trace sources for masonry of more than common interest in this part of Yorkshire Ripon should be kept in mind. There was a school of stone-carvers established there between the years 850 and 1000 whose carved crosses and grave slabs can often be identified. There are two of them inside the church at Wensley.

Several large churches in Craven have pointed-arch windows, but the more usual type is, of course, the square-headed, which harmonise well with the general plan of churches in the old rural West Riding, most of which were either built or rebuilt in the fifteenth century with naves twice the length of the chancels: proportions that contribute further to the general effect of squareness and regularity which is consistent with the usual view of the Yorkshireman's character, and is represented in his farms and manor houses as well as in his churches. The feature that surprises discerning visitors from the South is that the walls of the nave arcades in many of the churches should be as thick as the outer walls, which appears to be so wasteful of good building material, and entirely inconsistent with Yorkshire frugality. The explanation is probably to be found in the church having been enlarged in stages. At all events we have evidence of how the problem of enlargement was tackled at Kirklington, near Masham, that support the theory. When aisles were added in 1330 the external walls were erected first so that worship could continue in the existing Norman church without interruption. When the new outer walls were completed and the roof fixed, the original walls were broken for columns to be inserted in order to convert them into nave arcades. In some places where this method of enlargement was adopted fragments of the original windows can be detected in the masonry above the arches. Where piers were not inserted, the cost of enlargement was kept to a minimum by retaining blocks of unaisled church walls to serve as supports for the arches, giving the church a cave-like appearance.

But economy was not the sole consideration in building so many northern churches so austerely. Many of those in the Yorkshire Dales were built by Cistercian sheep-masters who evangelised the dales from the great abbeys, and built in a style which in their view could bear witness to the stark simplicity of Christianity as they preached it. So their churches were built without towers, tracery, or any kind of ornamentation, to symbolise a concept of the good life entirely different from that of the Benedictines and Cluniacs, who revelled in raising stately churches filled with all the treasures that craftsmanship could accomplish. To the Cistercian abbots, with their thousands of acres of sheep walks on the fells, and granges with small chapels attached to them in the dales, true worship was workmanship, and the good life one of honest toil. Not for them the luxurious living of the Benedictine abbots, flowing from wealth derived from the profits of fairs and markets, the ownership of fisheries, and the altar dues to be collected from craft guilds, or monopoly

87 Bolton Priory, Yorkshire: local in every feature and Cistercian in character

rights enforced dutifully by their faithful followers in local courts, as well as from pilgrims kneeling before the relics enshrined in their churches. Cistercian services were conducted with the simplest ceremonial. There were no processions, no special services on saints' days, no singing of litanies. Instead, from their abbeys at Rievaulx and Fountains they preached what became the Yorkshire gospel of salvation by hard work and regular study of the Scriptures. The abbot lived as frugally as his monks and eschewed even intellectual superiority. It is not surprising that the soil was so well prepared for George Fox and his Quakers in the seventeenth century or Wordsworth in the eighteenth. In one of his letters, Bernard of Clairvaux wrote:

'You will find in the woods something you never find in books. Stones and trees will teach you a lesson you never heard from masters in school. Honey can be drawn from the rock, oil from the hardest stone'. Pure Wordsworthian doctrine! And we shall see later how Wordsworth read it into the local style of Cumbrian churches.

The same coarse local stone continued to be used in the eastern foothills of the Pennines for churches, barns, byres, and cottages indiscriminately until the present century. But Yorkshire is not all of that character and never was. When we move out of the sphere of influence of Fountains and Rievaulx into that

88 Hemingborough, East Yorkshire: a Collegiate church built of white magnesium limestone from Tadcaster, with a spire twice as high as the tower

of York and Ripon we find an ecclesiastical system evolved from mother churches at Halifax, Dewsbury, Thornhill, Otley, and one or two others in churches in which art played a definite part under the guidance of schools of masons and carpenters from the cathedrals. Tracery and standards of furnishing found nowhere in Craven, Bowland, or the northern Dales, were introduced and affluence again became evident.

Again, stone no less than liturgy played its part. In the Vale of York churches could be built of magnesium limestone obtained from the quarries at Tadcaster, which had been worked by masons under the patronage of the abbots of St Mary at York and St German at Selby since the twelfth century. We see their work in decorative features at Stillingfleet, Birkin, Brayton, and Barton-le-Street, which scholars tell us had been introduced into England by the Benedictines from western France. But the main interest in decorative motifs over most of Yorkshire is that they are strongly Scandinavian in character. This pre-Norman influence is found in the Viking ship, dragons' heads, and plaitwork at Stillingfleet, where the south door of St Helen's church is justifiably held to be 'a national treasure of folk art'.*

In the villages of the Wolds such names as Kirkburn and Weaverthorpe indicate Scandinavian settlement, while others, which are known to be of earlier Anglian origin, have churches rebuilt in simple Yorkshire style after the wholesale destruction by the Conqueror during the terrible harrying of the North. As always in coastal regions, racial origins are complicated here. At Weaverthorpe the church built by Herbert the Chamberlain between 1108 and 1121 has pre-Conquest features which suggest the influence of Celtic missionaries.

Ornamentation is found in isolation in churches not very far from the hill country of the Cistercian sheep-masters. At Tickhill,

west of the Great North Road between Bawtry and Rotherham, for example, there is a decorative parapet which so far as I know is peculiar to Yorkshire, in which crocket-encrusted pointed arches break up the battlements in a style that has no artistic merit to commend it, but is certainly true to local character if only for the forthright strength of its construction.

The fewness of good screens in Yorkshire is often commented on. The explanation is again to be found in Yorkshire thoroughness, and in this case is to be debited rather than credited to local character. Between 1720 and 1737 Yorkshire archdeacons exceeded their legal powers by ordering that all screens should be either removed entirely or cut down to pew height. The order actually made by Dr Dering, archdeacon of the East Riding, who led the movement against them, was for the screens in all churches in his archdeaconry to be taken down 'from the balk or beam downwards as far as the tops of the pews, and the king's arms to be sett up in some more convenient place'.

The lack of better towers over the greater part of a county so well provided with stone might be more difficult to explain. Here again the deficiency is compensated for when we move nearer York and Ripon. And several of the towers in the east of the county are of peculiarly local interest. Instances of these are the defensive towers at Bedale, where the newel stairway inside was formerly protected by a portcullis that could be lowered when danger threatened, and at Masham, Middleham, and Thornton Watlass, where the towers have upper chambers with fireplaces for the comfort of those who took refuge in them when the Scots were on the rampage.

For those in search of architectural distinction rather than local character the main field of study in Yorkshire lies east of the Pennines. That is where the money has always been. The major glories must be mentioned presently; but in a search for the specifically local minor churches are often the most revealing, particularly when they have not

* P. V. Addyman and Jan H. Goodall, *Archaeologia*, vol. CVI, p. 104.

89 Old Malton, Yorkshire: the south-west tower, carved doorway and façade of a Gilbertine priory founded *c*. 1150

suffered unduly from restoration or local self-glorification. The austere twelfth-century church at North Newbald on a western scarp of the Wolds is probably the finest church in the old East Riding, while at Holme-upon-Spalding Moor, west of Newbald, there is another of those inexhaustibly interesting churches found in so many parts of the lowlands of eastern England, built of a motley variety of stones and pebbles to bear eloquent witness to the geological complexity of the region. The main body of the church was built in the fifteenth and sixteenth centuries, brick parapets and a porch were added in the seventeenth century, and in a niche in the tower is a representation of a crowned figure holding souls in a sheet.

90 Whitby, Yorkshire: Cliffside church of Norman origin with eighteenth-century fittings: galleries, box pews, and three-decker pulpit that it would be sacrilege to modernise

The Augustinian priories in the east of the county, such as Bridlington and Guisborough, and the Benedictine Abbey of Whitby owned groups of village churches in the Wolds behind them; but as many of the village churches in the East Riding were rebuilt in the nineteenth century we have to rely more on documentary evidence than visual to account for what we find. The church of St Mary, Whitby, however, originally Norman, is one on which no restorer should ever be allowed to lay disfiguring hands. Its eighteenth-century interior, with galleries,

box-pews, and three-decker pulpit should stand for ever as a memorial to the spiritual life of a Yorkshire fishing port with roots in the seventh-century monastery of St Hilda, where Caedman composed the first English hymns. Perched on a high cliff overlooking the sea, its site is among the most spectacular in England.

On the fringe of the county round Bridlington Bay is Tunstall, with a village church built of pebbles set in mortar in Lincolnshire style. At Skipsea, east of Great Driffield and west of Hornsea, the pebble-built church in an almost circular churchyard has a south aisle built of Tadcaster stone that must have been brought down the Ouse to the Humber estuary.

In the south of the county the churches in the east are closely linked with those of Lincolnshire, in the middle with those of Nottinghamshire and Derbyshire, and in the

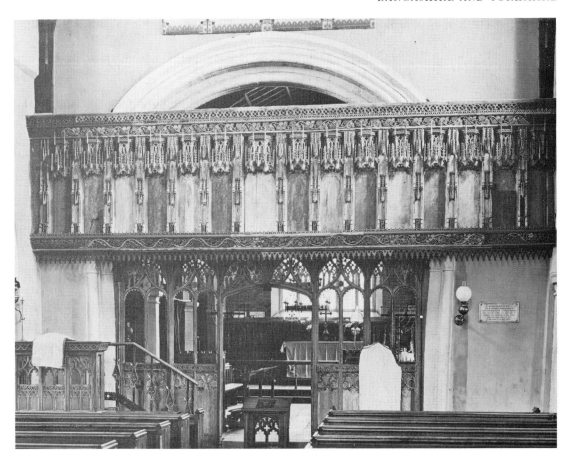

91 Flamborough, Yorkshire: one of the few rood screens in England retaining its loft

west with those of Cheshire. Apart from the facts of diocesan control already mentioned at the beginning of this section, these links were inevitable since communications were so much easier in the lowlands of the south than in the Pennines. There was also the fact that in the south there was magnesium limestone, which runs across Yorkshire from the Nottinghamshire–Derbyshire border to the County Durham border near Darlington. So it is in the south-east of Yorkshire that the best medieval churches are found.

The width of the River Ouse, which crosses a plain geologically so remote from the Yorkshire of the Pennines, provides clues to early settlement which place-names confirm. In the low landscape of the region Riccall, Cawood, Drax, Adlingfleet, and other places clearly derived much benefit from the proximity of both Selby and York. The most striking evidence of this is in the towers, some of which are larger than even the largest in either Somerset or East Anglia. Among the finest are the two west towers of Beverley Minster, the great central tower of Beverley St Mary, and the towers at Cottingham, Howden, Hedon, and Hull, all built in a region that lacked local stone, but could have it brought by barge from the quarries at Tadcaster, while timber for roofs could be hauled by draughts of oxen from the forests beyond the marshes.

Beverley is as distinguished for its carpentry as for its masonry, and we have a delightful footnote on family history in this region where craft guilds flourished and families followed the same occupations for centuries, in 68 of the misericords on the stalls being the work of members of family named Carver. The Beverley misericords are among the finest in the country. Among the subjects are a shepherd with his crook and two farmworkers shearing. Another shows two woodcarvers quarrelling, which may well record an incident of family violence, since one threatens with a raised mallet, the other with a chisel. Another depicts a man shoeing a goose.

The local development of tower styles in the affluent south-east of Yorkshire, to which wool brought prosperity not enjoyed so early in the Dales, was interrupted by the importation of Somerset styles by two Yorkshiremen who rose to be bishops of Bath and Wells: Walter Skirlaw, who died in 1406 while Bishop of Durham after being Bishop of Bath and Wells for the short period 1386–8, and Nicholas Bubwith, who was Bishop of Bath and Wells for the much longer period, 1407–24, and was responsible for the building of the west tower of Wells. The first importation from Somerset was at Skirlaugh, the birthplace of Walter Skirlaw, as his name is usually spelt now; but Bishop Budwith's influence was much the greater of the two since he sent one of his master masons from Somerset to direct operations in the North. Eventually the Somerset style spread from Skirlaugh to Beeford, Fishlake, Thorne, Hatfield near Doncaster, Wadworth, Conisborough, Sprotborough, Preston-in-Holderness, and Great Driffield.

It would be too much to expect that even Yorkshiremen so distinguished as these two would get away with importing south country styles into Yorkshire unmodified. In fact, they didn't. In most of these churches modelled on Somerset styles, what were to become Yorkshire features broke through. The parapet and great west window at Skirlaugh and Preston-in-Holderness, the large windows in the middle stage at Hatfield near Doncaster, and so on, belong to Yorkshire, not Somerset.

What were to become distinctively Yorkshire parapets and windows are fully developed as local style in the stately tower at Hedon, which expresses so well the directness of the Yorkshire character by relying entirely for its effect on good proportions and sound workmanship. Decorative features are kept to a minimum until the parapet is reached. This is arcaded in two tiers, the upper one perforated. Crocketed pinnacles rise from the corners, with smaller ones midway between them. Even Professor Allen, in his classic work *The Great Church Towers of England*, forgets for a moment his tendency to attribute all good features in towers to Somerset influence and says of Hedon's: 'In point of composition this tower is as perfect as any in England.'

The latest medieval style of Yorkshire parapet, which has the distinction of being battlemented with a small crocketed arch over each embrasure, is seen in perfection at Tickhill, where the tower was still in course of construction in 1429, since in that year John Sandford bequeathed a cart and four horses 'to the makyng of the stepall'. The upper stages of the tower are beautifully designed. The large top windows are in pairs with weather mouldings rising into the parapets in the style seen at York, Beverley, Bridlington, and Hull; but there are niches for statues, and in place of the usual gargoyles, animal grotesques resembling those on the Quantock towers. Essentially Yorkshire features are best studied in the towers of the west front of York Minster, those at Beverley, which are held by some to be superior to York's, and in the south tower of the west front of Bridlington Priory.

In the undulating plain of Holderness, where cobbles from boulder clay provided the main material for building during the Middle Ages, we find a group of churches that are as different as they could be from those of the northern dales. They are confined to the broad valley through which the rivers Derwent, Ouse, Aire, Don, and Trent flow into the Humber near Howden. These are the Yorkshire 'wool churches', built in the fourteenth century with the wealth derived not from the

92 Patrington, East Yorkshire: of a magnificence that transcends boundaries, due to its being built on one of the manors of the Archbishops of York during the period of the Church's greatest affluence

sale of woven cloth, like those of East Anglia and the central Cotswolds, but from the sale of wool from the backs of sheep by the Church. Two thirds of Yorkshire wool sold during this period of great prosperity went to Italian merchants, who continued to buy it right through to the Dissolution because they found the Cistercians not only far and away the best breeders of sheep, but also the best farm managers and business men.

The wealth acquired by the Church at this time enabled the builders of these great churches to get stone from quarries at Anston, Roche Abbey, Doncaster, Pontefract, Huddleston, and above all Tadcaster. The churches built during this period are the famous nine: Patrington, Hedon, Meaux, Beverley, Kingston-upon-Hull, Howden, Hatfield, Tickhill, and Laughton-en-le-Morthen. Of these, Hedon, Howden, Hull,

Beverley Minster and Pocklington are distinctively Yorkshire in character, Patrington transcends all boundaries. It belongs to that exclusive category of great cruciform churches of which the other two best-known members are St Mary Redcliffe, Bristol, and Melton Mowbray, Leicestershire. Patrington's magnificence is probably due to its being on one of the manors of the Archbishops of York. In comparing it with the two just named it becomes significant that while Melton Mowbray was built over a period of 50 years from 1290 to 1340, St Mary Redcliffe from 1355 to 1450, Patrington was built over the period extending from 1310 to 1410, which means that it exhibits a remarkably comprehensive range of tracery from the early curvilinear in the transepts to the Perpendicular in the chancel.

11 Northern England

WESTMORLAND – CUMBERLAND – COUNTY DURHAM – NORTHUMBERLAND

Apart from a few places, like St Bees, with churches dedicated to saints seldom if ever met with elsewhere, saints disappear as prefixes to place-names in the far north of England. Instead they have the Scandinavian 'Kirkby', and the Kirkbys usually have the most characteristic churches of the region. They are to the North what minsters are to the South; but as a rule with less freedom to work out their destinies unhampered by higher control. The North is far more authoritarian ecclesiastically than the South, although it now tends to be much less so politically. To take four of the most important northern churches, those at Kendal – formerly Kirkby Kendal, Kirkby Lonsdale, Kirkby Stephen, and Appleby, the ancient capital of Westmorland, we find that they were all appropriated to St Mary's Abbey, York, and for centuries suffered neglect. Nearer home, the bishops of Carlisle seldom showed the interest in Westmorland that bishops of Durham showed in Northumberland, where they owned vast estates. So in the fourteenth century, when there was so much building in the South of England, the North West got little. Nor could the people do much for themselves. They were so poor that tithes were not worth collecting. In 1302 Bishop Halton of Carlisle, who ruled the diocese for more than 30 years, directed that nothing should be collected from the parishes along the Scottish border and only two-thirds from such parishes as Cliburn, Bampton, Shap, Askham, Low-ther, Morland, Clifton, and Barton.

In 1337 his successor recorded that he could not get his tenths because all the clergy had fled, and from 1346 there is a seven-year gap in the episcopal records. Border warfare had combined with the Black Death to lay waste the entire region, and long after the Union of England and Scotland Cumberland continued to be exposed to raids and forays without the protection enjoyed by Durham and Northumberland of the private army of the prince bishops of Durham and the liegemen of the Percies of Northumberland.

The largest of the Kirkby churches is Kendal's. Its low, massive, austere fabric, with five lateral divisions instead of the normal nave with north and south aisles, is still tremendously impressive, despite the drastic restoration of 1850–52. With a width of 103 feet it is only three feet narrower than York Minster. In place of the emblems of saints there are the tombs and memorials of great feudal families: Parrs, Stricklands, and Bellinghams, and these like the church are to be seen in relation to the martial spirit inspired by the occasion in 1129 when the townspeople rushed into the church for refuge from the marauding Scots, only to be pursued over the threshold and massacred in the supposed place of sanctuary.

Kirkby Lonsdale, the 'kirk-town' of Lonsdale, or Lunedale, has a magnificent north arcade, c. 1100–25, which is reminiscent of Durham Cathedral. The facing piers are later, but still twelfth century. The chancel is *c.* 1200. All these features are so impressive that we instinctively ask why a church planned on such a scale was not completed in uniform style. Pevsner calls it 'the most powerful Early Norman display in Cumbria'. The answer to the question may be its remoteness from its owners, the monks of St Mary's Abbey, York.

In all the larger Cumbrian churches we find ourselves less absorbed with architectural features than with their all-embracing defensive air and martial character. This is most strongly felt at Appleby, where that valiant lady, Anne Clifford, Countess of Pembroke, Dorset, and Montgomery, ruled throughout the Commonwealth from her castles at Appleby, Brough-under-Stainmore, Brougham, and Pendragon, which she toured in regal progresses after coming into her Clifford inheritance. After restoring her castles she restored the churches on her estates, starting with St Lawrence, Appleby, in 1655, followed by St Michael in 1659. Finding the church of St Ninian above the River Eamont near her castle of Brougham in an advanced state of decay, she rebuilt it entirely, and it remains today as she furnished it, with the exception of the nineteenth-century cupboards in the south wall, and the 1841 porch. In all, she restored seven churches and chapels, two of them – Skipton and Barden – on her Yorkshire estates. The Book of Common Prayer, which was banned from use in public worship during the Commonwealth, continued to be used in all her churches during what she judged 'the worst of times'.

What the great monastic Orders had done in the South in establishing schools of masonry, Anne Clifford did more practically in the less affluent North, finding work for her tenants and keeping the clergy up to scratch. By her influence she started a movement for rebuilding that slowly spread across Cumbria. And none too soon! Armathwaite's Norman chapel was used as a shippon before Richard Skelton rebuilt it in the seventeenth century. The dating of the churches rebuilt at this time

is difficult because – like the Countess's – they were all done in a style that was long out of date, with a minimum of furnishing, but with an unpretentious dignity that cannot fail to impress anyone with a feeling for what is well-made and functional.

The other churches appropriated to St Mary's Abbey, York, had the same feudal character. Kirkby Stephen's fine church is built of the new red sandstone that runs from Maryport to Wigton, and down the Eden Valley to Appleby, instead of the slatey material of which the central Lake District churches are built. In the Musgrave chapel we are reminded of the hunting traditions of this ancient Royal Forest in the sculpturing on the fifteenth-century tomb of Sir Richard de Musgrave, of whom it is told that he killed the last wild boar in Westmorland. When the tomb was opened in 1847 a wild boar's tusk was found with the bodies. Near the font is a piece of sculpture called the 'Bound Devil', which used to be said to represent Satan, but is really a fragment of a grave cross, bearing – like the one at Gosforth – the figure of the Norse Loki, chained and horned.

There are abundant expressions of the traditionally northern concept of life as one of incessant strife and combat in carvings on innumerable crosses and pieces of symbolic masonry incorporated in church fabrics. The church of St Mary and St Bega at St Bees, Cumberland, has a lintel depicting St Michael slaying the dragon in a design with Viking interlace, and above the Norman doorway of the church at Bolton, five miles north-west of Appleby, is a carved relief of *c.* 1100 depicting two mounted knights with kite shields and lances charging each other. Bishop Nicolson of Carlisle, 1702–18, correctly attributed the origin of the fighting spirit of his flock, and the deep-seated conservatism of the northern character, to the lingering influence of Viking ancestors, who 'were anciently gross idolators and sorcerers'. But he was not, of course, the first to recognise Viking influence in the Lake District character. When the monks of Furness made Hawkshead their favourite hunting ground they found descendants of the Viking settlers farming in traditional fashion, and took steps to remedy it.

The monks of Furness, in fact, created the scenery round Hawkshead as we see it now, by clearing forest and draining marshes on the banks of Windermere and Coniston Water, and as far south as Morecambe Bay so efficiently that this northern outpost of the old geographical county of Lancashire enjoyed prosperity earlier than any other part north of the Ribble. Hence the siting of Lancashire's ancient capital at Lancaster. The monks of Furness also left valuable records of their agricultural pioneering. In 1219 the abbot of Furness, who had a grange at Hawkshead Hall, constituted Hawkshead the ecclesiastical centre of the whole of the hill country between the Duddon and the Leven. What kind of church there was at Hawkshead at that time we do not know. The present building is fifteenth-century, and shows the usual Cumbrian disregard for period conventions in having Norman-style arches on nave piers of so simple a form that they have neither capitals nor footings. The church at Hawkshead, however, has a special place in the affection of Wordsworthians as the one commemorated nostalgically in the lines:

The snow-white church upon her hill
Sits like a thronèd lady, sending out
A gracious look all over her domain.

The lime that made it 'snow-white' was stripped off by Victorian scrapers in 1875.

The church that played the minster role over the region as we see it today was Cartmel Priory, built for Augustinian Canons, which owes its preservation primarily to having been spared destruction in the Scottish raid of 1322, and later to the townspeople having been allowed to take it over at the Dissolution, although at the time they were so poor that rain continued to pour through the roof until it was repaired 80 years later by George Preston of Holker Hall. The walls are built of limestone mixed with slate rubble, and Cumbrian disregard for convention is shown here in the top stage of the tower being set diagonally on the stage below it, possibly to reduce wind pressure. Sandstone and millstone grit were used for the pillars of the interior arcades; but for the great east window of nine lights Caen stone was imported. The misericords are fun. One has a doctor represented as an ape, holding a flask.

On the hills behind Cartmel is a little church dedicated to St Anthony, where convention is flouted by leaving the floor to slope down to the altar instead of being built up to it. Scratches on the porch are said to have been made by using the stone to sharpen arrows, apparently in defiance of St Anthony who was the protector of beasts of chase!

Slate is almost invariably the building material in the Lake District; but it varies greatly in quality. The quarries round Morecambe Bay, in Borrowdale, and along the side of Honister Pass produce a kind that is volcanic in origin and much superior to the blue slate of Hawkshead. But everywhere churches and farmsteads are built of locally quarried material, with deep-sweeping flag roofs matching those of the older farmhouses and shippons, and wide-gabled porches identical with those on the fellside farmhouses, which, like the churches, were always lime-washed.

The earthy character of the old Westmorland churches must have been in no small measure due to the county having so few monastic foundations when Cumberland was rich in them. There were Benedictine priories at St Bees and Wetheral, nunneries at Armathwaite and Seaton, Cistercian abbeys at Holme Cultram and Calder, Augustinian priories at Carlisle and Lanercost, Dominican and Franciscan friaries at Carlisle, and an Augustinian priory at Penrith, when Westmorland had only one abbey: the Premonstratensian abbey at Shap. The other monastic foundations in Westmorland amounted to no more than a Carmelite friary at Appleby, and hospices (guest-houses) at

93 Hawkshead, Furness: basically late fifteenth and early sixteenth century. Built of grey Silurian stone, formerly whitewashed like most Cumbrian churches

Appleby, Brough, and Kendal. With so little monastic leadership the parishioners could hardly be expected to put more labour into the care of churches than they put into that of farm buildings, particularly as the Cumbrian parson in the seventeenth century was unlikely to be 'passing rich with forty pounds a year'. Most of them were getting a paltry five pounds a year from their 'cure of souls' at the end of the century. So it is not as shocking as it appears to be that when Bishop Nicolson made his Visitations in 1703–4 he found that of the 106 churches he inspected a score were 'in scandalous condition', 17 in 'bad order', and only three in fully satisfactory condition. These last, as we should expect, were in the

Countess's countryside round Appleby, with the best at Kirkby Thore, where Thomas Machell, 'the father of all Westmorland and Cumberland antiquaries', held the living from 1677 to 1698. The bishop reported of this church: 'The church, Quire, and Parsonage House are in the best Repair of any in the Diocese; a good part whereof is oweing to the late Incumbent Mr Machel'.

Bishop Nicolson noted that 16 of his churches had day-schools held in them, usually in the chancel. This holding of day-schools in churches has been represented in recent times as itself 'scandalous' by those who take what some of us would regard as too esoteric a view of the Church's function, forgetting that the Church pioneered universal education, and nowhere more enthusiastically than in Westmorland. There is a reminder of this in the fact that more traces of games being played in churchyards are found in Cumbria than in any other part of England.

The link between education and the Church is most impressively shown in the exceptionally large number of endowed grammar schools in Westmorland. I believe it has more than any other county of comparable size, and not only did the pupils come from the farms, the link between Church and education remained so strong that a large proportion went on from grammar school to university and from university into the Church. One headmaster of a Westmorland grammar school – I think it was Bampton – boasted that he had trained 200 boys for the ministry of the Church. Interesting research into this could be done by examining the records of Queen's College, Oxford, and Trinity College, Cambridge, to which most of these boys gained scholarships. Many of them attained eminence in the church, most of them went into North Country livings, where they farmed their glebe, ran the church school, and held the parish together through their leadership of the social as well as the religious life of the community. If it is asked what this has to do with the styles of Cumbrian churches the answer is 'Everything'.

Nowhere is this better expressed than by Wordsworth where he wrote in his *Guide*: 'Many of these humble sons of the hills had a consciousness that the land which they walked over and tilled, had for more than five hundred years been possessed by men of their name and blood'. Wordsworth's *Guide* was first published in 1810, by which time most of the churches in which children had formerly been taught in the chancel had an annexe built on to the main building, which Wordsworth called 'a sort of anti-chapel to the place of worship'. These are often said to be rooms built for the officiating priest to pass the night in before riding back to his abbey or priory the following day. No doubt they did serve that purpose in many places. In others they were 'marriage rooms', where wedding feasts could be held when cottages were too small to accommodate the guests. They could be used for other purposes. In the North, however, they were most often school rooms, as the carved names and initials of pupils continue to testify – as Wordsworth's do in his old schoolroom at Hawkshead.

Again it is to Wordsworth that we turn for a perfect evocation of the character of these buildings:

The architecture of these churches and chapels, where they have not been recently rebuilt or modernised, is of a style not less appropriate and admirable than that of the dwelling houses, and other structures. How sacred the spirit by which our forefathers were directed: the *religio loci* is nowhere violated by these unstinted, yet unpretending works of human hands. They exhibit generally a well-proportioned oblong, with a suitable porch, in some instances a steeple tower, and in others nothing more than a small belfry. ... A man must be very insensible who would not be touched with pleasure at the sight of the chapel of Buttermere, so strikingly expressing, by its diminutive size, how small must be the congregation there assembled, as it were, like one family.

This simplicity continues into the fells beyond the Lakes, where we may still rest in a wayside chapel after hours of tramping, and look through the clear glass of square-headed windows towards the whitewashed farmsteads from which generations of 'statesmen' have driven down with their wives and families to worship together in buildings that were sacred to them – not so much because of what happened in Palestine 2,000 years ago as because their children were baptised in them, they themselves were married in them, and their forebears were buried in the graveyard outside.

The three great churches in northern Lakeland are at Crosthwaite, the mother church of Keswick, Greystoke, and Penrith. All three are rooted in pre-history. The nearly circular churchyard at Penrith tells its own tale. Crosthwaite and Greystoke are dedicated to St Kentigern, commonly known as St Mungo, a man of prodigious vigour who maintained contact with every part of his vast diocese. Ten churches in Cumbria are dedicated to him, including those at Caldbeck and Castle Sowerby. The present church at Crosthwaite is the fourth on the site. The first was a small wooden chapel founded in the sixth century by St Kentigern himself. Greystoke was rebuilt in the fifteenth century. Originally cruciform, it has a typical Cumbrian tower at the west end. Penrith was rebuilt in 1720–22 in the pseudo-classical style that had been introduced into the district by Edward Addison of Kirkby Thore, who was associated with the Rev Thomas Machell in his building enterprises. Fortunately, the builders at Penrith had too much respect for the square, battlemented tower to try to modernise that. They would have found it difficult anyway as the walls are six feet thick at the base and four at the belfry stage.

Again we must go to a village church for a real understanding of local character. In this case my own choice would be Barton, three miles west of Penrith, another mother-church standing on a mound in a circular churchyard close to a spring that became a feeder of the River Eamont, in which early converts would be baptised. The south porch has a panel above the archway bearing the arms of Lowther, Lancaster, and Hartsop. Of these, the Lancasters held the barony of Kendal and married into the Salkeld, Strickland, Musgrave, and Lowther families, so between them the three were linked with all the landowning families of Cumbria, while the families of the 'statesmen' buried in the graveyard produced two Provosts of Queen's College, Oxford, as well as other eminent divines. But Barton is to be visited because we can be introduced there to a feature that we shall find common in Northumberland: the tunnel vault, the local name for a series of low arches built into the full width of the tower to provide a defensive passage from the nave into the chancel. The plan is believed to have come from France, but to have reached the North of England from Scotland. At Brough-by-Sands the [Burgh] church is close to a tunnel-vaulted pele-tower, with access from the church at first-floor level, confirming the defensive purpose of tunnel-vaults.

From the fertile valleys of the River Eden and its tributaries we strike across Stainmore from Brough to descend into the valleys of the Upper Tees and its tributaries, the Lune, the Balder, and the Greta, all basically of the same character as those we left behind in Westmorland, but bordering a county that is now universally associated with coal mining and the pride of Durham, the most spectacular of our great cathedrals. Fortunately the main industrial part of Durham need not concern us. Its churches are too much over-restored to offer clues to local style.

The Tees forms the boundary between the geographical counties of Durham and Yorkshire, with most of the settlements along its upper reaches on the Yorkshire bank, and associated with lead mining financed by Quaker bankers rather than coal mining, which was financed by the Durham landowners. Consequently Nonconformity has always been strong in what are the most northerly dales of Yorkshire and their villages.

It used to be said that Cotherstone was inhabited by Quakers, Mickleton by Primitive Methodists, Middleton by Wesleyans, and only Romaldkirk by churchpeople. Romaldkirk is certainly the one church to be visited in this region for local style. It is yet another northern church dedicated to a saint unknown in the rest of England. No-one appears to be certain who he was; but his church served a parish that extended from the outskirts of Barnard Castle to Holwick and the far bounds of Lunedale, making it one of the half-dozen or so claimants to being the largest in England. There was a church at Romaldkirk at Domesday, which would no doubt suffer when the Scots under King Malcolm made their devastating raid into these parts, destroying everything in their wake. The present church has features of twelfth, thirteenth and later centuries, and is a fine building, but much of its local character has been lost – not least in the drastic renovation in 1926.

North Riding-style churches cross the Tees into Durham; but not notably much beyond Yarm. Farther north we become conscious of how much longer the mineral wealth derived from a relatively narrow belt of land enabled the great landowners, seated in their castles, to continue in a style of life long after it had been modified in other parts of England. No doubt the main part of the explanation is that whereas in other parts of the country life became less feudal when the threat of invasion from the sea diminished, in the North cattle thieves – called rievers – continued long after the Union of Scotland with England to make their forays, burning down churches and farmsteads and intimidating the people in lonely farmhouses.

This feudal tradition has its strongest roots in the Bishopric of Durham. The prince-bishops had their castles in every part of their domain. Their tenants had military obligations and the bishop himself had a private army. The parishes were vast. Several, including Bamburgh and Rothbury, both of which encompassed more than 20 townships,

were royal estates. The enormous Simonburn parish, which was an estate of the pre-Conquest earls of Northumbria, extended from the Border to the Roman Wall. In 1082 the great mainland estates of Lindisfarne – 'the lands of St Cuthbert' – were granted to Durham. In fact, the unique prefix of 'County' to Durham's territorial name has its origin in boundary distinctions made between the estates of the bishops in Northumberland and those in the new county of Durham.

The delay in splitting up these ancient parishes demarcated by widely separated streams and other natural features was mainly due to their few settlements being separated from each other by sparsely populated areas of moorland and waste. So it was not until late in the eighteenth century that Allendale, for example, was constituted a separate parish by giving it boundaries defined by a series of straight lines arbitrarily drawn across the moors. The effect of this resistance to change, however motivated, has been the survival of architecture which Pevsner describes as being 'of a very northern and primeval kind'.

But before we can properly relate these primitive buildings to the present rural landscape dominated by castles, we need to look back beyond the Norman Conquest to the evangelisation of Northumbria in the last quarter of the seventh century, when the first churches were built on the Celtic plan by the missionaries of St Aidan, first bishop of Lindisfarne. Their characteristics, as described in the Introduction to this book, are long narrow naves, small square-ended chancels, and high walls. As they were built of the carboniferous stone that was later to produce the Durham coalfields they have survived every form of attack, and stand today as memorials of the Celtic evangelisation of Northern England 1,300 years ago. The most important were built by masons brought over

94 Escomb, Co. Durham: interior of a seventh-century church built of stone from Roman *Vinovia*

from Gaul by Bishop Biscop (629–90), abbot of Wearmouth. Escomb, County Durham, is the best-preserved complete Saxon church not only in Northumbria but in England, and the oldest. It is built of squared masonry believed to have come from the Roman military station of *Vinovia*, two miles to the north, with smaller stones at the top of the walls. Today it is a small blackened church in a decayed pit village one mile west of Bishop Auckland. The others are at Monkwearmouth and Durham.

In the last quarter of the seventh century St Wilfrid, Bishop of York, either built or restored four churches – one of them at Ripon – on the orthodox Roman plan seen at Hexham and Corbridge, where the Northumbrian kings had a manor. Parts of the Saxon church are incorporated in the structure of the present church. Other places in County Durham where Saxon memorials are treasured – if only as memories – are Chester-le-Street, where the body of St Cuthbert was enshrined in a timber Saxon church for 113 years before the present church was built, before the final removal to Durham.

One of the best places in Durham to see Saxon work is Aycliffe, now incorporated in the new town of Newton Aycliffe on the banks of the Skerne five miles north of Darlington. There is Saxon masonry to be seen at the west end of the nave; but Aycliffe's greatest treasures are the fragments of richly-carved crosses from the time when Ecgfrida, daughter of Bishop Ealdhun, married an earl of Northumbria and received Aycliffe as part of her dowry. A cross in the south aisle is carved with writhing monsters and interlace, and another shows St Peter being crucified head downwards. Celtic tallness continued to be characteristic of Northumbrian churches, as we see at Haltwhistle, with lancets in every wall, at Corbridge, Rothbury, and Bamburgh, which has blank arcades on shafts round the church.

The great age of building in these north-eastern counties followed the building of Durham Cathedral and Lindisfarne Priory in 1093. The twelfth century saw many churches rebuilt in Norman style, the finest at Warkworth, which Pevsner says is 'unique in Northumberland in being a large fairly complete Norman church'. Norman and Early English work overlap in the two counties. Lindisfarne had been refounded as a Benedictine Priory of Durham towards the end of the eleventh century. The Augustinians had founded a house at Hexham in 1113, followed by others at Brinkburn and Bamburgh in the twelfth century. The Premonstratensians had established themselves at Blanchland in 1165. So, as themselves builders of churches, all had their influence on local styles; but Durham's influence inevitably remained the strongest. How could it be otherwise? This meant that whatever styles the monks introduced into either Durham or Northumberland the Norman continued to dominate. We see the effect of this in the sturdy piers of the nave arcades and the rib-vaulted chancels at Heddon-on-the-Wall and Warkworth, both of which have heavy zig-zag in Durham style. Perhaps the motif most distinctively associated with the Northumbrian churches of the period is the 'nutmeg' seen at Hexham, Bolam, and Embleton among other places.

The influence of Durham in the thirteenth century is shown in the reluctance to depart from depressed arches. Even where they are slightly pointed they often carry Norman decoration. We see this at St Andrew's, Bolam, where Norman and Early English styles are combined in a remarkable church with a Saxon tower that was plainly built for defence. The tunnel-vaults already mentioned as being common in Northumberland are seen at their most cavernous at Kirknewton, where there is no vertical wall in the transept, and in the chancel so little that the place resembles a crypt. The tunnel vault at Bellingham, which runs through 15 narrowly set transverse arches in the nave, and seven in the transept, was actually repaired in the seventeenth century, showing that the passion for security in these northern counties continued to dominate building styles for 300 years or more. At Embleton the base of the tower is tunnel-vaulted with heavy single-chamfered transverse arches, while at Ancroft in the far north of the county a fortified tower house was built into the west end of the church.

Such defensive work brings home to us the vulnerability of Northumberland, and shows how much more violent and destructive the Scots were than the Welsh. This is confirmed by entries in the account books of the earls of Northumberland referring to money spent on repairing towers for the protection of the earl's tenants against the Scots. In 1450, for example, the earl's steward contributed a sum towards the building of a tower to the chapel of North Charlton in Ellington parish, and there are references in the *Victoria County History* of Northumberland to the people being warned to keep their towers in good repair. In these circumstances it is not surprising that roughness of construction continued to characterise church building in the North long after more sophisticated styles had been introduced in the rest of England.

But it must not be thought that these primitive northern churches were entirely destitute of art and adornment. Perhaps their most fascinating feature is the vernacular element in stone carving derived from that on the seventh- and early eighth-century crosses that are as common in the far North as in the far West. A particularly interesting feature is what has come to be called 'the Anglian Beast' because it is found so frequently on crosses in Anglian settlements in Cumberland, Durham, and Northumberland. Experts tell us that many of these designs appear to be eastern in origin; but that the flowing, graceful lines, both in the forms of the animals and birds represented on them, and in the interlacing of the background, is peculiarly local. Among the most important cross-shafts is the one from Spital, known as Acca's Cross, now at Durham, which commemorates the bishop who contributed so much towards the beauty of the church at Wrexham. What is not local in these carvings is the vine scrolls which may have been copied from illuminated MSS. We see them at Croft on the Tees, and at Bishop Auckland where they have vernacular characteristics which suggest that they are the work of local pupils of the craftsmen who came into the county in the seventh and eighth centuries. In the late eighth century the work deteriorated as the North entered into the dark age architecturally, from which it emerged in the twelfth century, and then only temporarily. Away from Newcastle, Alnwick, and Staindrop there is very little good medieval architecture in Northumberland. Even the furnishings of the churches – fonts, screens, and monuments – are seldom comparable with those in other counties.

Taking the two counties together, the most satisfying church from the point of view of continuous development of parish church style is the cruciform church of St Cuthbert, Darlington, originally designed by Bishop Pudsey in the twelfth century to succeed an existing Saxon church. Its chief interest is that it shows how Norman architecture in the North East was then evolving a characteristic style. The soaring spire was a well-designed fourteenth-century culmination to what had been so admirably accomplished elsewhere in the thirteenth century. Bishop Langley gave the church 18 oak stalls, with traceried bench-ends carved in the fifteenth century with seraphim and human faces.

But if the Church in the North East had lagged behind the rest of England in providing medieval adornment for its buildings it came to the fore with a flourish under the influence of the flamboyant Restoration Bishop of Durham, John Cosin, who actually used his ex-officio powers as lord-lieutenant of Durham to employ the militia to drive Nonconformists to church, and levied dues to raise money for his buildings at Bishop Auckland and Durham, for a library at Durham, scholarships at Cambridge, and other charities he favoured with his patronage. But his greatest passion was for ornate

95 Staindrop, Co. Durham: a church of all medieval periods on the site of one built in the eighth century. Its castellated tower relates it to the feudal North, as do its memorials to the lords or Raby

Gothic woodwork that had long gone out of fashion in the South of England when he began introducing it into his northern churches. So great was his enthusiasm for it that he founded a school of woodcarvers with himself as patron, and commissioned new stalls for the Cathedral in styles as near as possible to those destroyed during the Commonwealth. Similar work was commissioned in other places, most notably at Brancepeth, a living he had held before becoming bishop, where the Nevilles had held sway until they lost the castle after the Rising in the North of 1569 described by Wordsworth in 'The White Doe of Rylstone' in the lines:

From every side came noisy swarms
Of peasants in their homely gear;
And, mixed with these, to Brancepeth came
Grave gentry of estate and name
And captains known for worth in arms.

The showpiece is the chancel screen of five bays, with richly-carved tabernacle work and clustered pinnacles. The oak pulpit has a sounding board above it elaborately carved with fruit and cherub-heads. It is all most

96 Corbridge, Northumberland: like Escomb, built of stone from a Roman military station, including a complete gateway for an arch between the tower and the chancel

impressive. But does it belong? It may have its place at Durham, where castle and Cathedral rule in splendour. Perhaps it could be argued that Bishop Cosin was so clever in raising money for his workshops that he was able to create a local style and impose it on his parishes. Anyway, Bishop Cosin woodwork is a feature of the parish churches of Durham that must figure in any study of local style, although I personally would not regard it as reflecting the true character of the North East.

That leads me to the question: 'Is there a parish church that reflects the character of the people and sums up the local history of a parish in the way so many do in the South?' I think my answer would be that Staindrop does this for Durham and Corbridge for Northumberland, although I acknowledge that I make the choice with inadequate knowledge of either county, albeit with the happiest memories of hospitality in both.

Sir Walter Scott's

Staindrop who from her silver bowers
Salutes proud Raby's battled towers

was originally dedicated to St Gregory, which should immediately alert us to the probability of Saxon foundation, since every church with that dedication seems to have something Saxon about it. But Staindrop is now dedicated to St Mary, and the traces of Saxon origin are confined to a sundial and fragments of Saxon windows. The present church, as we approach it across the churchyard, is broad and low, with an unbuttressed battlemented tower in two stages, the lower one thirteenth-century, the upper one fifteenth-, and is in every respect strongly North-Country in character. The south aisle and porch are fourteenth-century. The fifteenth-century chancel has four sedilia and carved stalls dating from the time when the church was collegiate. In a county with fewer monuments of first rank than might be expected in one so proud, Staindrop pays full tribute in both tablets and tombs to the memories of the Nevilles and Vanes of Raby Castle who built the present church.

In Northumberland the choice is more difficult. In southern and midland England nearly every village has its parish church in which the entire character of the place is summarised. The pattern in Northumberland is very different. When William Cobbett rode from Morpeth to Alnwick in his *Rural Rides* he found 'only two churches, I think, in the whole twenty miles'. In the sixteenth century, when Devon had 45 market towns and Cumberland 16, Northumberland had only eight. Whatever the population may be today in relation to those other two counties, the north of Northumberland is still sparsely populated. So again we must look for the place or places where local history rather than architecture has determined the style of the parish church.

Approached from this angle, I am advised by my friends in the North that my choice of Corbridge is not likely to be challenged, although it now has the unusual distinction for an ancient Northumbrian town of lacking a castle. As at Escomb in County Durham,

the church was built of stone from a Roman military station, including a complete gateway for an arch between the tower and the nave. The chancel has a group of stepped lancets in true Early English style, and for defence there is the Vicar's Pele in the churchyard, built mainly of Roman stones: a fortified parsonage in three floors, of which the basement was used for cattle, the middle floor as living quarters and the upper floor for shelter and defence by parishioners when the Scots attacked. Happier relations with the Scots are now evidenced in Corbridge having in Stagshaw Bank Fair the most famous in the North of England for the sale of sheep and Scots cattle. At the end of the eighteenth century, when the fair was in its prime, 100,000 head of sheep would be sold there. The fair was abolished by a Home Office Order dated 5 March 1927 and Corbridge has assumed a more tranquil air. But every vital aspect of Northumbrian life, from the building of the Wall, through all the turbulence of the Scottish raids to the full maturity of a prosperous agriculture is represented in a church that so completely fulfils the obligation of 'belonging'.

It is consistent with the northern character, and evidence of the strength of local stone, that the two styles introduced respectively by the missionaries of St Aidan from Ireland and St Wilfrid from Rome in the seventh century should be so nobly represented in the twentieth. The Christianity of the North East is muscular, and its local style rock-like. There is symbolism in the churches at Escomb and Corbridge being built of Roman masonry. In the lands of St Cuthbert the faith has been guarded with the vigour displayed by the private armies of the prince bishops of Durham and the liegemen of the Percies in guarding the land. Both the spiritual and the physical possessions have been held through every assault and local style conserved.

Select Bibliography

Allen, Frank J., *The Great Church Towers of England*, Cambridge Univ. Press, 1932

Anderson, M. D., *History and Imagery in British Churches*, John Murray, 1971

Atkinson, T. D., *Local Style in English Architecture*, Batsford, 1947

Atkinson, T. D., 'Local Style in the Ancient Architecture of Cambridgeshire', *Proc. Camb. Antiq. Soc.*, vol. 40 (1944)

Betjeman, Sir John, *Collins Guide to English Parish Churches*, Collins, 1958

Blatch, Mervyn, *Parish Churches of England*, Blandford Press, 1974

Bond, Francis, *Screens and Galleries in English Churches*, Oxford Univ. Press, 1908

Braun, Hugh, *Parish Churches*, Faber & Faber, 1970

Brown, H. Miles, *What to Look for in Cornish Churches*, David & Charles, 1973

Budden, C. W., *English Gothic Churches*, Batsford, 1927

Cautley, Munro, *Suffolk Churches*, Batsford, 1938

Clapham, A. W., *English Romanesque Architecture*, Oxford Univ. Press, 1930–4

Clifton-Taylor, Alec., *the Pattern of English Building*, Faber & Faber, 1972

Clifton-Taylor, Alec., *English Parish Churches as Works of Art*, Batsford, 1974

Cook, G. H., *The English Mediaeval Parish Church*, Phoenix, 1954

Cook, G. H., *English Collegiate Churches of the Middle Ages*, Phoenix, 1959

Cox, J. Charles and Ford, C. B., *the Parish Churches of England*, Batsford, 1935

Crossley, F. H., *English Church Craftsmanship*, Batsford, 1941

Crossley, F. H., *English Church Design, 1040–1540*, Batsford, 1945

Fisher, E. A., *The Saxon Churches of Sussex*, David & Charles, 1969

Hewett, Cecil A., *Church Carpentry*, Phillimore, 1974

Hewett, Cecil A., *English Historic Carpentry*, Phillimore, 1980

Hoskins, W. G., *The Making of the English Landscape*, Hodder & Stoughton, 1955; Pelican Books, 1970

Hoskins, W. G. (ed.), The Making of the English Landscape Series, Hodder & Stoughton

Howard, F. E., *Mediaeval Styles of the English Parish Church*, Batsford, 1936

Hutton, Graham and Smith, Edwin, *English Parish Churches*, Thames & Hudson, 1952

Jones, Lawrence E., *The Observer's Book of Old English Churches*, Warne, 1973

Kendrick, T. D., *Late Saxon and Viking Art*, London, 1949

Lambourn, E. A. Greening, *The Parish Church*, Oxford Univ. Press, 1929

Nye, Thelma M., *Parish Church Architecture*, Batsford, 1965

Pevsner, Sir Nikolaus, *The Buildings of England*, all counties, Penguin

Poole, M., 'The Domesday Book Churches of Sussex', *Suss. Arch. Soc. Coll.*, vol. 89 (1948)

Salzman, F., *Building in England*, Oxford Univ. Press, 1952

Smith, Edwin, Hutton, Graham, and Cook, Olive, *English Parish Churches*, Thames & Hudson, 1976

Stoll, Robert, *Architecture and Sculpture in Early Britain*, Thames & Hudson, 1967

Thompson, A. Hamilton, *The Historical Growth of the English Parish Church*, Cambridge Univ. Press, 1911

Thompson, A. Hamilton, *The Ground Plan of the English Parish Church*, Cambridge Univ. Press, 1911

Tyrrell-Green, E., *Parish Church Architecture*, S.P.C.K. 1924

Vallance, Aymer, *Old Crosses and Lychgates*, Batsford, 1920

Verey, David, *Cotswold Churches*, Batsford, 1976

Wickham, A. K., *Churches of Somerset*, David & Charles, 1965

Glossary

abacus flat slab on the top of the capital of a pier, added to support the architrave

acoustic jars earthenware jars embedded into church walls to act as amplifiers. They were inserted in chancel walls to add resonance to the voices of priest and choir. In rural districts animal skulls were used for the same purpose

ambulatory arcade, cloister, or aisle provided for processions and sheltered walks

annulet a ring encircling a pier or shaft

apse vaulted semi-circular or polygonal recess at the end of the nave or chancel of a church

arabesque surface decoration in fanciful flowing lines interspersed with formal motifs

arcade range of arches supported by columns or piers

ashlar masonry of squared or sawn stone

aumbry cupboard or recess to hold sacred vessels

ballflower globular flower decoration with three incurved petals, carved along fourteenth-century moulding, sometimes referred to as 'sheep-bells'

baluster short 'turned' pillar used by Anglo-Saxon builders in window-openings, especially in belfries

balustrade series of balusters

barrel vault fully lined arched under-roof, called waggon or cradle roof if unlined

battlement indented parapet along the top of a wall, originally for purposes of defence, used in Gothic architecture for ornamentation

bay space between two piers of an arcade

beakhead Norman motif formed by setting bird or beast heads in a row with beaks biting into moulding

belfry roof turret to hang bells in

billet short cylindrical or squared motifs introduced to decorate hollow moulding by the Normans

boss projecting ornament or carved keystone at the intersections of ceiling ribs

brattishing ornamental cresting on late Gothic screens, usually naturalistic in design

broach half-pyramid covering the four angles of a square tower without a parapet. Used to form the base for a spire

buttress masonry projecting from a wall to resist thrust

cable moulding Norman moulding shaped like twisted rope

camber tie-beam bent so that it is higher in the middle than at the ends

canopy of honour the enriched section of roof over an altar or rood

capital head of a column or pier

cartouche inscribed tablet with an ornate frame

celure panelled and decorated section of a waggon roof above the altar

chancel from *cancelli*, 'screens', because the eastern limb of a parish church was isolated by a screen

chevron Norman zig-zag moulding

clerestory side wall of a nave rising clear of the roofs of the aisles, usually with windows to provide the church with extra light

corbel supporting stone bonded into a wall, usually carved or moulded

corbel table row of corbels

credence small stone table on which stood the water and wine before being consecrated for Holy Communion

cresset stone stone with hollow cup to be filled with oil to carry a floating wick for lighting a section of the church in the manner of a candle

crockets leaf-shaped decorative features placed equidistantly along the angles of spires, pinnacles, or canopies

crossing space at the intersection of nave, transepts, and chancel of a cruciform church

crypt church basement or cellar

cusps small pointed intersections at the openings of tracery to form trefoils, quatrefoils, etc

diaper work surface decoration in square or lozenge shapes

dog-tooth raised pointed stars set continuously along Early English hollow moulding

dripstone projecting hood-mould over doorways or windows to carry off rain water

Easter Sepulchre canopied recessed tomb-chest for holding the sacraments for Easter celebrations

embrasures openings between merlons of a battlemented parapet

encaustic tiles glazed earthenware tiles used in flooring and paving

fan vault tracery in Gothic vaulting in which the curvature of the ribs forms a series of fans

fillet narrow band running along shaft or moulding

finial decorative apex of roof pediment or gable, common feature on the corners of towers

flèche spirelet, French for 'arrow', from which the surname Fletcher is derived

flushwork patterns formed by setting knapped flints in frames of dressed stone to form tracery or lettering, a feature of East Anglian churches

flying buttress buttress arched from a wall

foliated carved with leaf shapes

four-centred arch depressed arch of a form struck from four centres

freestone stone of grain fine enough to be cut freely in any direction

gargoyle water spout projecting from the parapet of a roof or tower ending in a human or animal head and mouth

graffiti markings cut into the stonework of churches usually by stone masons as their personal signature

hammer-beam wooden roof in which the tie-beam is replaced by projecting beams. A second beam may be added to form a double hammer-beam. The ends may be enriched with carvings of angels etc.

hatchment an armorial painting on a square board carried in the funeral procession at the death of the head of an important local family and afterwards hung in church

hood-mould dripstone

Host the wheaten wafer consecrated at the altar for administration in Holy Communion

impost capital of pier from which the arch springs

Jesse window window with a representation of the genealogy of Christ

label-stop ornamental feature at the end of a dripstone

lancet narrow pointed window in Early English churches, so called from the resemblance to a lancet blade

ledger stone carved floor slabs of hard bluish-grey stone let into the floor of the church, usually bearing an inscription surmounted by a coat of arms

louvres sloping boards fitted into belfry openings to allow the sound of the bells to come through

lozenge diamond-shape

lucarne an opening, or light, in a spire

lychgate wooden canopy with open sides at the entrance to a churchyard, built to provide shelter for the coffin and mourners before the funeral procession formed on the arrival of the priest

mensa the stone slab of an altar

merlons the solid part of battlements

minster mother church from which missionaries went out to serve chapels-of-ease, most of which are now themselves parish churches

misericord tip-up seat of a choir stall, often carved with amusing representations of local characters

moulding masonry forming continuous rounds and hollows to enrich piers and arches into which they are cut. The hollows are often ornamented with motifs useful in dating the work

nail-head squared ornamentation with raised centre set continuously in late-Norman moulding

narthex porch extending across the west end of a church

niche canopied recess in a wall to hold a statue

ogee compound curve, partly convex, partly concave, the two flowing into each other

parclose side screen enclosing a chantry chapel or chancel

pier masonry built in courses to support an arch

piscina shallow basin with drain set in a niche south of the altar for washing sacred vessels

plate-tracery early form of tracery with apertures cut into slabs to form circles

plinth projecting base of pier or monument

poppyhead *fleur-de-lis* termination of bench-end. Properly Poupée-head

pyx the receptacle in which the Host is reserved for the administration to the sick and dying

quoins wrought stones at the angles of buildings

rectilinear tracery window tracery with straight lines largely involuted for curves in Perpendicular architecture

reredos ornamental screen above and behind the altar

respond half-pillar or corbelled termination to an arcade

rood-loft gallery above the chancel screen providing access to the crucifix, or rood, with flanking figures of Our Lady and St John

rustication placing of large blocks of cut stone in door and window surrounds to give an impression of strength

saddleback gabled tower roof

sanctuary the part of the Chancel or Choir in which the High Altar stands

sedilia canopied recessed seats built into the wall of a chancel for the use of officiating priests

shaft long thin quasi-column

soffit underside of an arch

spandrel triangular space formed in the angle between two arches or one arch in a rectangular close fitting frame or moulding

stoup basin near a church door provided to hold holy water

string-course projecting band of moulding along walls to mark stages in building

sword-rest   receptacle to hold the swords of civic dignitaries during church services

tabernacle work   ornamentally carved canopy-work over church stalls, fonts, niches etc.

tie-beam   stout beam with ends resting on the top of opposite walls

tracery   curved patterns in stone at the head of Gothic windows

triforium   an arcaded passage along a wall, or blank arcading below the clerestory

tympanum   space enclosed between the lintel and the arch of a doorway, often filled with sculpture

waggon roof   roof formed with wooden rafters resembling the frame supporting an old-time waggon, also called a cradle roof, and when fully lined a barrel-roof

wall plates   timber along the top of a wall to take the load from the roof rafters

weather boarding   overlapping boards nailed horizontally as wall covering

web   stone filling between ribs of vaulting

zig-zag   Norman ornamentation, also called chevron

Index